How to ADHD

An Insider's Guide to
Working with Your Brain
(Not Against It)

Jessica McCabe

RODALE
NEW YORK

This book aims to provide useful information based on the author's personal experience and research, but it is not intended to replace your doctor's diagnostic expertise and medical advice. Please consult with your doctor if you believe you have any medical conditions that may require treatment.

The "Self-Improvement" diagram on page 330 is reproduced here with permission, © 2019 by Dani Donovan.

Library of Congress Cataloging-in-Publication Data
Names: McCabe, Jessica, 1982– author.
LC record available at https://lccn.loc.gov/2023036480
LC ebook record available at https://lccn.loc.gov/2023036481

ISBN 978-0-593-57894-0
Ebook ISBN 978-0-593-57895-7

Printed in the United States of America

Book design by Andrea Lau
Chapter-opening illustrations by Stephen Foster and Palestrina McCaffrey
Jacket design by Irene Ng
Jacket art by Ann1911/Shutterstock
Author photograph by Dan Montgomery

10 9 8 7 6 5 4 3 2

For the curious, the innovative, the wandering.

For the project-starters, the risk-takers, the problem solvers.

*For those doing too much,
and those who are worried they're not doing enough.*

*For those who do things differently,
because it's the only way they know how.*

*For the alternate-universe version of my past self,
who might have made her dreams of going to
a university come true if she had stumbled across this book
in her community college's library, which she loved.*

*For my mom, who would have had an easier time understanding and
supporting me if she'd known what's in this book.*

For my dad, who may have found himself within these pages.

*For ADHD Brains and the Hearts who love them.
May this book empower you to be who you are and
achieve what you want to achieve.*

Contents

Introduction

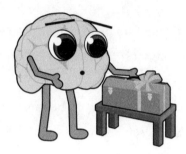

You don't write because you want to say something;
you write because you've got something to say.
—F. SCOTT FITZGERALD

Hello, Brains!

You found my book! A BOOK! How did that happen? Well, first I had to write one. So why did I, someone with ADHD, do such a long and forever-taking thing? Because I lose and forget things, and what I have learned over the last seven years is too important to do that with. As I'll explain in Chapter 1, my intention in starting the YouTube channel How to ADHD was to put everything I learned about ADHD in one place so that I could actually find it again when I needed it.

Well, it's years later. Over the course of building the channel, I've developed a deep and detailed understanding of the invisible obstacles those with ADHD tend to run into, as well as our options for dealing with them. The (almost) weekly videos in which I've shared what I learned, every step along my journey, have helped me and millions of others learn to work with our brains, not against them.

In fact, my team and I have made so many videos that even I'm a little overwhelmed by the amount of information we've put together! Sometimes I wish I could just flip to a table of contents, or control-F my channel or my brain.

Until that is possible, I'm putting the most important information I learned—what's been the most helpful for me and for my community—in a book. Something tangible, with a cover and a table of contents and an index. A reference to remind myself of a tool I can use when I'm feeling stuck. And if I accidentally leave it on the bus like half my school notebooks, I can just buy a new one—wherever I am in the world. (Hello, International Brains!!)

More importantly, though, I wanted to write a book that would give people the experience they'd have if they saw my TEDx Talk, binge-watched my videos, hung out in the comments section, and went to coffee with me. I wanted to give others, if I could, what I had found on my own journey: a deep understanding of how our brains work, a sense of solidarity, and a toolbox full of strategies tailored to the specific challenges we face in achieving what it is we set out to achieve. I wanted to make our invisible obstacles visible for

> Think of this as a user's guide to ADHD full of insights, research, strategies, and validation, one that both explains and accounts for how our brains work.

as many people as possible, so we stop blaming ourselves for trip-ping over them and understand how to navigate them. And I wanted to do it all in one book.

It was an ambitious project, and I wasn't sure how to make it hap-pen. I was pretty sure it wasn't even possible many, *many* times while creating it. But I used the book I was writing to push me over the finish line—tapping into the tools, reading the ending anecdotes for each chapter when I felt discouraged, and . . . well, here it is!

What you are holding in your hands right now is the book I needed and didn't have. Maybe it's the book *you* needed and didn't have.

Think of this as a user's guide to ADHD full of insights, research, strategies, and validation, one that both explains and embraces how our brains work. You won't find definitive solutions for managing ADHD, but a menu of tools I've collected from the community, ADHD experts, lived experience, and research. You'll also find deep dives into why we even need these strategies, so you can choose the ones that fit your unique life and brain. The information and strate-gies I share in these chapters are meant to empower those with ADHD, enlighten and support the efforts of those who love some-one with ADHD, and be helpful and insightful for anyone who is simply human.

How to Book

This book was written by and for ADHD brains. That said, ADHD brains often struggle to read books. We tend to get distracted (or bored), forget what we just read, lose our place, or stare at the same wall of text for five minutes, unable to actually read it.

For this reason, I was determined to write this book in a way that is ADHD-friendly. The pages have a lot of white space, the paragraphs are short, and it even feels good to hold. I included many reading "shortcuts" throughout the book, too: there are pull quotes, bullet points, and bold subheadings that you can scan to catch the main ideas. I worked closely with my (very patient!) editor to make the text as ADHD-friendly as possible for a book this jam-packed with information.

I have included quotes from Brains within the How to ADHD Community. They share their personal experiences, including how they find ways to navigate around obstacles and how they work with their brains, in case you need ideas for how to apply any of these tools. I have also written the chapters so that you can read them sequentially or skip to the ones that interest you without missing important information. (We are interest-based learners, after all!) Almost every chapter is divided into four sections.

1. THE EXPERIENCE OF . . .

At the beginning of every chapter, I describe my lived experience of the topic of the chapter, which tends to be relatable to those with

ADHD. Sometimes I get a little literary in these sections. I may use metaphors, hyperbole, or jokes to make them more fun to read (and, let's be honest, to write). If you don't enjoy reading this kind of thing—or if you prefer literal language to figurative language and just want to get to the facts—skim (or skip) the chapter introductions.

These sections sometimes deal with emotionally heavy topics, especially the ones that begin the "How to Feel," "How to Heart," and "How to People" chapters. It was important to me to be honest about my experiences here, because the struggles we face in these areas can be profoundly painful, but feel free to step away or skip ahead if you need to.

2. WHAT I LEARNED

In this section, I share the information that helped me the most on my own journey, as well as the information that resonated most with my community. If you like the easy-to-understand science communication in my lecture-style videos, this part of the chapter is for you.

I've compiled facts and insights from credible sources, such as peer-reviewed studies, books by ADHD coaches, doctors, and researchers, and conversations with experts in the field. That being said, there is so, so, so much more to know about each of these topics than I could possibly include in a single book, and there is new research being published all the time. If you are extra curious, please consider this information as a jumping-off point for more learning— and check out the research papers cited in the link on page 422 if you want to take a deeper dive.

3. THE TOOLBOX

In each toolbox section, you'll find strategies that work *with* your ADHD brain, rather than against it. The strategies I've included are research-backed, commonly recommended by ADHD coaches, and/or ones that have been helpful to my community and me. Each toolbox section has four or five main evidence-based strategies (tools), as well as a few ways each one can be used.

It is important to note that none of these tools are magic wands that will painlessly eliminate the obstacles that those with ADHD face. Everyone has go-to tools that work more often for them and a couple tools they only use occasionally. And we all have days when nothing seems to work. My hope for you is that by the end of this book, you'll have a personal toolbox full of options. This, in my experience, is better than a toolbox with nothing but a sticky note that says "try harder." Even if you never use some of these tools, they're there for you when you need them.

On page 415, you can find a shiny new toolbox page—make copies, tear it out, write in the book, whatever you like. On it, you'll find space to list three tools you want to try, how long you'll commit to trying them out (it can take time for some strategies to become comfortable/routine enough to make our lives easier), and for what purpose. It's limited to three tools for a reason. I built up this toolbox over seven years, learning one tool a week. And even then it got overwhelming sometimes. We have brains that want to do all the things, but I suggest adding more tools slowly as you get comfortable with (or decide you hate) the ones you're currently trying.

4. THE ENDING ANECDOTE

After spending months and years studying a particular topic, my perspective on it often changes. The final section in each chapter shares this perspective shift. I include these stories to remind you (and myself) that there is no single way to look at any topic, and that we can always learn something new—not just new information but new ways to view it. It's one of the awesome things about having a brain.

IS BOOK? IS BOOK.

So here it is. *How to ADHD: The Book.*

This whole journey started as a personal project—an attempt to understand how to work with my brain more effectively.

It quickly became a group project. My community jumped in to help me before I even thought to ask. I learned a lot of what I've written here from talking with Brains, Hearts, ADHD experts, and researchers.*

Over the years, we've shared long, deep discussions about what it means to have ADHD. About how being "normal" isn't a realistic goal but being functional *is*. About how sometimes, paradoxically, being functional means behaving in *less* (neuro)typical ways, so we can be more mentally healthy, happy, and generous humans for ourselves and for those we love.

I offer all that I've learned back to you, the reader. I'm really proud of how this book has turned out. Thank you for making your way to these pages. Allow your brain to explore this book however it wants. This book was written for your brain, and I hope your brain enjoys it. And if you are finding us for the first time here?

Hello, Brain!

Welcome to the community.

---

*   I call my viewers "Brains" (Hello, Brains!) because it's their brains that brought them to my channel. Plus, they're here to learn about their brain. When people find their way to my channel because they love someone with ADHD and want to understand them better, I call those people "Hearts" (Hello, Hearts!) because their hearts are what led them there. (In addition to what you may learn throughout this book, I wrote a whole chapter for Hearts; see page 323.)

A Note on Language

What I prioritize when it comes to language is *accessibility*. So many of us have run into issues of access—access to information about how our brains work, access to the supports we need, access to one another, and access even to ourselves and our own voices.

There is language that decreases or denies access, which I do not use or allow in my community: language that attacks, shames, or silences.

There is language that creates access. For example, "disability" gives us access to legal protections and accommodations. "Impairments" explains what we might need and where we might struggle. Research-based terms such as "response inhibition," "divergent thinking," and "working memory" give us and our healthcare providers access to information about our deficits and strengths relative to neurotypical brains so we can access treatment tailored to our needs. Colloquial language like "doom spirals" and "brain smoothie"

xvi   **A Note on Language**

makes discussing our challenges more accessible to those of us who did not go to grad school and helps us build community.

There is language that people use to identify themselves or their loved ones: identity-first language, person-first language, or terms such as "neurodivergent" or "neurotypical." People hotly debate which type of language is appropriate, and some communities ban the use of one term or another, including in how people refer to themselves. I do not.

While the language we use matters, rigidly enforcing the use of specific language can deny access to those who need it most: those with the least cognitive flexibility or the least ability to remember and get it "right," or those living in places that have the least understanding of ADHD. It can alienate or isolate those who are more comfortable using different terminology for themselves or are at a different place in their self-identity and self-acceptance journey. What's more, some people may maliciously wield the "correct" language in a way that actively stigmatizes our community, while others might use the "incorrect" language in an accepting, supportive context.

My policy is to use the language that an individual person prefers: "brain-holder's choice," I call it. Because of this, I also use the language a particular community tends to use when there is a clear preference. In our community, people often use different terms to refer to the same thing. In these cases, I use these different terms interchangeably.

Ultimately, my hope is to combat the underlying stigma surrounding ADHD through education and understanding, and normalize the experience of having ADHD enough that the meaning can, eventually, be assumed to be respectful regardless of the particular language used. Just as I can be characterized as a girl with green eyes or a green-eyed girl without anyone, including myself, think-

> My policy is to use the language that an individual person prefers: "brain-holder's choice," I call it.

ing less of me. I'm hoping my use of language in this book will help advance this goal.

In terms of how I refer to myself, I use person-first *and* identity-first language, depending on context. I also enjoy casual, community-created terms like "neuro-spicy," especially when speaking about my anxiety or trauma. It took some time for me to adjust to some of the words I now use. I shied away from the term "disability" for a long time. Ableism is deeply entrenched in our society, and I internalized a lot of it. But the bigger issue, for me, was that I didn't feel I was "disabled enough" to claim that identity and the protections and accommodations that come with it. It took me a long time to understand that it was my internalized ableism telling me I "should" be able to do without them.

My hope is that using the word "disability" helps me let go of my internalized ableism, and that it helps others accept themselves and access the supports and protections they need. For what it's worth, many things can be considered a disability, even pregnancy. According to the Americans with Disabilities Act (ADA), "disability" means you have a "mental or physical impairment that substantially limits one or more major life activities"—which can include focusing, working, or communicating. It was helpful for me to learn and embrace that.

As for the stigma around disabilities and the willingness to speak openly about mine? I had a head start on that one.

Being disabled is an identity I share with my mother. She was born with one leg shorter than the other, and after several unsuccessful surgeries, she moved through this world using a special shoe, crutches, and/or a wheelchair. She was also a talented special education preschool and kindergarten teacher, and the strongest, most capable woman I've ever known. I can still hear the baffled tone in her voice when she was told she'd be excluded from something she cared about. "What do you mean I can't teach in that room because I'm on crutches? Put some carpet down!" (And they did!)

My mother spoke openly about her disability to anyone who was curious. Children would gawk and stare at her at the grocery store. When they asked questions like "What's wrong with your leg?" their parents would turn red, rush their child away, and begin scolding them.

My mom would respond, "No . . . let them ask!" She'd then patiently explain her scars, show them how to touch them ("See? It's fine!"*), and help them to understand how her mobility aids worked.

---

*   When you encounter someone with a disability, it's a good idea to ask about their preferences: If it's okay to ask questions. If you can touch their service dog or their mobility aids. If there are types of support they'd like you to provide. Everyone has different needs and preferences. It's important not to assume.

She knew that these explanations would normalize her experience for them and help them understand that there are differences in how bodies work. She knew that this exposure combats the stigma

> Language evolves through conversation.

that results in biases about people who are "different." She encouraged every curious person to participate in those conversations, however awkwardly they could.

This was because she knew that while people may always communicate differently, language evolves through conversation.

As a trained speech and language pathologist, my mom's job was to help students with disabilities learn to communicate, and she encouraged augmentative and alternative communication systems to meet each student where they were, giving them a path to having their voices heard and their needs met as they learned to speak.

She knew that, contrary to popular opinion and concerns from others, these different ways of communicating would not make it harder for her students to learn how to speak; they would be a path toward it. I volunteered in her classroom every summer starting when I was five, and her classroom rules are ones that guide my own work: We are here to learn. We make space for differences. And we allow all voices a chance to be heard.

My mother modeled language for her students and let them speak back how they could. This increased their sense of safety and efficacy—which made it easier for them to stay in the conversation and learn how to communicate in more nuanced ways over time. This is what my mom—Mrs. McCabe, or "'abecca" to many of her students—modeled for me, in her classroom and outside of it. In my mom's memory, it's what I still do now, in this book and beyond its pages.

Chapter 1

How to Fail at Everything

Be yourself! . . . No, not like that!

—SOCIETY

POTENTIAL

My whole life, I felt like I was failing to be the person I was supposed to be.

When I was little, my mom would drop me off at school—my hair braided, jacket clean and warm from tumbling in the dryer, quietly reading a new book. At the end of the day, my dad would pick me up—dirty, disheveled, backpack left unzipped and messy, anxiously shivering because I'd forgotten my jacket.

I went to school looking like the person I was supposed to be. I went home looking like . . . me.

And I wasn't what anyone expected.

When you are eight, people expect you to be able to dress

yourself, keep your shoes tied, and keep your backpack zipped. The basics. When you are thirty, people expect you to show up to work on time, pay your bills, and put gas in your car *before* it runs out.

I've never been great at meeting basic expectations.

I could, however, *exceed* them.

In school, I took standardized tests every year. These tests measured my performance in each subject by grade level. In third grade, my reading comprehension came back "PHS." I asked my teacher what it meant. She didn't know, so she asked the principal. He told us, "Post high school." (I really liked to read.)

In high school, I was assigned an essay to write. I do not remember what the topic was, but I decided that—to research it properly—I needed to go to a duck farm, buy some eggs, incubate and hatch those eggs, raise the ducklings, and then teach them to swim in my bathtub. This wasn't for a science fair project, by the way. I did this for *English* class. I'm not sure why I felt I had to go to those lengths, but the day I presented my paper to the class, I was the only student walking around campus with three ducklings in tow.

In college, I signed up for multiple classes on the music business because I wanted to support my then boyfriend, who was a musician. I had no plans to be a composer, but I took a composition class where I learned how to write music using math. I was pretty good at it, too!

The teacher gave me the same feedback that I had heard throughout my entire life: "You have *so much* potential!"

The teacher gave me the same feedback that I heard throughout my entire life: "You have *so much potential!*"

EXPECTATIONS

The fact that I could *sometimes* exceed expectations made it even more frustrating for me—and everyone around me—when I failed to meet the basic ones.

Be a Good Daughter

As a daughter, I was supposed to make my parents proud.

But I struggled to meet most of my parents' expectations for me: clean your bedroom, do your homework, and behave at the dinner table. So I tried to earn their respect in other ways.

When I was in middle school, my mom survived a car accident that killed two of her friends. The accident left her with a broken back that never healed completely. With both drivers uninsured and my mom—a special education teacher—suddenly unable to work, our family went from financially comfortable to broke. Mom needed to go back to work sooner than she probably should have.

I started my acting career at fifteen because, as a kid growing up in Los Angeles, I knew it was a path where someone my age could make enough money to support their parents. I didn't want my mom to have to work anymore; it was clear how much pain she was in. I couldn't take away her pain, but I could try to make her life easier.

When my parents struggled with their marriage, I tried playing therapist.

When my little brother experienced significant mental health issues, I tried to mediate between him and my parents. Sometimes, I parented him myself.

After quite a bit of therapy, I now understand that this was not healthy, but I so desperately wanted to be a good daughter and make my disabled mom's life easier that I did whatever I could, especially because I felt like such a "difficult" child.

Pay Attention in Class

As a student, I was supposed to know what was happening in class.

In elementary school, I could get away with staring out the window or getting distracted during tests because I was smart, we stayed in one classroom all day, and there were sticker charts and prizes to motivate me to do my work. By middle school, when I was responsible for motivating myself to do my work, bringing the right books to the right class, and managing assignments on my own, my academic life fell apart.

Around twelve, I was struggling so much that my mom brought me to a doctor, who diagnosed me with attention deficit disorder (ADD).* I was prescribed daily stimulant medication, and it helped

---

*   This is an abbreviated version of the story. In reality, she took me to a doctor who said I couldn't have ADD—I was "too smart." My mom thanked this doctor for his opinion and asked to see a specialist. The specialist knew that "not smart" isn't on the list of symptoms and gave me a proper evaluation.

me focus. My GPA went up a whole point without me doing anything else differently. The effort I was already putting in suddenly *worked*. As far as everyone I knew was concerned, my ADD had been successfully treated—and that was supposed to be the end of that.

But medication added new expectations. Now, "Stop messing around, are you ready for school yet?" was followed by, "Did you take your meds?" Now, I figured there was no excuse for me failing to be what everyone wanted me to be: the gifted student who received straight A's and was a "delight to have in class."

On top of completing my schoolwork and finding time for extracurriculars, I also needed to remember to schedule my doctor's appointments every month, go to them, pick up my prescription, refill it within the two-day window, and then take my meds at the right time (after I woke up but not too late if I wanted to go to sleep that night).

And when my meds wore off or I forgot to take them, I struggled even harder than I did before.

Get a College Degree

As a gifted student, I was supposed to graduate college.

Though I had completely missed every deadline to apply for universities, I did very well on my community college entrance exams. My counselor told me she wasn't worried. I'd be able to transfer to a four-year university, no problem.

Somehow, despite her confidence in me, I missed another expectation: the part of college where you make a plan to complete your course requirements. I wanted to be a journalism major, but instead of writing classes, I took fencing. And those music business classes I mentioned. And ballet. And opera. And Italian, so I could understand what I was singing in opera. One semester, I decided to take statistics, a class I actually needed to graduate. I forgot to register for the course in time,* but the professor told me to show up for class anyway. Once I completed the course, he said, he would give me whatever grade I got when I officially registered for the class next semester.

Statistics is *tough*. I went to every lecture, spent two hours a day doing homework, and aced the class. The next semester, however, I forgot to sign up—*again*. I spent the rest of the year looking for bushes to hide behind when I saw this professor on campus. By the time I worked up the courage to admit my mistake a year later, and ask if I could still register for his class and get that A, he told me it had been too long; I'd need to take it again. I was so discouraged, I dropped out shortly after. Statistically speaking, I knew my odds of graduating anytime soon were not great.

Be Successful

I couldn't reach my potential as a student, so I tried to reach it in my career.

After dropping out of college, I decided to give acting another

---

*   Honestly, forgetting to register for classes in time was half the reason I ended up taking so many courses I didn't need. They were the only classes left because the students who signed up early for courses took all the spots for the required ones.

shot. My theater teacher had previously introduced me to his acting manager, who also believed in me.

I pursued acting the same way I pursued everything—with total enthusiasm! Unless I got distracted . . . or had to do something boring like memorize lines, listen while someone else spoke, or hold relatively still, which turns out to be 90 percent of being a professional actor.

I had a handful of early successes, but as time went by, there were fewer and fewer opportunities. (Heads-up: you'll find a frank discussion of disordered eating. Feel free to skip ahead to the next page.)

My manager and agent had ideas to boost my career: "Lose ten pounds, and we can get you a pilot!" I'd try a new diet or a different workout, but I could never sustain my efforts long enough for them to matter. I'd get discouraged and give up, or run out of money from paying for personal trainers I couldn't afford or purchasing dehydrators and other equipment so I could follow the latest diet. I'm not sure if I would have qualified for an eating disorder, but I definitely ended up with disordered eating (see "Let's Talk about Eating Issues," page 295).

I carried my shame and frustration with me into the audition room. I hadn't lost ten pounds. I saw other girls walk in, competing for the same role, who I thought were thinner or prettier, or who seemed more confident in their preparation. I couldn't even remember my lines.

I'd work for days preparing for a role, only to give an audition that said to the casting director, "I'm sorry for wasting your time."

It wasn't just acting I struggled with. In the ten years after I left college, I quit, or was fired from, fifteen jobs and abandoned *several* careers.

My performance as an employee was wildly inconsistent. Sometimes I was a superstar. At my first job as a server at a retirement home for millionaires, I noticed that they didn't have an organized system for order-taking, so I created one. I got to work early, did all my side work before going home, and stayed as late as they needed me to.

At another job, I left at lunch to see my boyfriend and didn't return. I assume they fired me. I don't know for sure. If I remember correctly, I didn't pick up the phone when they called, and I never went to that McDonald's again.

Take Care of Your Home—and Everyone in It

As a child of the nineties, I watched my mom raise three kids, build a career, keep her house clean, manage the finances, and put dinner on the table every night.

At thirty, I couldn't even keep my car clean. My glove box was full of unpaid parking tickets. My acting career had stalled, and I paid rent by working part-time jobs waiting tables.

I was ashamed of how messy my house was. There were times I got so overwhelmed that my mom would come over and help me clean. *My mom had mobility problems and chronic pain! She carried things to the rooms where they belonged and put them away, did my dishes, and cleaned out my car on crutches.* I was perfectly able-bodied. Why couldn't I do this myself?*

---

*   Yeah, we'll come back to that. See Chapter 4, "How to (Executive) Function," page 73.

Desperate to prove my worth as an adult and a woman, I married my long-term boyfriend. I planned a beautiful wedding, signed up for dance classes, found the perfect ball gown–style wedding dress, and memorized a waltz. The marriage lasted four months.

I saw women my age with dazzling careers, stable relationships, and perfectly manicured nails. Meanwhile, I was broke, divorced, and working in restaurants so my hands were a mess (cutting lemons during the dinner rush because you underestimated how many you'd need for the shift is hard, especially when you're clumsy! But hey, that was my sidework . . . gotta do it, Jess, *don't be lazy . . .*).

WHAT I LEARNED

I knew I wasn't the person I was supposed to be, at least not consistently, and in lieu of other explanations, I accepted and internalized the ones given to me.

I'm "Irresponsible"

"Responsible people follow through," I thought. "They don't bail, procrastinate, or avoid things they are supposed to do." But me? I spent money I didn't have on things I didn't need or couldn't find— and then forgot to pay my bills. I showed up late or unprepared to classes, meetings, and work. I made promises to friends and broke them when I became distracted or overwhelmed.

I don't think anyone ever called me irresponsible to my face, but I heard what people said when others failed in similar ways. It wasn't hard to put two and two together.

I'm "Messy"

Growing up, I had a nickname—"Messy Jessie"—and I earned it. My room generally looked like something had exploded in it. My backpack and desk were constantly disorganized. I spilled things on myself regularly.

Even though I grew out of the nickname, I never grew out of the mess. I dreaded having company over because I didn't want people to see the state of my apartment. When friends asked if I could drive them home, my decision was never based on how far they needed to go or what else I had planned that day. It was based on how much stuff I had in the front seat and whether I could shove it into the back seat quickly enough so I wouldn't leave them standing on the curb for five minutes with nothing to do but watch and judge.

My thoughts, my emotions, and my speech were just as messy. I'd get confused about where I was supposed to meet someone and show up at the wrong time or place. I skipped steps in relationships, like making sure you *like* the person before you start dating them. I overshared with complete strangers and didn't think to mention important stuff to the people I cared about.

I wanted to be the cool, fun friend and girlfriend. I wanted to be put together and witty and succinct, but I had big emotions and too many thoughts, and when I tried to express them, the words would tumble out together, always ending in a slew of apologies. *"I'm sorry I'm such a mess."*

I'm "Careless"

My teachers were the first to point out how "careless" I was. I'd neglect to turn in my homework, miss deadlines, and forget my lunch. My tests came back marked up in red with "careless mistakes" scribbled in the margin. I was the kid who always won second place in the spelling bee but "could have done better" if I'd "actually studied." I would have been able to answer the teacher's question if I'd "bothered to pay attention."

As an adult, small oversights like this had more significant consequences. I interviewed for a corporate job, and it went *well.* The company offered me a salary that was more than I'd ever made in my life. I quickly accepted, and they started clearing out a desk for me. I was going to have a company car! I was going to be a real adult! I was so excited, until I got the call.

The background check they'd run on me showed that I had a suspended license. They couldn't hire me anymore because they couldn't let me drive a company car.

The suspended license was over a broken taillight from months earlier. I'd fixed the taillight, but I'd forgotten to follow up on the ticket—another "careless mistake."

The Echoes of These Beliefs Linger

I still say these negative things to myself sometimes, even though I know better now. These judgments—even once I learned how inaccurate they are, even now that I understand the biology behind the invisible obstacles I kept tripping over and blaming myself for—are long solidified by decades of neural pathways wiring together and firing together.

The day I wrote this section, I was scheduled to moderate an online panel that had taken months of preparation. I'd glanced at my calendar too fast and missed the fact that I was supposed to log on half an hour early. As soon as I realized my mistake, I raced to my office, jumped on the video meeting fifteen minutes late, and breathed a sigh of relief that at least I was there before the event started—only to realize in slow horror that my laptop's battery was at 3 percent and *I forgot my charger.*

I knew how it would look. I knew the assumptions people would make.

"How irresponsible," I imagined them saying, as I dug through my mess of a backpack, fighting back tears, hoping I was wrong, hoping my charger was here somewhere. It was not.

"She must not care."

But I *do* care, and I desperately want to be the person I was supposed to be. I've tried. In fact, I have tried everything suggested to me by well-meaning teachers, doctors, friends, parents, professionals, and strangers on the internet, as well as what I've learned on my own. I've evolved past the largely maladaptive coping strategies I'm listing in this chapter, but I'm including them because this is how many of us go through life when we aren't getting support and don't have strategies that make sense for us. They were my very first set of "tools."

THE "TOOLBOX"

When you boil it down, there were five strategies that I used to use. Constantly. I've compiled them here for your convenience.

1. DENY

Very few people ever knew how much I was struggling because I became a master of pretending everything was fine. Anxiety helped mask my forgetfulness. (*Did I do the thing? Better check. And check again.*) I covered my anxiety with a mask of cheerfulness. (*I'm fine. This is fine.*) I pretended I remembered people's names while wracking my brain for clues. I pretended I'd absolutely started on the project that was due next week. I pretended I'd stuck to my budget and could totally afford to go out to dinner that night. I pretended I didn't have needs, or at least that it was fine that they weren't getting met. I pretended I hadn't forgotten my laptop for class. I just *preferred* to take notes by hand. I pretended I didn't need help.

2. APOLOGIZE

If people had to know I couldn't meet basic expectations, at least I could feel properly bad about it. It got to the point where I regularly apologized for things that weren't even remotely my fault because *I assumed that they were. Because they always were.* I apologized for whatever it was they were upset about, and I accepted the moral judgments that came with it. After all, I wasn't "supposed to" be struggling to this extent, certainly not at the age I was at the time. I knew better. It must be my fault.

3. BEG

I begged. For forgiveness, for a loan, for another chance, for an extension on a deadline. To be let out of a ticket, for my boss not to fire me, to not be judged for the state of my house or car. For help, even, once it was finally clear that I needed it. For a chance to "make up for it," to "do better next time."

4. TRY TO DO BETTER NEXT TIME

If I couldn't meet expectations, I could try to exceed them. I could overgive, overwork, overplan. Forgot to buy someone a $30 birthday gift? Fix it with a $100 gift card. Got to work fifteen minutes late? How about I stay two hours late. I pulled all-nighters just so I didn't have to let someone down again. I made lists—and lists to help me keep track of those lists. I started getting ready to go somewhere hours in advance just so I'd have some hope of arriving on time. I thought through everything that could go wrong and tried to plan for all of those scenarios. Inevitably, I still missed something.

5. TRY HARDER

I never forgot the line I saw on so many report cards right after "so much potential": "needs to try harder." So when I wasn't reaching my potential, that's what I did. I tried harder. But as life got more complicated, and there was more to do than just homework, the belief that I wasn't trying hard enough morphed into a more insidious belief.

I'm "Not Doing Enough"

I constantly felt like I was supposed to be doing *more*. My meds allowed me to do that. At fifteen, I was going to high school, taking courses on writing children's books, attending swim team practices, working at the local fast-food joint, and dating a string of boyfriends, all while trying to be a professional actress. I pushed the limits of what my brain and body could handle, even with the meds.

As an adult, I kept the same pace. There was always more I could be doing . . . for my career, for my parents, for my partners, for my friends, for my financial health, for my physical appearance, and for my future. I pushed myself to get that second (or third) job, finish that extra workout, take that class, and show up for whoever needed me. I tried self-help books, seminars, and every organizational strategy anyone ever suggested. Whenever anyone needed something from me, my needs went out the window. When I failed to do the things I set out to do, I chastised myself: "Stop being lazy. You're flaky. You give up too easily."

After watching me struggle ineffec-tively with some task, one of my friends asked me, "Have you ever asked yourself if there's an easier way to do this?"

> "I'm just used to things being hard."

I looked at him. "No. I'm just used to things being hard."

The more I tried to meet everyone's expectations, the less I seemed to be able to. I tried harder and moved faster, until my efforts were frantic. I would memorize lines while driving and doing my makeup. I ate while I worked. I sent my boyfriend a text after another fight while I was supposed to be hanging out with friends, or I canceled on them at the last minute to pick up an extra shift at work. The only time I ever stopped was when I physically couldn't keep going and passed out from exhaustion.

Eventually, I burned out.

THE ONE THING I HADN'T TRIED

At thirty-two years old, I was broke, divorced, and living with my mom. My credit was terrible. I couldn't remember the last time I'd actually spent time with my friends, and I wasn't entirely sure they even liked me.

It was as if my brain had gone on strike. I was exhausted. I was disillusioned. I didn't care anymore. I didn't know how to keep going.

I didn't know how to do better, make everyone happy, or lose those ten pounds. I just knew what I was doing wasn't working.

I was ready to accept that I couldn't be this person everyone wanted me to be. I was no longer someone who had so much potential. I was quickly becoming someone who hadn't reached it.

I was trying so hard to force myself to fit the stencil cutout of who others expected me to be that I never got to know the person I *was*. I thought I was working to "meet my potential" and "be my best self," but what I was actually doing was trying my hardest to *be someone I'm not*.

The first person to challenge me on the belief that I had to change to be successful wasn't a therapist, or a doctor, or my mom. It was Alison Robertson, a life coach for actors.

At this point, I had been struggling to get traction as an actress for over a decade.

I went to one of her acting workshops, where she explained her role as a life coach and let us ask her questions.

I raised my hand. "How do I lose ten pounds?"

She smiled at me. "Why? You don't need to lose ten pounds."

I shook my head. "You don't understand. Yes, I do. If I want to be a successful actress, I need to lose ten pounds. How do I do it?"

What I was really asking, in retrospect, was, "How do I meet these expectations my agent and manager have of me? How do I be the person everyone is telling me I'm supposed to be?"

She responded, "You don't need to be smaller. You need to be bigger." I was confused. "You think you need to be small, so you're making yourself small. And maybe it made sense ten years ago, when you were trying to play a teenager, but you're a woman now. You're allowed to take up space."

> "We don't know where you need to put your effort yet."

This answer annoyed me.

I was *sure* she was wrong.

But the more I thought about it, the more I realized that she was the first person to tell me I didn't have to keep struggling to accomplish something that I couldn't achieve despite my best efforts. I decided I needed to hear more of what she had to say, even if I could only afford a couple of sessions.

I showed up to my first session with my grocery money in hand and asked, "So, what do I need to do?"

"Nothing," she said.

"What do you mean *nothing*?"

Alison told me to stop doing everything. Stop taking acting classes, stop going to auditions, stop trying to lose weight, stop reading self-help books, stop responding to other people's demands and crises, stop trying to make up for lost time in my career, my friendships, my relationships.

"We don't know where you need to put your effort yet."

After a lifetime of trying harder, it felt terrifying and wrong to just *stop trying at all*. But I had tried everything else.

So, as behind on life as I believed I was, as much as it felt like *I didn't have time* to stop, I stopped. No auditions. No calling my manager. No diets. No making up for my past failures with family and friends.

And it worked.

In the space of a month that *felt* like a lifetime, I realized where I needed to be putting in my effort.

It wasn't trying to do *all the things* I was convinced I needed to do to be successful. I finally saw that it wouldn't work. If it could have, it would have. I'd been doing it for so long, and all I'd gotten out of it was levels of exhaustion. Instead, I realized, I needed to put my effort into figuring out *why it wasn't working* when everyone around me kept telling me that it should.

I went back to Alison with an idea. "I need to put my effort into figuring out what's getting in my way, and what to do about it." She agreed.

"I was diagnosed with ADD as a kid, so maybe there's something to that? Every once in a while, I've come across a strategy that helped, for a bit, until I stopped using it and then couldn't find it again when I wanted to. Maybe I can figure out what I'm struggling with, find strategies that can help, and put them somewhere I can actually find them again."

"Like, a notebook?"

I shook my head. I lost notebooks. I lost *everything*.

"YouTube."

I knew I wouldn't lose YouTube.

Alison's advice worked so well for me, I've included a permission slip in the back of this book (page 416) for you to do the same. Whenever the efforts you're putting in aren't working, you have permission to just, for a little while, *stop*.

Chapter 2

How to ~~ADD~~ ADHD

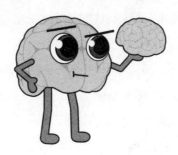

We know what we are, but know not what we may be.

—OPHELIA, FROM *HAMLET*,

BY WILLIAM SHAKESPEARE

I DON'T HAVE ADD

The first thing that happened when I started my YouTube channel, which I was planning to name "How to ADD," was learning I do not, in fact, have ADD.

What? It's all called ADHD now?!

I thought about the stereotype of someone with ADHD—a Bart Simpson–type boy bouncing off the walls—and compared it to my staring-out-the-window, daydreamy self. Saying I had attention deficit *hyperactivity* disorder felt . . . weird.

I soon learned that there was an "inattentive presentation" of ADHD. I learned that hyperactivity can show up differently based on biological sex. I learned it can look like tearing voraciously through a book series, or interrupting in class, or SpeakingReallyQu icklywithNoSpacesBetweenYourWords!

I also discovered you could qualify for both the inattentive and hyperactive presentations of ADHD. It was called "combined type."

Huh.

At my next doctor's appointment, I asked which presentation I had. He glanced at his copy of the *DSM* (*The Diagnostic and Statistical Manual of Mental Disorders*).

"See how your leg is fidgeting? Yeah, you have ADHD combined type." He checked his watch and wrote a prescription. "See you next month?"

Thanks, Doc.

I turned back to Google.

Executive function? What's that? Working memory? Define, please! Motivation deficit? Oh, man.

Maybe everything I dealt with wasn't all in my head. Or more accurately—I wasn't imagining it. The struggle was *real*. (I mean, it technically was in my head because that's where your brain is.)

I had no idea that all of the showing up late, difficulty staying organized, "irresponsible" spending, and feeling like a hot mess were related to the condition I'd been diagnosed with twenty years ago.

> I had been seeing a doctor every one to three months for two decades and none of them had told me *any* of this.

I knew I struggled to focus, which is why I took meds, but as I read about the executive function challenges (which I didn't know I had) associated with ADHD (which I also didn't know I had), I wondered how it was possible that I had been seeing a doctor every one to three months for two decades and none of them had told me *any* of this.

> It was like reading error codes on a printer *and actually knowing what the error codes meant!*

I felt relieved, angry, delighted, sad, *vindicated.* There *was* more to having ADHD than I'd thought. I found article after article sharing strategies and explaining why we needed them. You might think learning about your brain's impairments would be depressing, but for me, this information gave me hope. If these were real impairments, there must be real solutions, too.

In my earliest videos, I explored one aspect of ADHD every week: I researched and explained one ADHD-related challenge, and I presented one possible strategy that could help.

Gaining this knowledge about my brain—from ADHD experts and researchers—empowered me in a way I'd never experienced before. I learned about the specific deficits involved, which meant I could now "see" the invisible obstacles I kept tripping over, label them, and understand how to navigate them. It was like reading error codes on a printer *and actually knowing what the error codes meant*! If I knew it was out of paper, I could refill the empty tray—which was *way* more useful than banging on the printer. It *definitely* worked better than "trying harder."

I found joy and validation in what I learned, but also grief. How much suffering could I have avoided if I had known this information?

How many failed relationships? Could I have finished college? Could I have saved all the money I spent on purchasing self-help books that never seemed to help?* Could I have been a better daughter?

Sometimes, I sat reading research papers with tears streaming down my cheeks, mourning my past self. That little girl who thought she was doing everything wrong had no *idea* what obstacles she faced. She spent her whole young life blaming herself for struggles that, according to researchers and ADHD experts, were *totally normal* for those with ADHD.

But my grief was overshadowed by my passion—my fierce determination to tell everyone what I had learned. Needless suffering is my least favorite thing in the world. But I could live with my regrets if I could give meaning to my pain—if I could use my experience to help others not have to go through what I went through.

I talked about the channel to my tables at the restaurant where I worked. I gave them fidgets and glitter bottles and asked them to subscribe.

I learned about website promotion and started hosting giveaways of sticky notes and fidget toys to encourage people to watch the videos, to get more people the information they needed. The information I'd needed, anyway. The information I hadn't even known I needed because I thought I understood my condition.

I wasn't just *learning* about ADHD. I was also *unlearning* all the assumptions and misunderstandings that I had accumulated in the

---

* Yes, I realize the irony of writing one of these books myself, but this one takes into account my ADHD!

years since my diagnosis. As excited (and shocked and sometimes saddened) as I was by what I discovered, the viewers in the comments were just as enthused—and confused. "How come I never knew this?" "Why did nobody tell me this about my ADHD?" Or even, "*Wait . . . do *I* have* ADHD?"

How could a condition that is so well known be so poorly understood? Why were so many of us still struggling so much, even after years or decades of diagnosis and treatment? And why were so many people learning about their medical condition for the first time from some college dropout on YouTube?

WHAT I LEARNED

ADHD is incredibly misunderstood, both by those who have it and by many professionals who treat it.

Why? Research and publishing peer-reviewed papers takes time, and it takes even longer for new information to trickle down to those who need it. This means a lot of what we *think* we know about ADHD (and what our doctors know) is already outdated.

Many people also think ADHD is less serious than other mental health conditions, so much so that even health professionals frequently aren't taught much about it. After all, its symptoms describe tendencies that everyone experiences sometimes. Comedic media portrayals of ADHD, comments like "Isn't everyone a little ADHD?," and dismissive friends and/or relatives (who may have undiagnosed ADHD themselves because it runs in families) reinforce the notion that ADHD is nothing more than a funny quirk. *"Ooo, look, butterfly."*

Plus, misinformation is everywhere. Inaccurate information about ADHD spreads on social media and by word of mouth—and often more quickly than accurate information. People tend to gravitate toward simple answers, and . . . well, the truth is usually annoyingly complicated.

Even though the truth is often complicated, it's infinitely more helpful to have an accurate understanding of your own (or a loved one's) mental health condition. Let's start our updated understanding by correcting some common misconceptions about ADHD.

ADHD DOESN'T INVOLVE AN ATTENTION DEFICIT

ADHD is a terrible name for the condition, because "attention deficit" implies a lack of attention. However, our brains can focus quite well sometimes—particularly on things we find engaging, such as our hobbies, crushes, video games, and so on. The trouble is, we can't control the intensity of our focus or what we focus on. (We'll learn more about this in Chapter 3, page 47.) This big misconception makes people less likely to seek a diagnosis because they are able to focus . . . sometimes.

YOU DON'T HAVE TO LOOK HYPERACTIVE TO HAVE ADHD

Many people believe if you don't look hyperactive, you must not have ADHD. This leads to missed diagnoses and leaves those who were originally diagnosed with ADD (hi!) confused about how they could possibly have ADHyperactivityD.

There are three presentations of ADHD:

- Primarily inattentive (ADHD-PI)
- Primarily hyperactive/impulsive (ADHD-HI)
- Combined type (ADHD-C)

Most people with ADHD are combined type—which means they have enough symptoms of the inattentive presentation and the hyperactive/impulsive presentation that they qualify for both.

For the primarily inattentive presentation of ADHD, however, you don't need to have *any* symptoms of hyperactivity to qualify for the diagnosis (because, turns out, same condition, different presentations). Also, even those who do have symptoms related to hyperactivity and impulsivity aren't always *physically* hyperactive. Verbal hyperactivity is a thing, and it's one way hyperactivity in girls and women tends to show up. (I get a lot of comments about how quickly I speak.) Physical hyperactivity also often evolves into *mental* restlessness. Plus, presentations can change over time.

In short, ADHD *can* look like a kid bouncing off the walls. It can also look like a full-grown adult unable to sleep because of racing thoughts or a child staring dreamily out a window.

ADHD IS A NEUROLOGICAL ISSUE—
NOT BEHAVIORAL

While ADHD used to be considered a behavioral condition (and it can sure look that way!), it's now understood that the behavioral issues related to ADHD exist for neurological reasons.

ADHD is a neurodevelopmental disorder, which means the nervous system, including the brain, develops and functions differently.

Fundamental differences in brain development and structure contribute to differences in behavior. This is why behavior strategies that work for neurotypical people are frequently unsuccessful for ADHDers. Our behaviors happen for *different reasons*.

In fact, research shows that—compared to neurotypical children—punishment is *less* effective for ADHD kids, while immediate positive feedback and salient rewards are *more* effective.* Unlike punishment, rewards can address the motivational deficits inherent to ADHD (see "How to Motivate Your Brain," page 156, to learn more).

ADHD HAS A SERIOUS IMPACT

While individual ADHD symptoms might not seem like "that big of a deal," the *extent* and *consistency* with which those with ADHD struggle *are* a big deal.

---

* This is one of the reasons it can be so frustrating for parents of ADHD children to be judged by strangers when their kids misbehave. It might *look* as though they need discipline—what they actually need is *support*.

ADHD affects multiple aspects of our lives on a daily and even moment-by-moment basis. While there's much I personally value about my ADHD brain, life outcomes on average are worse for those with ADHD, especially if it's untreated. Those with ADHD are more likely to get divorced, be fired, and get into car accidents.

Research by psychologist Dr. Russell Barkley, a prominent ADHD researcher, demonstrates that ADHD has a significantly negative impact on life expectancy—by *12.7 years, on average.* ADHD makes our lives harder—and shorter. And when combined with the effects of gender, race, socioeconomic status, and coexisting mental health conditions, many of which are also more common with ADHD, the outcomes can be even more dire (see Chapter 11, "How to Make ADHD Harder," page 282).

These factors and the interplay among them make ADHD a lot more serious than people think—and definitely more serious than just being a cute quirk.

THERE IS NO "ONE" SOLUTION

Every time I went to my doctors, they asked if my stimulant medication was working for me (it was) and if I was having any negative side effects (I was not). They'd give me another prescription and send me on my way. ADHD treated! Except that it wasn't. Not entirely.

In the words of one of our team members, also named Jessica, "There's no magical rainbow unicorn tool that will solve all of your ADHD woes."

According to research, the optimal treatment for ADHD is multimodal and involves more than one type of treatment option.

In fact, the National Institute of Mental Health conducted an enormous study about ADHD treatment (and gave it an equally enormous name)—the Multimodal Treatment of Attention Deficit Hyperactivity Disorder Study, or MTA Study for short. The MTA Study found that medication alone was not enough to effectively treat ADHD, and the most successful treatments combined therapy *and* medication.

While the MTA Study only looked at two treatment options, there are many ways to effectively treat ADHD. A multimodal approach can include some of the following:

- **Medication**
  Stimulant medication is the most common treatment for ADHD, although there are non-stimulant options available as well. Every brain is different, so it can take some trial and error to find the right medication and dose. However, medication is typically highly effective for ADHD and offers the greatest immediate improvement in ADHD symptoms out of all the available treatment options. The effects are temporary, wearing off when the meds do, but for many, the difference they make in our focus, productivity, and even emotion regulation can be profound.

- **Psychoeducation**
  Psychoeducation means providing information and education that helps someone understand and cope with their

mental health condition. While not specific to ADHD, research across multiple diagnoses shows there are significant benefits of psychoeducation—not just for individual client outcomes, but for family members as well. It also improves self-awareness, which is helpful for those of us who struggle with that. Turns out, it helps to understand the brain you're working with. Who knew?

- **Skills training**

  Skills training can focus on many things (e.g., social skills, parenting skills, life skills, and organizational skills) and can benefit both the person with ADHD and their caregivers. For parents of children with ADHD, parent management training (PMT) can help them learn how to parent in a way that accounts for and supports their child's ADHD challenges. For adults, skills training can also focus on things like ADHD-informed training in career development, personal finance, communication, goal-setting, and prioritization.

- **Therapy**

  Several types of psychotherapy have been proven highly effective for ADHD, including cognitive behavioral therapy (CBT), dialectical behavioral therapy (DBT), and acceptance and commitment therapy (ACT). All of these can help us untangle our unhelpful thought patterns and adjust behaviors that worsen our functional impairments and make our emotions more difficult to manage. Therapy is most successful when you develop a good therapeutic relationship with your therapist, meaning you trust them to help you toward your goals.*

- **Coaching**

  An ADHD coach is someone who offers accountability, guidance, insights, and practical strategies that help minimize the functional impairments related to ADHD. They can be an incredibly helpful resource for setting and achieving goals. Often, ADHD coaches have ADHD themselves and work exclusively with ADHD clients, which means they have a wealth of personal experience and knowledge specific to ADHD.

- **Support**

  Having ADHD is *hard.* One of the most important factors for successfully managing it is having support from family, friends, work or school, and our peers. Connecting with other ADHDers can be particularly helpful, because it can normalize the struggles of having a brain that works differently from the vast majority of the world. I'll talk more about how to develop a support network in "How to

---

* This is easier to do when our therapists have a solid understanding of ADHD and other important factors in our experience, because they're more likely to understand our struggles and offer guidance that works for us.

People," page 248. "How to Heart," page 323, covers how to offer support to someone you care about—even if that person is you.

Unfortunately, there are barriers that often make one or more of these options inaccessible. Thankfully, many professionals offer free resources (some of which are listed on page 429), and I started to learn about my ADHD by digging through them.

A *LOT* OF PEOPLE STRUGGLE WITH ADHD

Because I didn't know anyone with ADHD outside my own family, I *assumed* everyone around me was neurotypical. (I have since learned not to assume.)

The more I learned, the more I shared on my channel. The more I shared on my channel, the more I realized I wasn't alone.

People from all over the world started commenting and openly sharing their ADHD struggles after hearing me talking openly about mine. For the first time, I didn't need to explain why I had trouble doing something to someone who looked at me as if I were defective or weird. There were so many others who were nodding along and saying "me too!"

Not only was ADHD a lot more common than I realized—the struggle was *real*, and not just for me.

If this condition is this common,* where had everybody been hiding? How did the struggles of so many people go unnoticed and unspoken—and why?

There's a Ton of Stigma Around ADHD

Many ADHDers don't feel comfortable disclosing their diagnosis because of the stigma (misunderstandings and misconceptions) around it. While it is illegal, discrimination—from employers, by professors, even medical professionals—does happen. Some people don't even realize they have ADHD; many parents either don't get their kids evaluated or don't tell their kids about their diagnosis, because they are afraid of what will happen if they have a "label." (More on that in "How to Make ADHD Harder," page 282.)

There is also serious stigma regarding the medications used to treat ADHD, which leads to prejudice and discrimination against those who take them. Those with ADHD sometimes feel the need to hide the fact that they take them, even from those closest to them. Parents of children with ADHD are accused online, in person, and even by healthcare providers of "drugging" their children into compliance. When I shared a heartfelt letter to my mom on an episode, thanking her for "drugging" me, it wasn't long before I saw a picture of myself on the internet with the word "EVIL" written across my forehead.

---

* Depending on the study, between 3 and 8 percent of the population has ADHD.

We're Held to the Same Expectations as Our Neurotypical Peers (and We're Punished for Not Meeting Them)

Regardless of our level of impairment and whether we're receiving treatment and/or accommodations, ADHDers are often expected to meet the same standards as our neurotypical peers—and punished when we don't.

So we learn to mask our ADHD behaviors and do what's expected of us—be quiet, sit still, *pay attention*—when we're in public. We pay the price later—melt down, feel exhausted, stare blankly at a wall, or scroll through social media for hours just trying to recharge.

Even when others are aware of our diagnosis, we're often taught how to hide our struggles rather than effectively cope with them.

We might suppress our too-big emotions by overeating.

We may force ourselves to sit still, even though the effort means we can't focus on the lesson.

We clean our house in a whirlwind of panic when someone is coming over, often at the expense of being able to find our stuff again when they leave. (Why did I put the good frying pan under the bed?)

We pull all-nighters trying to get projects done on time, then sleep through the class where we were supposed to turn them in.

We often develop anxiety, depression, or both. Many of us self-medicate using alcohol or other drugs. And these conditions, too, can mask the ADHD.

No One—Including Us—Realizes How Much Harder We're Struggling

A lot of our individual symptoms are something "everyone struggles with sometimes," so we think what we're struggling with is normal.

Likewise, others may not realize the extent to which we're struggling, because the behaviors they can see are only the tip of the iceberg. We're trying so hard to meet neurotypical expectations, it might seem we're doing okay—even when we're not. The soul-crushing effort it took for us to *meet* those expectations isn't obvious.

When I was in college, what people saw was a self-sufficient student who made the Dean's Honor Roll, worked on campus, and had a boyfriend.

What no one saw was that I was eating lemon cookies for lunch every day, signing up for classes that weren't going to help me graduate, and choosing my boyfriends based on who could help me with my math homework.

I learned later that others in my life had similar tip-of-the-iceberg experiences. People who impressed me with their accomplishments, who seemed to have their lives together in ways I *definitely* didn't, revealed to me years later: "Hey, guess what! I have ADHD!" and poured out the litany of struggles beneath the surface.

Someone with ADHD can be *highly* successful. I've spoken to ADHD entertainers, doctors, and CEOs. But it's critical to understand that success doesn't mean they don't have ADHD, or that it isn't impairing. We *can* accomplish great things—but without appropriate support, it tends to come at great expense in other areas of our life, or at the expense of ourselves.

For those with access to all the supports they need, ADHD can feel like a superpower. They can lean into their creativity and hyper-focus without worrying about drowning in the sea of life.

For those without enough supports, ADHD can be a nightmare. They constantly need to defend themselves against criticism and shame from their families and friends. They burn out at work and struggle through tasks that everyone tells them "should" be easy. They take longer to succeed, and it comes at a much greater cost.

 Shawn T., 39, California

"I've assumed I had ADHD for the past twenty years but didn't realize a diagnosis would make a difference until I discovered Jessica's channel and started learning. I got diagnosed two months ago and am now trying out medication. This diagnosis has been very powerful for me already because I now have such a wealth of knowledge about the nature of my struggles in life. The solidarity of other ADHDers has probably been an even bigger help than meds (but don't take my meds, they help too!)."

Daniel C., 36, Kansas

"I was diagnosed with ADHD as an adult. I am a college professor. I had a month to prepare for a challenging class. Instead, I binged an entire season of a Netflix show in a single day sitting at my desk. I decided I was depressed and reached out to a therapist.

"She almost immediately asked if I had ever wondered if I had ADHD. I looked back on my life and started remembering things, like how I locked my keys in my car eight times the first year I had a car. I remembered how the only time I ever got detention was when I forgot to get my straight-A report card signed.

"My therapist went through the diagnostic criteria with me. I went to my primary care doctor, and he agreed with my therapist's assessment. The diagnosis was such a relief."

Brody S., 26, Pennsylvania

"It's really hard to explain to others when I'm having an ADHD struggle, because I don't want to sound like a broken record, where my whole personality starts to become 'Hi, I have ADHD. Did you know I have ADHD?' I also don't want to sound like I'm making excuses. It took me a year of knowing I have ADHD to actually figure out what that means. Being fully open about it is difficult when I know others won't understand the experience of living with a brain that behaves the way mine does. That said, I try to be open about it while taking responsibility for the impact it has on those around me. It's still just difficult."

Jill C., 32, Virginia

"I was diagnosed with ADHD when I was seven but didn't actually know that it was a medical disorder until I was fourteen (I think I saw it as a kind of personality trait). I thought that it was normal to spend hours and hours on homework every night. I thought it was normal for everything to be hard, for your teachers to be constantly frustrated with you, and to feel like you were in the way of everyone else's progress because you couldn't do anything right.

"I'm not the stereotypical picture of ADHD. I'm pretty neat and organized on the outside, but inside my head is a mess. As an adult, sifting through the mental clutter to find what I need takes a lot of time and effort.

"I realized recently that my whole life has been watching people get frustrated with me for not moving fast enough or not understanding something fast enough, and that is probably not going to change. I have been able to make my life much more pleasant by expecting this reaction, not hating them for it, and not hating myself for it."

THE TOOLBOX

It now made sense why my old approach to ADHD didn't work terribly well for me. Trying harder didn't account for how hard I was already trying. It also didn't account for the fact that *I have ADHD,* which affects many aspects of my life and much more significantly than I'd realized. Now that I understand this, I take a much different approach to my struggles—and it's what I recommend for anyone with ADHD.

1. TAKE ADHD SERIOUSLY

It's easy to dismiss unseen disabilities, but ADHD can be incredibly disabling. If it's not clear by now, our invisible obstacles can keep us from reaching our goals, even when we try our hardest.

Even "mild"* ADHD significantly impacts multiple aspects of our lives. (If it didn't, it wouldn't qualify for a diagnosis.)

Reassurances of how great it is to have ADHD or pretending the struggles we face don't exist might feel good in the moment. However, our impairments exist whether we acknowledge them or not. Just like the assignments we're avoiding. Our sense of self and sense of empowerment ends up being much stronger if we are able to accept and understand ourselves as we are, not as we feel we should be. Some people think that acknowledging your impairments means placing limits on yourself. I've found quite the opposite is true. Learning to recognize them and figuring out how to navigate them has made me more functional, not less.

Taking ADHD seriously starts with recognition. The only way we

---

* This is an example of clinical language not meaning the same thing as everyday language, even when the same word is used. Imagine a "struggle scale" from 1 to 10, and typical struggles are 1 to 7. Diagnoses would be 8 to 10, and a "mild" diagnosis would be an 8, which is already a big deal!

can recognize and work with our challenges is by being honest about them, whether or not we think they're a "big enough deal." None of the treatments, strategies, accommodations, or environmental changes I lay out in this book will be as useful if we deny the extent of our challenges and don't think we "really need" help.

2. CONNECT WITH OTHERS

As much as reading the research helped me understand my impairments and take them seriously, being around others with ADHD helped normalize them.

Something magical happened when we swapped stories about the struggles we felt ashamed of and the times we needed supports that others thought were childish. (Sticker charts work for adults, too!)

The stencil of who we were "supposed to be" fell away, and what was left was who we *were:* curious, passionate, divergent thinkers, struggling to exist in a world not built for us.

In myself, I only saw deficits. I didn't see the ways in which my ADHD traits could be valuable. In others, I *could.* They were funny. Caring. *Fascinating.* Generous. Creative. Silly. Passionate. Ambitious. And they *were like me.*

Because I liked *them* so much, I finally started to like *me.* Maybe I had value, too, despite my struggles.

Spending time with people whose brains work the way yours does is an incredible experience. The shame begins to fall away, and we begin to see ourselves through one another's eyes—as the funny or talented or curious or ambitious humans we are, with struggles that are perfectly normal—because while they might not make sense to those who are neurotypical, they *are* normal when you have ADHD.

3. WORK WITH YOUR BRAIN, NOT AGAINST IT

Whenever you experience that gear-grinding feeling that tells you something isn't working, don't try harder. Try different.

Trying different starts by learning how to work with your brain. Those of us with ADHD often work far better and faster when we're not forcing ourselves to do things the "right" (read: neurotypical) way. When our brains are engaged, our performance can be exceptional. It can be worthwhile to spend a little extra time figuring out how to do something in a way that works for your brain—even if it seems unconventional.

Here's what working with my brain looks like for me:

- Focusing on what *does* work for me rather than what "should."

- Building a toolbox of strategies I can use for tasks with which I struggle.

- Doing my most challenging work at times when my brain works best.

- When possible, choosing ADHD-friendly products and services.

- Asking for the tools/accommodations I need—or providing them myself.

- Approaching tasks as a negotiation. What do I need to get The Thing done? What does my brain need for that to be able to happen?

KEEP GOING

I failed so often, at so much, and so consistently throughout my life that I was riddled with self-doubt while I was building my channel. There was a near-constant voice in the back of my head telling me, "You can't do this. You'll fail. You're just going to give up someday, just like you always do."

When I was just starting out—and still hustling as a server—it was really hard *not* to give up. Because I was running into obstacles constantly.

Some weeks, I'd fall behind and need to skip shifts at work to catch up.

Sometimes I wouldn't notice the battery in my camera had died. Because I had to go to work, I couldn't reshoot the video until midnight, sometimes one or two a.m.

Once, I couldn't get myself to write a script for weeks because the research on the topic was so painful.

Another time, I was trying to steam my new backdrop from underneath and the lid from the steamer came off, pouring scalding hot water onto my face. I ended up in the ER with face burns on the day I was supposed to shoot.

A litany of things went wrong, but I fought through all of it, partly because I cared so deeply about what I was doing and partly because I wanted to prove that voice wrong.

But one week, I couldn't argue with it anymore. I hadn't written an episode by the time it was supposed to have been shot *and* edited. I wasn't just failing; I had *failed*. I posted a tweet formally communicating this failure, explaining to my community: "Maybe that voice was right. Maybe I can't do this."

I waited for my community to agree with me and release me from the promise I'd made to help them. I expected them to tell me it was okay to go do something else now. Maybe they would berate me, which I figured I deserved.

Instead, I got encouragement.

"What? No. You're doing great. Keep going."

Keep going.

. . . I didn't know that was an option.

It sounds ridiculous, but living with ADHD and grappling with its challenges left me believing that you could only fail so many times before it was game over. Before I'd run out of time, out of understanding. Before I'd get fired or someone would stop being my friend. Before I'd hit my limit of disappointing

> I expected them to tell me it was okay to do something else now.

people. Before I'd hit my limit of disappointing myself. Before I could give up.
Once you've *failed* failed, you had to move
on and try something else. That's how it
went, right?

> What I got was
> permission to
> keep going.

I had been given permission to stop. Now, I expected permission
to quit.

What I got was permission to keep going.

My community's encouragement inspired me to make a video
about how success isn't about avoiding failure—it's about continuing
despite it.

Does that mean you should always keep trying to do something
you keep failing at?

No, sometimes we fail because something isn't a great fit for us.
And continuing to bang your head against the wall won't get you
anywhere or anything. Except a headache.

But if something is important to you, you *can* keep going—even
if you fail. Failing doesn't make you a failure. It isn't the opposite of
succeeding, as I'd feared. It's something that happens—and *will*
happen—all along the way.

What allows us to keep going when the failures pile up is the encouragement of others. It's like the quarters you use to keep playing
an arcade game after you run out of lives.

Sometimes, someone says something
so perfect, so powerful, that it's like a
magical quarter—one you can use again
and again.

> Failing doesn't
> make you a
> failure.

I've failed hard, utterly and undeniably, a few times since that day. Every time shame and despair almost derailed me, I used that magical quarter, given to me by someone in my community telling me I was doing great. "*Keep going.*"

If anyone thinks they're unimportant, or that it doesn't make a difference to offer encouragement to someone they believe in—know that this book you're holding wouldn't exist if it weren't for someone who did.

I hope this book leaves you with pockets full of quarters.

For now, I'll lend you mine.

You're doing great. *Keep going.*

Chapter 3

How to (Hyper)focus

I can't blame modern technology for
my predilection for distraction, not after all the hours I've spent
watching lost balloons disappear into the clouds.

—COLSON WHITEHEAD

FOCUS

"Jessica. *Focus.*"

People have told me to focus, to pay attention, as if it is a choice I can make or an action I can take. Something I should be able to just do.

But focus, for me, wasn't a verb. It was a noun. Not something I could *do* so much as an elusive, unreliable creature I attempted to *capture* over and over again. It felt as if I were on a relentless quest for some mythical animal—one that was magically bound to me but also had a penchant for mischief and liked to play hide-and-go-seek. The Focus Beast.

More often than not, I didn't have enough focus (*noun*) to be able to focus (*verb*). At least, not on whatever task I was trying to accomplish at the time. When I managed to find it, I learned quickly to take advantage of it.

As a kid, I would *try* to pay attention to my teachers in class. I loved to learn, but it was never long before the words and dates would blend together. I can still recall the terror of being called on when I knew I wasn't focused, the teacher knew I wasn't focused, and the entire class was about to find out. The shame that followed.

"I'm sorry. I got distracted."

When I was told to focus, what I actually heard was that I should stop hunting for my focus and pretend I'd found it. Like the riders in *Monty Python and the Holy Grail,* I would perform all the gestures one does when riding a Focus Beast, without actually having one to ride.

It felt ridiculous, but at least pretending to focus was doable to a certain extent. I could sit relatively still by digging my fingernails into my palm. I could stare at my book. In reality, I was about as focused as a potato, but hey, it kept me from getting called on in class. It kept teachers happy. It kept me from getting yelled at.

When I'm focused or starting to find my focus, I often don't look as if I'm doing

> But focus, for me, wasn't a verb. It was a noun. Not something I could *do* so much as an elusive, unreliable creature I attempted to *capture* over and over again.

it at all. I'm probably eating something or playing with my hair. I might be listening to music, swaying, or rocking. Or my eyes are closed. Maybe I'm texting my friend because I can't wait to share what I just learned. If I'm in class, I might be raising my hand every five seconds to ask a ques-

> When I'm focused or starting to find my focus, I often don't look as if I'm doing it at all.

tion, or picking up my phone to google what I just learned.

In stories, you can capture and tame a magical creature by casting a spell. I tried to make my own magic, experimenting with different ingredients and incantations. Occasionally, if I happen on the right combination and no one interrupts my spellcasting, my focus appears. I can tune out all the other things pulling on my attention—the clock ticking, the squeaky chair, the tags in my clothing—and ride my focus long enough to get where I need to go.

Unfortunately, casting the spell involves some weird ingredients, and they seem to change every time. One time, I cast a focus spell by doing my work while eating animal crackers, in a kigurumi, on a swing set. The next time, though, the swing set hurt my hands, the kigurumi was too hot, and the animal crackers reminded me that I'd been wanting to go to the zoo. (And hey, where even is the nearest zoo? I should look it up!) Like so many junior wizards, my spells sometimes backfired on me.

Other times, I wasn't the one charming the beast—it was casting its spell on me. I'd sit down only to find myself hours later, pretzeled up in my chair, having missed lunch but having planned an entire wedding (despite the fact that I was not, in fact, engaged). My laptop

would be almost dead, sticky notes everywhere; I'd gotten seventeen text messages,
and I hadn't heard any of them ding. If I
ran out of steam and came out of this state
naturally, if I had the chance to ride hard
and slow down, it was an incredible experience. If, on the other hand, I rode right

> Other times, I
> wasn't the one
> charming the
> beast—it was
> casting its spell
> on me.

past the time I was supposed to leave for work or meet the friend I
was supposed to have lunch with, it would get me into trouble. Ironically, not only did I have to learn to hunt down focus, I also had to
learn to rein it in so I wouldn't crash into things.

After I was diagnosed with attention deficit disorder and given
stimulant medication, it was like someone handed me a potion.
"Makes focus appear. Duration: four to six hours."

Something that would give me focus, even on things that were
boring? It was magical.

Finally, I wasn't burning all my energy hunting down focus, or
running out of spell slots (or animal crackers) trying to summon it.
I now *had* focus, and I could spend my energy on *using* it.

Meds weren't a perfect solution. I still had to be careful about
what I was doing once my focus potion kicked in. Once, it kicked in
while I was in the bathtub scrolling through social media, and I
didn't get out of that bathtub for four hours.

Sometimes I couldn't afford my meds because I didn't have insurance, or my new insurance didn't cover them. Occasionally, the
pharmacy didn't have them in stock, or I'd get to the pharmacy but
couldn't pick them up because they are a controlled substance and I'd

forgotten my ID. (Have I mentioned I have ADHD?) I might forget to make an appointment to get a new prescription (again, controlled substance, you can't just refill it). There were times I couldn't find a provider willing to prescribe ADHD meds *at all*.

When I didn't have my meds, everything seemed even foggier than before. Having a focus potion didn't make me any better at focus-casting, and it made me fall out of practice. I'd gotten so used to having focus when I needed it, it felt even more frustrating and discouraging to have to search for it again.

I was grateful to have found a "potion" that worked for me and one that I had access to most of the time. But I didn't like feeling so powerless without it. Trouble with focus was an ongoing, lifelong battle I was incredibly tired of fighting. So when I started digging into ADHD research, my first focus was on focus.

WHAT I LEARNED

For twenty years, I thought I had a deficit of attention. I mean, it's in the name of my diagnosis: attention deficit disorder. Brains need a full tank of attention to work properly, so I must be a few quarts low. Right?

Wrong. The reality is, we have plenty of attention. What we lack is the ability to regulate our attention. You know how lizards can't internally regulate their body temperature? ADHD brains have difficulty regulating their focus (and emotions, and sleep, and . . . okay, yep, we'll get to that later).

The ability to control our focus—also called top-down attentional control—relies on the prefrontal cortex. It is the last part of the brain to develop, and it develops even more slowly in those with ADHD. And even once it is fully developed, it's still impaired.

This is why we often have to go to great spellcast-y, potion-y lengths to support our ability to focus. It's easy to assume we're not focused because we're closing our eyes, or doodling, or shuffling things around on our desk. But we're often doing those things because we're trying to find focus. Just as lizards externally regulate their temperature, we try to externally regulate our attention.

IT'S LIKE SOMEBODY LEFT THE DOOR OPEN

In the first video I ever watched about ADHD, a woman posting under the name "Just Jen" described her doctor's explanation of attention as a door that was always open. Other people could close their door and focus, but in ADHD brains, the door lets *everything* in. We can't ignore the things other people might be able to tune out.

Remember how often you heard a teacher say "keep your eyes on your own work"? In laboratory studies, scientists used eye tracking to measure how often people with ADHD shifted their attention away from the task they were working on, and, uh . . . wow, *we can't keep our eyes on our own work*. At least, not to the extent that our non-ADHD peers are able to.

It isn't just external distractions that are hard to tune out, either. Our brains also have a harder time "shutting the door" on our anxieties, negative thoughts, or brilliant new ideas. We also have a harder time remembering things (see "How to Remember Stuff," page 187).

Sometimes what's distracting us is our effort to remember or communicate something we don't want to forget.

SOMETIMES, FOCUS IS MORE LIKE A TUNNEL

The flip side of the open-door-distractibility is hyperfocus—the experience of being *so* engaged we don't notice anything outside our hyperfocus-tunnel and often can't pull our attention away. A lot of missed diagnoses can be attributed to the phenomenon of hyperfocus. People think someone can't have ADHD because they can focus *so well* "when they want to."

But hyperfocus is a function of the wonky attention regulation typical of ADHD brains. We don't *choose* to hyperfocus on something—we get sucked in. When that happens, we lose track of time, and we don't come out of it until we're done, dead, or someone or something pulls us out.

Sometimes, hyperfocus works out great for us—and sometimes it doesn't.*

Hyperfocusing on that paper we need to get done when we've got nowhere else we need to be? Fantastic.

Hyperfocusing on a book you're reading and missing the book club meeting you were reading it for? Not so much.†

Because focusing is so hard for us, hyperfocus on something

---

* Dr. Russell Barkley calls this perseveration—the inability to pull ourselves away from things we don't even want to be doing, or doing anymore.

† True story. My aunt Suzy, who also has ADHD, told me that this just happened to her. "I was really looking forward to talking about the book!"

we're supposed to be working on can feel like a get-out-of-struggling-free card. For once, we don't have to fight with our brains!

Still, it's important to remember that *any* focus comes at a cost. The time may have flown by, but if our brains were working for ten hours straight, we're going to feel it the next day—and probably have a harder time focusing.

OUR ABILITY TO FOCUS IS INTEREST-BASED

ADHD brains are chronically understimulated, which is why treatment involves stimulant medication. When something isn't interesting to us, it's harder for us to pay attention to it. Even if we care about learning or doing the thing we're being asked to do.

There's a clip from *Parks and Recreation* that perfectly illustrates this phenomenon. Lovable goofball Andy Dwyer interrupts his boss's instructions to enthusiastically exclaim, "I wasn't super paying attention to what you just said we would be doing, but I will give it 110 percent! As soon as you repeat yourself in a more interesting way."

Andy doesn't mean to ignore his boss. His brain was likely operating in what brain scientists call the default mode network (DMN). It was on autopilot, "listening" without actually listening while his attention wandered off in search of something more engaging. His amusing outburst is honestly quite insightful: he's trying to self-advocate for an accommodation that will allow him to focus on his boss's request.

The default mode network is more active in ADHD brains than

neurotypical brains.* This tendency isn't a choice; it's due to our brain structure. There is more gray matter in the default mode network of ADHD brains than neurotypical brains. Because of this, it's easier for this part of the brain to be activated and stay activated—leaving the door open for distractions and shower thoughts. This is also why those with ADHD are better at divergent thinking!

---

divergent thinking (n.)

A cognitive process that generates creative ideas by exploring many possible solutions or bouncing from one thought to the next. Divergent thinking generally occurs spontaneously, is seldom linear, and tends to produce abundant and unique ideas.

WE OFTEN AREN'T SURE WHAT TO FOCUS ON

In addition to having difficulty regulating our attention, we have a harder time prioritizing what to focus *on*. The signal—the task we need to do—is harder for us to distinguish from the noise—which is everything else.

---

* One of my favorite explanations of ADHD I've ever seen in the research is "chronic mind wandering."

If something stands out as urgent, it's easier to see it as a priority. We may end up focusing on that, often at the expense of things that are more important.

When it isn't clear what is urgent, the signals can all sound the same, and we often just get stuck. Decision paralysis is a common experience for those of us with ADHD. When we try to narrow down our choices, a process that relies on convergent thinking, our divergent-thinking brains often keep handing us more options to choose from, and we can end up overwhelmed.*

On the flip side, if everything we need to do is urgent, we might try to get it all done at the same time—with mixed results.

A Note on Multitasking

Those with ADHD are more likely than our neurotypical peers to multitask. Unfortunately, research shows that multitasking is not the time saver we think it is.

As amazing as it feels to be doing multiple things at once, brains aren't actually capable of *focusing* on more than one thing at once. What actually happens when we're multitasking is either that one of the tasks doesn't truly require our attention or we're shifting our attention back and forth quickly between the different tasks. Each shift of attention costs a tiny bit of time; and getting fully

---

*   Anxiety about choosing the wrong thing can also play a role. As can our difficulties with how we perceive time.

refocused when we switch back to a task we've switched away from can take up to twenty-five minutes.

Mistakes are also more common while multitasking. And for us, so is completely forgetting about one of the tasks entirely. For tasks that don't require our full attention—like folding laundry for the thousandth time while watching reruns of a sitcom—multitasking works fine. It can even be beneficial because it makes the task less boring, which means we're more likely to do it. (More on this in "How to Motivate Your Brain," page 156.) Tasks that do require attention—like cooking a meal you've never made before while helping your kid with their calculus homework—can end in comedic disaster.

THERE'S A LOT OF NOISE

We are living in a world where we carry shiny supercomputers in our pockets that can access every book ever written in seconds and also play games. Our watches beep, and our phones bloop, and our web browsers show us pop-ups in pop-ups. We all deal with a barrage of stimuli competing for our attention, whether or not we have ADHD.

This incredibly distracting environment is leading even those without ADHD to struggle with focus—what Dr. Ned Hallowell calls the attention deficit *trait*. This is not the same thing as having ADHD. According to Hallowell, if you, an attention-challenged person, abandon all the distractions of modernity, go live on a farm, and finally find peace, you don't have ADHD. If, instead, you show up to the farm and get so bored you decide to build a carnival—congratulations, you are one of us.

> **Koen S., 33, Belgium**
>
> "My 'normal' focus feels like squeezing the last bit of toothpaste from the tube. If it's not really fun or challenging, it's really draining to have to focus."

> **Joshua S., 31, Germany**
>
> "Focus needs a lot of strategies or tools to work for an ADHD brain. It's like carrying a bucket of water up a hill. If you got the tools (the bucket), it can work, but it's exhausting. It's difficult to get started and easy to stop."

> **Miriam R., 30, Canada**
>
> "Focus and hyperfocus is the difference between riding a bicycle and riding a bullet train. Both will get me to my destination, but one requires exertion on my part and the other is effortless."

THE TOOLBOX

So, what's a brain to do? ADHD meds, if they work for you, can work wonders and are a good place to start, because they give our brains the stimulation they need and allow us to better regulate our focus.

But they don't work for everyone, typically wear off at the end (or even middle) of the day, and aren't always an option.

I have found developing other tools to support our attention to be critical. That way, when you need to (or someone tells you to) focus, you have options. My brilliant friend and middle school teacher Jo Meleca-Voigt teaches her students to think of focus using this acronym: Figure Out the Cause, and Use a Strategy (FOCUS). This changes focus from a noun—something we don't always have—to a verb—something we can actually do.*

1. BOOST THE SIGNAL AND DECREASE THE NOISE

Because the "signal" of what we're supposed to be doing easily gets lost in the "noise" of everything else, what can help is both to strengthen that signal and decrease the noise around it. That way, it's clearer what needs our focus, and it's easier to find our way back to it when we inevitably wander away.

- **Create clear cues.** ADHD brains are more sensitive to environmental cues than neurotypical brains. We can take advantage of this fact by intentionally adding reminders of what we're supposed to be doing into our line of sight—and moving reminders of things we *don't* want to be doing out of it. (More on this in "Use Cues—But with Caution," page 209.)

---

* Jo was kind enough to explain how teachers can support with this. Scan the QR code on page 432.

- **Lay down the tracks.** Thinking through the order of what you want to accomplish *before* you start doing it can make it easier to stay on track when there are a million distractions being thrown your way. Our operations director, J2, calls this "setting up her dominos." There are lots of ways to do this—make a list, review your calendar, imagine how you'd like your day to go before getting out of bed.

- **Fight distraction with distraction.** One thoughtfully chosen "distraction"—such as music, a TV show, or using a fidget—can provide our brains with enough stimulation so that they don't have to go searching for it and get distracted by something more exciting.

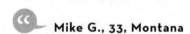 David A., 47, Canada

"I walk the dog, meditate and then journal (putting anxieties on paper so that I 'don't forget'), drink coffee, and make sure I have a work space that is quiet and private. I'm good for about four hours (until lunchtime) before I really drift."

Mike G., 33, Montana

"Hacking my focus is hard. Meds help me overcome the obstacles to focus, which helps me slide into hyperfocus more easily. Pomodoro timers [timers or apps that help break up tasks into doable portions] help overcome the 'switching/starting' problems. I can trick myself into doing something for ten minutes."

 Natasha L., 25, Florida

"Fill the stimulation meter. Listen to a podcast while doing dishes or play music while cleaning to increase stimulation. But find a balance. You want to fill the 'empty space' by adding whatever stimulation is needed for the meter to hit 100%, which helps me focus. If I am doing a high-focus task, I add low stimulation (like instrumental music)—and vice versa. That way there's no room for my brain to stray."

2. PRACTICE NONJUDGMENTAL REDIRECTION

Our brains are chaotic places. Our thoughts are going to wander. *No one* is able to control their thoughts entirely, and if you have ADHD, it's even harder. Thankfully, there are many strategies we can use to (gently) bring our attention back.

- **Practice mindfulness.** Mindfulness is the practice of intentionally bringing your attention back to whatever you're doing, thinking, or feeling in the present moment in a nonjudgmental, curious way. If you are doing the dishes, you might notice how the water feels on your hands. If you are avoiding doing the dishes, you might notice the feelings that come up for you. "Huh. Interesting. Moving on." Practicing mindfulness improves self-awareness and strengthens our ability to redirect our attention when we need to.

- **Install some bumpers.** My favorite low-tech way to do this is to create a "Doing" and "Not Doing" list on separate sticky notes. Put both lists where you can see them while you work, so you can notice if you've wandered off track. You can also install physical barriers. When I kept getting distracted while I was cooking, I put up a baby gate. I knew I'd forget about the pot on the stove as soon as I wandered away from the kitchen. Running into a physical barrier was an excellent reminder of what I was supposed to be doing, and brought my attention back, too.

- **If stuff pops up, put it down on paper.** If you suddenly think of something you *need to do*, write it down in a "parking lot" instead of acting on it right away. You can take a look at what you've written when you're done working on the task at hand and see if it actually needs tending to right away. Often, upon reviewing the thing that came to mind, you might realize that it wasn't quite as important as you thought. This strategy helps strengthen our distractibility delay, the ability to wait before responding to a distraction so you can stay on task, especially when it's one our brains want to avoid.

 Madalayne R., 24, Canada

"I do five minutes of meditation and ten minutes of easy yoga every single day. It's a practice. When I get distracted, I am now better able to simply be aware of what's happening, pay attention to my breath, and slowly veer myself back to the thing I want to be focusing on."

 Niki M., 35, USA

"I keep elastic coil bracelets around my house. Whenever I do something that would be dangerous to forget about, like cooking, I put on a bracelet. I will inevitably forget what I was doing and wander off, but will remember what I was doing when I start fidgeting with the bracelet."

 Free P., 78, Georgia

"I grab a small legal pad and write down whatever is distracting me. (I have them in each room.) Then I take the 'note to myself' and put it on my office desk. When I find ten minutes or so available, I go through my pile and ruthlessly discard most all of my notes."

3. MAKE SPACE FOR (HYPER)FOCUS—AND INSTALL GUARDRAILS

Hyperfocus is a bit of a double-edged sword. When we're in that kind of flow, we can get deeply absorbed in a task and forget about everything else. But also, when we're in that kind of flow, we can get deeply absorbed in a task and forget about everything else. Giving ourselves enough time to slip into hyperfocus—and guardrails that help us come out of it when we need to move on—can allow us to take advantage of it without driving straight off a metaphorical cliff.

- **Create the right conditions for hyperfocus to happen.** Different brains achieve hyperfocus in different ways, but most of us require a certain amount of dedicated time, plus an environment that is conducive to long periods of focused work. Before work, I try to avoid doing things that will get my brain spinning on something else and intentionally get my brain spinning on the task I want it to do instead.*

- **Establish a cutoff time.** Just because you might be able to hyperfocus for long periods doesn't mean it's helpful to keep working as long as you can. Sometimes, limiting your

---

* This is obviously not always possible. I'm currently learning to build in "palate cleansers" when I can't focus. These palate cleansers are activities I can do for a short period of time to unstick from one task so I can move on to the next.

intense focus—and having a cutoff so you can start winding down for bed, eat food, or do whatever else your body needs—can help you to be productive the next day, too. This can lead to more good brain days—and better productivity—overall. Just . . . make sure to set an alarm.

- **Leave yourself "breadcrumbs."** In some situations, we know we really need to stop, but we're afraid to stop because we're not sure if we can get started again. When it's time for a hyperfocus spell to come to an end, use a bit of that remaining mental energy to write down these two things: 1.) *What did I just do?* 2.) *What would I have done if I could keep going?* These clues, like the breadcrumb path in the story of Hansel and Gretel, can make it easier to find your way back into the task the next day. Unless they get eaten.

Pete W., 32, Arizona

"I can easily get into hyperfocus with the right sort of music (upbeat but no outrageous tempo or lyrics, video game music works great) and environment (low light, no distracting noises from other people, no notification noises)."

Miriam R., 30, Canada

"When I enter hyperfocus, unless I've prepared an alarm in advance, I simply won't break out of it. I'll keep reading or whatever until I reach the end or something really big jolts me out of it. I can block out any audio except for something totally unexpected when I'm deep in thought."

4. MOVE YOUR BODY

While we're often encouraged to sit still to help us pay attention, it's typically easier to focus when we build movement into our routines.

- **Exercise.** Exercise produces dopamine and norepinephrine, the same chemicals that stimulant medication does to help with focus. The focus-boosting effects of exercise typically last for about an hour afterward, so if you're trying to do something brain-heavy, working out beforehand can help!

- **Explore alternative "seating."** Walking while you work—by using a standing desk with an under-the-desk treadmill, for example—is a way to "fidget" while also getting some of the benefits of exercise. Special seating, such as yoga balls, rocking or swivel chairs, or stationary bike chairs, can provide additional stimulation to help focus your brain. You can even use a regular chair and add bouncing bands! It's often helpful to change it up based on our brain's needs that day.*

- **Go to another room.** When focus is hard, moving to a different room, building, or even state (I wrote this chapter in a vacation rental in Arizona) can help you reset and refocus. Sometimes finding focus is about the lack of distractions; sometimes it's about the novelty!

Ana Luisa, 26, Brazil

"I focus while moving. It can be on a bus, walking, or in a hammock; if I'm moving, I'm engaged. Usually, when I have an impossible essay to get through, I record myself reading it at night and listen to it during my daily exercise.

"I used to read on the go, but then I ran into a tree and, well let's just say, one split eyebrow is enough to learn my lesson."

---

*   My absolute favorite classroom ever was one that had desks and chairs close to the teacher and couches placed around the room. I sat at the desks when I needed accountability to focus, and I could relax on the couches during high-anxiety days or when I was deeply engaged. Being able to select seating based on my needs on that day was empowering, and I learned so much more than I otherwise would have.

cc **Alison B., 44, Virginia**

"I chose my professional path—education—because it allows me to move around. I am able to focus much better when I can move. Teaching virtually was agonizing because I had to stay seated. Thankfully, an under-desk elliptical machine allowed me to get some activity while still doing my job."

5. REST YOUR BRAIN

Focus takes energy, and any kind of focus comes at this cost. "Bad brain days" are a *thing* with ADHD, and while fighting through them is sometimes possible (and necessary), it's important to consider whether the benefits outweigh the drawbacks. If your brain needs a break, sometimes the best thing you can do is give it one, so it has a better chance of focusing later.

- **Take brain breaks.** If you are losing mental energy but want to keep going, consider a time-limited "brain break." Taking a walk around the block, playing a relaxing game, or just staring out the window can be the difference between continued productivity and a pooped and cranky brain. (Sleep is also a great brain break! More on page 100.)

- **Plan time away from your task.** If you have a long, cognitively intense project (like studying for finals or writing a presentation), make sure you schedule to take time away from it if you can. Visit the park on your lunch break or sign up for an exercise class. Put the thing in a drawer for a week. Not only will your brain get a chance to recharge, but time away from a stressor can also help prevent burnout.

- **Take a break from self-reg.** Many people with ADHD feel like they're "bad at relaxing" because while they're TRY-ING to relax, they end up doing something else. What I have learned is that, for us, taking a break from self-regulating IS a break. Sometimes, letting your brain do what it wants—even if that's starting a new project—is more restful than asking it to focus on a relaxing activity.

 **Lucila S., 30, Mexico**

"In college, the only way I could write my essays was by watching rom-coms. I'd work for twenty minutes, then watch like fifteen minutes, and then go back. It was a bit like the Pomodoro method [a time-management technique], but it had to be with a movie that had a really easy-to-track plot, and one I hadn't yet watched."

Emrys H., 32, California

"I take 'brain breaks' between lectures. I need them, or I cannot cram more information into my head. I watch a cat video or take a walk outside. They work incredibly well. There's a noticeable difference in how much I retain when I take brain breaks versus when I don't."

Jennifer S., 38, Michigan

"This might seem counterintuitive, but I rest my brain by doing something physically challenging and repetitive enough that my brain stops partying because my body is so tied up in the movement. Rowing, and sometimes just a circuit or intervals of something, works. Afterward, there's this tiny window of relative quiet."

IN DEFENSE OF THE NOISE

During an interview with journalist Aarushi Agni, I proudly explained how I boost the signal and decrease the noise. I described all the ways in which I set up my environment to help me focus: using different computers for gaming and work, limiting my to-do list so I don't get overwhelmed and avoid it entirely, putting sticky notes with a "doing" list and "not doing" list on my desk.

She nodded, thoughtful. "But sometimes the noise becomes the signal."

"What do you mean?" I asked.

She explained to me that sometimes when working on a task, the thought that distracts her becomes the new project she *wants* to focus on in the future. She grinned at the irony.

I nodded slowly, a realization dawning.

Once, instead of working, I was scrolling through Twitter and came across a thread asking people what their favorite musicals were. "*Into the Woods,*" someone said. I'd never seen it. I decided to watch it instead of whatever I was supposed to be doing that day. It was powerful. I ended up creating a video essay of sorts about it, and to date, it's one of my proudest accomplishments.

While it's great to focus, there's value in getting distracted. That's where innovation lives. And I'd forgotten that. Thinking back, I started seeing how my pursuit of focus made me considerably less creative.

When I started the channel, my brain was off-leash most of the time. It could sit in the sandbox and play. I came up with a lot of metaphors back then. The Paper Monster (my term for all the mail and paper clutter that piles up), (Magical) Quarters of Encouragement, Motivation Bridge. I dressed up like I was in the Matrix to explain why we focus on things that don't matter. I made finger puppets that kicked over dominos to explain how routines work. I danced around in a Homework Hat and ate giant pizzas on camera. As I got better at controlling my focus, I got more productive—but I lost some of that creativity.

If your brain can't wander off, it can't come back with something unexpected. If you're farming and planting corn, you're going to get corn. If you're off foraging, or

> While it's great to focus, there's value in getting distracted.

even just wandering through the woods, there might be berries. Or mushrooms. Or faeries. (Why not?) Our brains are *incredible* at divergent thinking, coming up with lots of ideas, new ways to combine things, and innovative ways to solve problems. This is why many of us are inventors, early tech adopters, industry leaders, and disrupters. And in the relentless pursuit of improving our ability to focus, we might forget to allow space for that.

It's normal to take what we have for granted while searching for what we don't. But there is a trade-off. You can't have metaphorical shower thoughts if you don't make time for metaphorical showers.

Now I'm aiming for more of a balance. I have tools to use when I need to focus, but I also give myself time to wander. I've done a good job taming my focus beast. I know how to direct it. Sometimes, though, I let it take me where it wants to go. I let it surprise me. And I'm excited by what we discover together.

Regardless of where we're at in our journey, our brains are *going* to roam. And maybe that's okay.

We can always (eventually) bring them back.

Chapter 4

How to (Executive) Function

And now that you don't have to be perfect, you can be good.

—JOHN STEINBECK, *EAST OF EDEN*

ADHD NEW YEAR'S

I'm about to move in to a new office space, and I find myself slipping into the same fantasy I had every time I started a new school year—the fantasy of *finally* being organized. Of finally getting it "right."

The fantasy that, *this* time, I'll be the person I'm supposed to be. That my space will look like it's supposed to look. This time it'll be perfect. Why not? I'm starting from scratch.*

I'd spend a whole blissful, optimistic week setting up my back-pack, new binder, tabs, planner, and all the folders I could ever need

---

* Here's the thing. I'm not really starting from scratch. I'm bringing my habits, my routines, and my brain. I'm bringing my chaos with me. You just can't see it yet.

to get and stay organized. My mom would show me how to set up my folders and explain how to maintain them. Two weeks into the school year, none of this mattered. I couldn't find *anything*. There'd be Cracker Jacks stuck to forgotten homework crumpled at the bottom of my bag, and my mom would *regularly* have to dump it out and help me triage.

> Trying to stay on top of things when I did not know how to stay on top of things came with a trade-off.

What happened? I couldn't explain it. The systems just fell apart.

As an adult, I celebrated ADHD New Year's with new purses, apartments, and desks. With new hobbies, friendships, careers, and credit cards. I'd move into a new place and buy organizing bins and cleaning supplies, putting everything where it belonged and feeling so proud of myself. Two weeks later, all the surfaces would be cluttered, the sink would be full, and I'd spend hours a day looking for things I swear I *just saw*.

Sometimes I'd come across a new system, and that, too, would offer a blank slate. "Okay, sure, my finances are a mess, and everything I've tried hasn't worked out. But I haven't tried *this* system yet. Maybe this is *the one*."

Almost every system I set up to manage the stuff in my life broke down almost immediately, usually due to some combination of the following: I forgot to use it. I forgot *how* to use it. I lost it. I got bored of it. I forgot it existed. I put it in a Very Important Place and now I can't find it. I promised myself I'd update it later. (I did not.) I got distracted. I broke my phone and hadn't backed it up. I accidentally deleted the app or couldn't remember my password. I couldn't afford it anymore. Life happened—I got sick or went to a friend's house on a day I was supposed to clean/cook/organize a thing, and I never went back to it again.

And when a system fell apart, so did whatever it was supposed to help me manage. My stuff. My time. My relationships. My finances.

There were instances (and areas in my life) in which I'd be perfectly organized and could stay that way, but only because I protected my systems fiercely. Obsessively. I didn't care how tired I was; I was folding my clothes Marie Kondo style, because the moment I didn't, I knew it would all collapse. No, I couldn't go out to dinner with everyone; it would throw off the meal plan I had made. Sometimes, having my colored pencils organized by color felt like the only thing holding back the chaos. So, no, sorry, you couldn't borrow one. In fact, even I wouldn't use them.

Trying to stay on top of things when I did not know how to stay on top of things came with a trade-off. I could do it as long as life didn't happen, so I didn't let life happen. This, of course, defeats the entire purpose of being on top of things—to make it easier to live your life—but it was a trade-off I felt I had to make.

WHAT I LEARNED

In retrospect, my need to be organized was a way to gain some semblance of control in a life that often felt far outside my control. I was constantly trying to find systems and rules to contain the chaos, to help me be able to do what I needed to do, when I needed to do it. I felt like a hot mess, and what do you do with a mess? You clean it up.

My usual level of disorganization had a snowball effect on my ability to function, too—I can't find the thing, which makes me late, which makes me rush and put something where it doesn't belong, telling myself I'll reorganize it later, which I absolutely forget to do. I had trouble functioning, and because I kept being told that being more organized would make me more functional, I put a ton of time, effort, money, and other resources into trying to be.

The truth is the opposite of what most of us were told: the reason those of us with ADHD have trouble functioning isn't because we haven't found the right system yet and/or don't "stick to it." It's actually the other way around. The reason we have trouble sticking to these systems—and why our stuff, time, actions, emotions, and words "spill over" onto those around us—is because we have trouble with executive function.

WHAT THE HECK IS EXECUTIVE FUNCTION?

Executive function (EF) is like the CEO of the brain. It's a set of top-down cognitive processes (executive functions) that help us self-regulate so we can effectively plan, prioritize, and sustain effort toward long-term goals.

executive function (n.)
A set of top-down cognitive processes (executive functions) that help us self-regulate so we can effectively plan, prioritize, and sustain effort toward long-term goals.

These cognitive processes originate from the prefrontal cortex, which is the last part of the brain to develop. In most people, the executive function system finishes developing by age twenty-five. This is why we associate a lot of skills reliant on executive function—such as being able to manage a career, make good decisions, pay our bills on time, and drive a car without crashing into things—with "being an adult."

While a lot of organizational, financial, and project management systems are designed to support executive function, they also *rely* on the executive function of the person using them.

You can probably see where I'm going with this.

EXECUTIVE FUNCTION IS IMPAIRED IN ADHD BRAINS

When I started the channel, I thought my inattention—which I now understand is difficulty *regulating* my attention (see "What I Learned" on page 51)—was the only impairment I had. Turns out, that is not the case. ADHD struggles are more broadly due to executive functioning difficulties.

Executive functions that tend to be impaired in ADHD brains include:

Response Inhibition

Response inhibition refers to the suppression of actions that interfere with a goal or are inappropriate (or no longer appropriate) in a given context. It creates mental and temporal space between a stimulus and an action. Have you ever shouted out answers without raising your hand as soon as a teacher asked a question, left your seat just when the meeting is starting, blurted out thoughts that popped into your head without thinking, or continued to overshare (or overexplain!) even when you know you should stop? These actions are all common—and frustrating—results of impaired *response inhibition.* Stimuli happened—and we responded.

Working Memory

Working memory refers to our ability to temporarily hold information in our mind, manipulate it, and produce a response or action. For example, when you're cooking dinner, you may use your working memory to hold the ingredients you saw when scanning inside your fridge, think of how you can mix and match those ingredients, then decide what you're going to make.* (We'll learn more about

---

* Or if you're like me and this overloads your working memory, you may order food or eat garbanzo beans straight out of the can instead.

working memory in Chapter 8, "How to Remember Stuff," page 187.)

Set-Shifting

Set-shifting refers to our ability to switch between tasks that have different cognitive demands, like reading a recipe and cooking it, or switching from being a speaker to being a listener during a conversation. When we multitask on tasks that require our attention, we're relying on set-shifting. It allows us to be flexible when demands change. Set-shifting is moderately impaired in ADHD. In situations where we're expected to shift between tasks, we often operate slowly or make more mistakes.

These executive functions work together to help us, well, function.

Research has found that impairments in set-shifting, for example, may be due to deficits in working memory and response inhibition. When we can't remember the "rules" of the task we're switching back to—say, writing an email to our boss—or we're still stuck following the ones of the task we were just focused on—texting our friend—it's harder to set-shift both quickly and accurately.

All of this explains some of my organizational difficulties as a student. In the five to ten minutes between classes, I had to stop taking notes, figure out what the homework assignment was, look for my planner to write that down, put my books away, go to my locker, remember what my combination was and what supplies I needed for the next class, and transition to the next class. Doing all of this *and* organizing my things required a level of executive function I hadn't yet developed.

EXECUTIVE FUNCTION DEVELOPS MORE SLOWLY IN ADHD BRAINS

Most human-built systems assume that the person using them has typical levels of executive function—whatever is considered normal for the target age group or audience. If a system is made for kids, it's probably simple to navigate or designed to be used with the support of a parent or teacher. If it's made for college students, it might assume its users have an almost developed executive function system.

People expect an eighteen-year-old going off to college to have the executive function abilities of an eighteen-year-old. They wouldn't be expected to be great at, say, running a company yet, but they should be able to handle registering for classes.

For people with ADHD, that's often not true.

With ADHD, executive function is delayed—up to *30 percent*. That means the eighteen-year-old you're sending off to college might have the executive function of someone who is twelve.

This is why those with ADHD can seem "immature." It's also why we can seem as if we're misbehaving intentionally when we're not. When we're not following instructions or meeting expectations, it doesn't necessarily mean we don't understand what the expectations are, or that we don't want to meet them. Often, we don't have the executive function (yet or right now) to do those things effectively.

THERE ARE "HOT" AND "COOL" EXECUTIVE FUNCTION SYSTEMS

What we do or say in the heat of the moment is often much different from what we'd *plan* to do—or recommend to someone else.

That's because there are two neural pathways underlying the executive function systems that help us make decisions and reach our goals.

The "hot" executive function system refers to affective and motivational processes; it kicks in when emotions and stakes are high.

When we're not in the heat of the moment, or the stakes are low, the "cool" executive function (EF) system kicks in, and our decisions tend to be much more logical. Cool EF refers to the cognitive processes such as response inhibition, working memory, and set-shifting.

We can switch quickly between these two systems. They can also both be active at the same time, although one typically overrides the other.

This is true for everyone.

But it's especially important to understand for those of us with ADHD. While executive function impairments explain many of our struggles, they don't paint the entire picture. Otherwise, ADHD would just be called executive function disorder.

Emotions run high in those with ADHD (see "How to Feel," page 216). There are also differences in our motivational processes that make us more likely to choose smaller rewards now over larger rewards later (see "How to Motivate Your Brain," page 156).

And successful problem-solving (which uses cool EF) relies heavily on one's motivational and emotional influences (our hot EF).

This explains why, when I ran into challenges setting up and initially maintaining my organizational systems, I was able to successfully problem-solve. I was *excited* to set the systems up and had the immediate *reward* of seeing everything look pretty and organized.

It also explains why, when I was running from one class to the next, I made the objectively illogical choice to shove my papers wherever they fit in my backpack, telling myself (contrary to all past experience) that I'd organize them "later." The emotions from the stress I felt about getting to the next class and the consequences of being late were more immediate.

Many people, regardless of whether they have ADHD, make choices that aren't exactly logical when their hot EF system is dominant.

But as research has demonstrated, tapping into our cool EF—through reflection, contextualizing, and analyzing abstractly—can make it easier to make logical decisions, even when our emotions and motivation are pulling us toward impulsive ones. And these are skills that can be learned.

Joshua S., 31, Germany

"With my ADHD, every day is different. I have amazing days and terrible days—but rarely 'average' days. I have tons of ideas or a blank mind. I am one hundred percent unproductive for most of the time, but then manage to catch up with everything I should have done in an extremely short amount of time."

 Madalayne R., 24, Canada

"I struggle with executive function every day. There are so many small things to remember for every task! Remember to take meds, turn the oven off after cooking, grab grocery bags before heading to the grocery store, save a cup of pasta water before straining, put the leftovers into the fridge after they cool down, go to this appointment, make plans to meet up with this friend, grab the clothes from the dryer. So. Many. Things!"

 Merle D., 21, Netherlands

"When I'm struggling with tasks and whatnot, almost everyone in my life has told me to 'just start.' It hurts me every time, because I feel like they don't take the struggles I have (because of an actual brain disorder!) seriously."

Magi K., 40, Pennsylvania

"Becoming a mom has increased my executive function challenges, because now it's not just my own life I have to manage, it's theirs too, their childhoods. I make sure that I'm on top of the essentials, but it's nowhere near the picture-perfect childhoods they're comparing theirs to. The worst are the 'whys': 'Why didn't we bake cookies for the holidays last year? Why did we get out late trick or treating? Remember that one time you made a spooky treasure hunt? Why haven't we done that again?' I answer them as best as I can, 'It's not that I don't want to. I am doing my best...' Deep down, I can't help but feel that I'm still failing them somehow."

THE TOOLBOX

Many mental health professionals focus on ADHD symptoms alone, or on our relative strengths and weaknesses in EF. But what's worth considering is how we function *given* our brain's differences. While we can't change the fact that we have these differences in EF, the impairments we face as a result *can* be minimized. There are many things we can do to help compensate for our EF differences.

1. HAVE LESS STUFF TO MANAGE

There's a common saying that regularly makes the rounds in the ADHD community: "If you want to do more, do less." The more you're trying to do, the more you have to keep track of—and the harder it is for your executive function system to keep up. That's true for everyone, but it's especially true for those of us with impaired executive function. Because we often take on way-the-f*ck more than we can handle, one of the most helpful ways for those with ADHD to better manage their stuff is simply having less of it.

- **Delegate areas of responsibility.** Delegating individual tasks often requires more cognitive resources than it saves for those of us with ADHD. Delegating entire *areas* of responsibility, however, can be more executive function efficient because it allows someone else to take over both the *doing* of a task and the *management* of it. Handing your partner a grocery list will save you one trip to the store, but mutually deciding that your partner is the one in charge of making sure there is food in the house frees up a ton of brain bandwidth.

- **Keep systems simple.** While it might be fun to set up an elaborate organizational system when we're hyperfocusing on it (see: issues with response inhibition), being able to maintain that system when we need to turn our attention to other things is another story. Simplifying your systems so they're easier to maintain can make it more likely to be—and stay—functional in the long term. An example of this is "books go on the bookshelf" as opposed to "books need to be put on the *correct* bookshelf, sorted by color and size."

- **Practice minimalism.** Minimalism essentially means owning less stuff. It's a lot easier to manage clutter if you don't have a lot of stuff to create it. Many ADHDers I've met swear by minimalism, because they can function more effectively when they have less to manage, lose, organize, and/or clean. This can work for projects, too; limiting the number of ongoing projects, especially long-term ones, takes pressure off our executive function.

- **Say no (to at least some things).** Limiting the number of ongoing projects, especially long-term ones, takes pressure off our executive function. The stuff-we-could-do-in-life buffet is unlimited. Our capacity is not. If your plate is full, don't get another plate.

Do we have to do less forever? Not necessarily. But because of our neurodevelopmental delay, adults with ADHD are often stretched to their EF limit. If our coping skills don't increase faster than the demands do, keeping up gets harder and harder, and we sacrifice more and more of ourselves and our well-being.

THE ADHD CYCLE OF OVERWHELM*

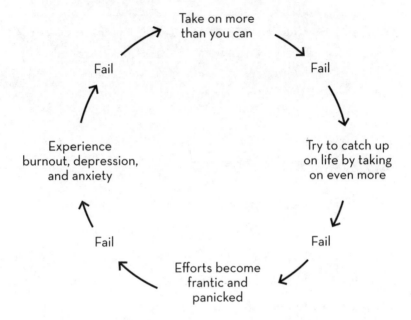

The way to step out of this cycle is often by starting to do less—ideally an amount that you can *currently* handle. And before committing to more, level up your skills.

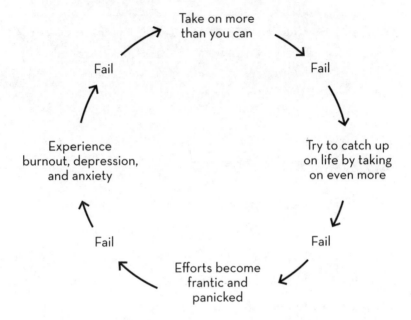 **Mark N., 66, USA**

> "As a Certified Financial Planner, I *only* see clients and offer advice. Someone else manages my calendar, records notes, builds client plans, manages revenue collection, and handles anything operational."

---

*   As someone pointed out when I shared this with our community, we can fall into the same cycle if we succeed because now we're given more responsibility and have more to manage.

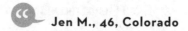

Jen M., 46, Colorado

"Lower the bar! Let the floors be dirty. Let the laundry sit in baskets for two weeks. Who cares? Make sure you and the kids/plants/pets are fed. Make sure there's time for sleep (if possible), and fun. Laundry will keep. Life won't."

2. ACCOMMODATE YO'SELF

When we face struggles that others don't, we need tools that others don't. For example, I am short. I can reach the top shelf of my cabinet, but if I want to do that safely, I'll need a step stool. In environments where stuff is on high shelves, it levels the playing field and helps me avoid struggling significantly more than someone who is taller. The same idea applies to ADHD. Accommodations are generally well worth the cost (and many are free!) because they make tasks and environments more ADHD accessible, which can make a huge difference in our ability to perform at the level we are otherwise capable of. It's ideal to put accommodations in place *before* we desperately need them, because finding the most effective ones can take time.

- **Add scaffolding.** Just as you use training wheels to learn how to ride a bike, you can put extra supports in place to help you learn a new system or take on new responsibilities. For example: first, I have someone sit with me and do a thing. Then I'll sometimes do it on my own. Once I get the hang of it, I'll do it totally on my own. Scaffolding benefits us because we get the support we need to learn a task—and as we become more confident with it, that support can be pulled away.

- **Self-advocate.** Speaking up when someone can make a task more doable for you lets others know how they can help you. For example, you can ask if someone can share a document so you can read and follow along. (If they need to know why you're making this request, check out "How to Remember Stuff," page 187.)

- **Ask for formal accommodations.** In the US, students and workers with disabilities (and, again, ADHD can qualify as a disability) are legally entitled to reasonable accommodations. Individualized Education Plans (IEPs) and 504 plans protect students, and the ADA (the Americans with Disabilities Act) protects those who are no longer in school. The Job Accommodation Network's website (askjan.org) lists accommodations by disability or impairment, and it even has a live chat option for those who need guidance.

Stephanie R., 33, North Carolina

"My sister and I both have ADHD and are roommates. We body double so we can get things done. If I'm washing dishes, she'll sit in the kitchen and grade papers, and we keep each other on task."

Jesse A., 42, Washington

"I live in fear of the surprise 'let's talk' meeting with my boss where I find out I'm falling behind or have been doing something wrong for six-plus months. So we started weekly check-ins where he would give me a quick, reassuring green light that everything was 👍 from his perspective."

Reese, 40, Virginia

"When I first had kids at school, I was shocked by the amount of baking they expected parents to do for class parties. I find baking simultaneously boring and stressful, which plays hell with my executive function, so I modified the expectations by telling teachers, 'I don't bake, but I would be happy to bring themed plates and napkins for every party!' *Boom. Accommodated.*"

3. ACCOUNT FOR THE ADHD TAX

The ADHD tax is a colloquial term used in the community to refer to the additional expenses we incur simply by having ADHD in a world that doesn't account for our challenges. While the term typically refers to financial costs, the ADHD tax can include energy, time, and other resources. And it is *expensive.* While we can't eliminate the ADHD tax entirely, accounting for it can help us avoid (at least some of) the crises we face. And we can lessen it by, when we can, paying the ADHD tax up front—investing our time, money, and energy in tools and systems that can reduce the cost in the long run. As many in this community (and those who love and work with us) have discovered, it is not only less stressful; it typically ends up being much "cheaper."

Examples of the ADHD Tax

- Late fees

- Rush shipping fees

- Fees for subscriptions and memberships we forgot to cancel

- Beverages that have gone flat or missing

- Replacements for things we lost or broke

- Last-minute tickets for traveling or missed flights because you were late / forgot your ID / went to the wrong airport

- Leads we forgot (or were too overwhelmed) to follow up on

- Car accidents we got into because we were distracted by billboards

- Time. Spent. Looking. For. Everything. *Constantly.*

- Vegetables. (Yup. Go check the drawer. I'll wait.)

- **Use services for tasks that aren't error tolerant.** Many people with ADHD hire others to manage important tasks they may otherwise forget or mess up. Accountants can help us pay taxes on time and catch deductions we might miss. Lawyers can read important documents or, depending on their specialty, help you plan the future of your estate or handle your divorce. Speaking of which, asking a lawyer to draft a prenup is an effective way of lowering the ADHD tax, too.* Many services that feel like a luxury are actually an accommodation for us.

- **Set up shortcuts.** For things you do often, learn—or practice—ways to cut down on the steps that they involve. This reduces the demand on your working memory and makes it less likely you'll get distracted or lose something along the way. Almost all programs have built-in shortcuts; it can be worth taking the time to learn them. We can create physical shortcuts, too; coatracks condense the process of putting your coat where it belongs from four steps (open closet door, find empty hanger, hang coat, close door) to one step (hang coat on rack).

---

* The number of documents you have to find and the amount of stuff you have to remember during a divorce—one of the most emotionally devastating experiences of your entire life and one that ADHDers are statistically more likely to experience—is ridiculous.

- **Invest in tools that can help.** If you know that you lose things, look into Bluetooth trackers like Tile or features like Find My iPhone. If you forget to take your medication, consider investing in timer caps. If you know you tend to abandon planners unless they're covered in shiny stickers or are colorful AF, you might as well buy the shiniest stickers and the most exciting colors you can find. It will be surprisingly cheaper than going without them because you won't spend as much money (and frustrated effort!) on planners that aren't accessible to you.

Traeonna W., 47, Ohio

"My smartwatch reminds me of *all the things*. My watch is always on vibrate, so I am tapped every time there is a reminder app notification or an alarm I set. I have repeating alarms for waking up, leaving for work, three breaks at work, leaving work, etc. Certain health apps remind me of things like when to fast, when to check blood sugar, etc. If I need to get poked at for some reason, I set my watch to notify me somehow. Having that physical feedback is essential because I miss a lot of notifications on my phone."

"My family (six people, three with ADHD) uses smart speakers and smart home technology to automate 'shortcut' routines that save time and brain space. For example, running the 'Goodnight' routine turns off all the lights, starts the robot vacuum, and tells us if our dishwasher has been started and our devices are charging."

Gin A., 40, Maryland

"My psychiatrist told me if you find a work-around that solves the problem, it's just as good as not having the problem. For example, I kept shoes in my car because I sometimes left for work still wearing my slippers. So instead of being mad at myself for forgetting to put on shoes, I could let it go because it didn't matter. When I got to the office, I still had what I needed."

4. BUILD WHAT WORKS FOR YOU

We often build systems for the person we'd like to be rather than the person we are. We already have habits, preferences, aversions, strengths, and a history of what does and doesn't work for them. If we build systems with them in mind, we'll often be more successful at creating a system that works than if we try to build one from the ground up.

- **Look at what's worked before.** We can often reuse and re-purpose strategies that have helped us in the past. Even if they're not a perfect fit, we can often tweak them to make them work better. New systems might be more fun and exciting, but that novelty wears off. The stuff that's lasted beyond the new and shiny phase is often worth adapting (as needed) and trying again because it's more likely to stick.

- **Look at what you currently do.** If you usually spend an extra half hour after an exciting meeting brainstorming and infodumping at the person in the next meeting, maybe let them know that's the plan and make sure they're cool with that? If they're not, give yourself a buffer between meetings to let your super spinny brain wind down and transition to the next thing.

- **Consider your preferences.** Motivation can be a huge challenge for those with ADHD. If you love *Doctor Who*, getting a *Doctor Who* key holder might make it more likely you'll hang your keys there. If you hate spending time in the garage, is that really a good place to put the elliptical, Jessica?*

---

* The elliptical is still in the garage. I still do not use it. I am thinking of putting a pretty rug down there, though, and making it feel less garage-y!

- **Remember that you have ADHD.** Current us isn't neuro-typical. Future us isn't neurotypical, either. While we can improve our skills and mitigate some of our impairments, this takes time, and progress isn't always linear. Plus, the deficits don't go away, even if some of the impairments do. I'm still working with the same brain even after some of my impairments have lessened through the use of strategies. There are still places where my brain is going to trip over itself. Ever run a three-legged race with someone much faster or slower than you? Yeah. You're out of sync. And I am both of those people.

 — **Ron W., 49, Michigan**

"I love using my riding lawnmower. I hate raking leaves. So after years of letting leaves sit on my lawn all winter, I figured out that by taking the bag off and running my mower over the thick fallen leaves, I can chop the leaves into mulch. Then, all I have to do is put the bag on and run the mower over the yard again. Done. The neighbors may think it's weird to mow leaves, but as far as I'm concerned, this all-season pain-in-the-butt now takes one afternoon . . . and it's fun!"

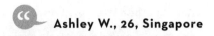
Ashley W., 26, Singapore

"I'm bad at remembering things, so I religiously take notes. I've set up a custom style sheet on my word processors because I once hyperfocused on typography, so now every time I look at my word processors, I get a dopamine rush just from how clean and good it looks."

MANUAL MODE

I was still waiting tables while working on the channel and learning about my brain. At this point, I had worked at restaurants for so long and gotten so good at it that I barely had to think about what I was doing. I was on autopilot.

I was one of the best servers at the restaurant. I could step out back to check YouTube, reply to comments, and still keep my tables happy. When I put in an order, my fingers flew over the computer screen. The sense of urgency, the stimulation—it was exhilarating. I loved doing that work because I'd get into flow. Sometimes I felt superhuman.

One day, the system was updated and the menus were rearranged. They didn't change completely, but they were different enough to keep me from relying on muscle memory or mental autopilot.

I was now in what I call *manual mode:* I had to think about each action, actively look for what I needed, figure out which category a menu item was in, and then scan the screen for what I was looking for. In other words, I had to rely on my executive function.

These changes were disabling.

Sometimes I went through the same folder three times before I could find the menu item I was looking for.

The other servers became impatient and stood behind me waiting for me to finish putting in orders. The anxiety of knowing someone was watching me wrestle with the new system made it even harder to think. It took me so long to put in a single order that I started to fall behind. My tables became angry, and needing to attend to them threw everything else out of whack. I couldn't keep up with the demands I'd so easily handled the day before. I was scared my managers would notice and decide I couldn't handle more tables, which would affect my income. I tried to make myself go faster, but it just made me more likely to make mistakes, which slowed me down further because now I needed to find a manager to correct them.

I started doing the rest of my job differently to try to keep up, which threw those parts into manual mode, too. Before, I could get everything done, no problem. Now, I needed to prioritize which tables to keep happy and figure out which steps of service to skip.

I went from being the quickest server in the restaurant to the slowest because of the increased demand on my executive function. Going from automatic mode to manual mode in just one aspect of my job was enough to make me struggle to even do my job. If the location of the menu items had changed every day, I would have gotten fired.

> In the effort to improve our lives, it can be easy to forget that some parts are already working for us.

Thankfully, my managers were understanding, and they didn't also change where the lemons were or what the sidework was. They expected that we'd have trouble with the changes (though I definitely had more trouble than most). They understood we'd need to get to the point where that system became automatic again before they changed anything else.

Now when I'm struggling to (executive) function, I check if any of the systems I rely on have been thrown into manual mode. And to remind myself that when a lot of my life is on manual mode, it's not a good time to add more to my plate.

When you're getting adjusted to something new, be aware of how many new systems are changing and try to keep as much of your life on automatic as possible.

In the effort to improve our lives, it can be easy to forget that some parts are already working for us. And keeping these parts the same—even if they're in areas we'd eventually like to improve—can provide a more stable foundation for the changes we're trying to make.

And if you are struggling with a new system, give it time. Even a system that will eventually work beautifully is often going to be a struggle at first.

Chapter 5

How to Sleep

I want to sleep, but my brain won't stop talking to itself.
—ADHD BRAINS EVERYWHERE

CHAOS THEORY

If sleep were a Dungeons & Dragons character, its alignment would be chaotic neutral.

Sleep doesn't care what you have going on the next day, what time you were supposed to wake up, or the fact that, in certain situations, sleeping is rude or even illegal.

For many of us, sleep does what it wants, when it wants, and doesn't care whose day it ruins.

And for me, it's been doing it since day one.

According to family lore, my mom kicked me out of her room on the first night I came home from the hospital because I was so dang noisy, even when I wasn't crying. And I wouldn't settle down no matter what she tried. She deposited me in my crib across the hall, which she hadn't intended to use for six months, and shut the door with a sardonic, whispered prayer: "*Please, God, don't let her die.*" Then she dove into her own bed to rest for the next day's battle.

> For many of us, sleep does what it wants, when it wants, and doesn't care whose day it ruins.

I often slept in weird places: only in my bouncy chair, or while being driven around, or on my dad's chest. "I can't get up—the baby is sleeping!"*

Some nights, as a kid, I'd lie awake for hours, staring at the popcorn ceiling in my bedroom or cracking the door open to peek down the hall at the TV. Other nights, I would wake up a few short hours after bedtime, my legs hurting so badly I needed ibuprofen and a hot bath to get back to sleep.

"Growing pains," the doctor said. "Not uncommon."

In the morning, though, I slept like the dead. I'd miss everything from my alarm to breakfast to an entire class.

Frequently, even when I *did* wake up on time, I was exhausted, my jaw sore, as if I'd been having fistfights in my nightmares.

"She grinds her teeth," the dentist said. "It's not uncommon."

My doctor and dentist weren't wrong. My symptoms weren't uncommon among children and adolescents. What deserved more attention, though, was how *significantly* I had struggled and *continue*

---

* This annoyed my mom to no end, but I am grateful for it. To this day, laying my head or face on someone I love is the most comforting thing in the world for me; it makes me feel safe and is often part of how I wind down for bed.

to struggle with sleep. Some kids grow out of their sleep difficulties. Mine persisted.

As a teenager, I would fall asleep before I made it to bed. Or even into the house. One night, I woke up in my parents' minivan, still in my marching band uniform—hat and all.

My boyfriend might suffer the most from my difficulties with sleep. Sleep problems can be the hardest aspects of ADHD to mask—especially from the people you live with. While watching TV before bed in the evening, I constantly shift positions or pace around the room. If I do manage to settle down, I might kick him as I doze off or wake him up with "bed yoga"* at three a.m. Last night, I scared him because just as he was falling asleep, my leg shot straight up into the air—and stayed there. (I don't remember this.)

My sleeping and waking behaviors have always felt oddly out of my control, and I was pretty sure many of them were *weird*. I was incredibly frustrated by them; I also had no idea what was causing them. As I described it in the episode on sleep that I created for my channel:

"I didn't know my sleep problems were related to my ADHD. I just thought I was a borderline narcoleptic night owl with restless leg syndrome who'd grind her teeth at night, fall asleep every time I sat down to relax, not go to bed so much as pass out from exhaustion, and sleep through every alarm short of the ice bucket challenge."

---

* I do actual yoga positions in bed, not because it's a great time to get in a workout but because my brain and body are too restless. Sometimes I find the right position to calm my nervous system, or get enough energy out to finally fall asleep.

WHAT I LEARNED

Sleep disorders are common with ADHD. *Really* common. Like, if-you-have-ADHD-you-probably-have-one common.

My doctors never looked more deeply at my sleep habits, but they should have. Sleep problems are so prevalent with ADHD, *they used to be part of the diagnostic criteria.*

According to the first edition of *Sleep and ADHD: An Evidence-Based Guide to Assessment and Treatment* published in 2019, 73 percent of children and adolescents and 80 percent of adults with ADHD experience sleep disorders.

These conditions commonly coexist with ADHD:

- **Obstructive sleep apnea:** This sleep disorder, characterized by snoring and pauses in breathing during sleep, is more common among adults, but it does occur in children, especially children with ADHD.

- **Restless leg syndrome:** This condition causes an intense, often irresistible urge to move your legs, particularly when sitting or lying down. Unlike ADHD-related hyperactivity, it happens mostly at night and often gets worse with age.

- **Periodic limb movement syndrome:** You know how your leg kicks or your arm flops all of a sudden when you're falling asleep? *It has a name.* At least, it does when it keeps happening every twenty to forty seconds and long enough to interfere with sleep.*

- **Sleepwalking and night terrors:** These sleep disorders occur when the lines between awake and asleep are blurred. They are often first observed in childhood by parents.

- **Insomnia:** You've probably heard of this one. Insomnia occurs whenever you *want* to sleep but *can't* sleep, due to difficulties falling asleep or staying asleep, and it is also one of the criteria for delayed sleep phase syndrome.

- **Delayed sleep phase syndrome:** This syndrome occurs when your body's internal clock, or its circadian rhythm, is delayed by two or more hours. For example, you might naturally want to sleep from three a.m. to noon.

- **Excessive daytime sleepiness:** This condition is exactly what it sounds like. If you're falling asleep in the middle of a movie at your friend's house or missing a shift because you can't stay awake, it doesn't mean you're a bad friend or a lazy employee. It could be a sign that something is wrong.

---

*   This is different from the hypnic jerk, the sudden movement of your entire body that happens as you're falling asleep. Those don't usually interfere with sleep.

Current research suggests that more severe ADHD symptoms are associated with more severe sleep disorder symptoms (and vice versa). Sleep disorders are also more prevalent with certain ADHD presentations. For instance, excessive daytime sleepiness is more strongly associated with the primarily inattentive presentation, while restless leg syndrome is more strongly associated with the primarily hyperactive/impulsive presentation. Those of us with combined presentation are at higher risk for both conditions. (Whooooo.)

WE'RE MORE LIKELY TO MISS SLEEP

There are all kinds of reasons people sacrifice sleep—grad school, caring for a baby, or meeting book deadlines. ADHDers, however, are more likely to regularly experience the following reasons for staying awake:

We're not tired yet.

Those with ADHD tend to have a later chronotype—that is, the time we're naturally inclined to sleep is later than usual. For those with these chronotypes, melatonin (the sleep hormone) is released later, delaying our bedtime. Dr. Stephen Becker, an expert in both ADHD and sleep who shared his insights with me, says this is especially problematic in adolescence when chronotypes are naturally later and more sleep is required.

> **chronotype (n.)**
> Your body's natural disposition to be awake/
> alert or sleepy/asleep at certain times of the
> day, based on your circadian rhythm.

We're not done yet.

Because we have difficulty focusing, homework, chores, and bedtime routines can take longer for us to finish. We might find ourselves staying up late to take care of things we forgot, cramming for tests at the last minute, or finishing projects the night before they're due. Time management, motivation, and focus also pose significant challenges for those with ADHD—and our struggles in these areas often cut into our sleep.

We're too stimulated (or not stimulated enough).

Stimulant medications and caffeine are commonly used to treat ADHD (or self-medicate, in the case of caffeine). They can also keep us awake. However, for some with ADHD, stimulants have the opposite effect. Many doctors report some patients have an easier time making the transition to bed when they're medicated and find it more difficult when their meds have worn off. Understimulated brains might race with a million thoughts, pick a fight with their bedmate, or bounce out of bed for one more bedtime snack.

We experience revenge bedtime procrastination.

Revenge bedtime procrastination is a phrase that describes the experience of staying awake to play video games, message friends, let our brains dive down Wikipedia rabbit holes. You know, the things we didn't get to do while we were awake.

Bedtime? What's a bedtime?

Research has found that inconsistent sleep schedules can make it harder to get enough sleep, and a lack of routine is associated with inconsistent sleep schedules. Since ADHD brains tend to have trouble sticking with routines, it isn't surprising that we have trouble sleeping at the same time every night. But sometimes, our lack of routine might be due to our *difficulties sleeping*. After all, what's the point of going to bed at a certain time when you know you're just going to stare at the ceiling for three hours?

Going to bed is boring.

Boredom is *painful* for ADHD brains, and sleep can be boring, especially if we need to transition from doing something fun to a tedious bedtime routine. When we finally make it to bed, we often deal with the distress that boredom causes by distracting ourselves with activities that don't support a good night's sleep. (What's up, blue light?)

WE NEED SLEEP

Skipping sleep can, in some circles, become a point of pride and even earn you bragging rights. Certain phrases from college and from living with other neurodivergent brains come to mind: "I'll sleep when I'm dead." "Sleep is for quitters." "Pfft, I don't need sleep—sleep is for the weak." When sleep often isn't an option, *not* sleeping can become an identity. A lifestyle. You lean into it. Unfortunately, all this bravado doesn't change the fact that we *need sleep*.

Out of all the self-care practices that support brain function, such as eating well and exercising, getting enough sleep is *by far* the most crucial. When we forgo sleep, it's at the expense of our energy levels, alertness, cognitive capabilities, and emotion regulation. Missing out on sleep makes our ADHD symptoms worse. Research on children with ADHD has found that as little as a *thirty-minute reduction* from normal sleep duration is enough to impact their daytime functioning and behavior.

Inadequate sleep impacts many of the same executive functions affected by ADHD:

- Attention regulation

- Recall and working memory

- Processing speed

- Response inhibition

While it's tempting to tell ourselves we can make up for missed sleep on the weekend, it doesn't work that way. Sleep is not a side quest. Human beings need to sleep *consistently,* and those of us with ADHD aren't exceptions. It might be harder for us to sleep well, but the consequences are greater for us when we don't.

 Shelley S., 49, Canada

"I am an active sleeper both physically and mentally. When I sleep, I rub my feet together—we call it cricket feet. I jump when I flip over, I roll up in the blanket, and I flip my pillow about four times a night. Mentally, I am very alert and wake up easily to noises. Sometimes I wake up with my heart pounding if I hear people outside being too loud. I also do a ton of problem-solving through dreams and come up with ideas for art projects I am working on."

 Kristen H., 33, USA

"Procrastination, sleep, and I are in a toxic mid-2000s love triangle. Logically, I know an adequate amount of sleep will help me think more clearly and lead me to make better decisions. It's the safe, reasonable choice. But bedtime procrastination lures me back in with promises of excitement and adventure!"

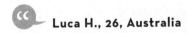

Luca H., 26, Australia

"For me, getting to bed is a constant struggle against the dopamine slot machine that is my phone."

Adrian G., 20, Norway

"I've had trouble sleeping for as long as I can remember. My overactive brain also used to give me a lot of night-mares as a kid, to the point of me waking up screaming every night for a long period of time. My biggest problem now is falling asleep. Weighted blanket, medication, and trying every single advice available. Nothing works. Simply put: sleeping is stressful."

THE TOOLBOX

While there are effective treatments available for every single sleep disorder associated with ADHD, there are many practices that you can do for yourself or your loved ones right now.

1. PRIORITIZE (THE RIGHT AMOUNT OF) SLEEP

While there are times when we have trouble sleeping, there are other times when we skip sleep to have extra hours in our day to get stuff done. Prioritizing sleep means no longer seeing sleep as optional, or less important than whatever else needs to happen in our day. None of the other strategies will matter much if we throw sleep out the window the second something comes up.

You might be wondering, *But isn't that six a.m. yoga class / gym session worth waking up early for?*

If you can do that and still get enough sleep, sure. But according to Dr. Patrick LaCount, "If you need to pick between exercise and getting enough sleep, *sleep*." This is coming from someone who researches the positive impacts of exercise on ADHD.

However, prioritizing sleep doesn't mean getting as much sleep as possible, or even getting eight hours. The amount of sleep we need varies from person to person and changes over our lifetime.

According to experts, you should aim to sleep long enough to fulfill your intrinsic sleep needs. In other words, we should be aiming for enough sleep so that we feel refreshed and alert, not dull and sleepy.

 Daniel C., 36, Kansas

"I absolutely love the quiet nights. I love that I get to forget about deadlines and requirements, as the day is usually over and just about the only time I don't feel like there's a demand on me. I also enjoy those nights because I'm alone and don't have to mask in any way. But losing sleep makes me more impulsive. When I stay up (as an impulsive decision) and then continue to make impulsive decisions in the following days, I regret it and try to adjust my habits."

❝ **Shizue T., 23, Oregon**

"I've trained my body to go to sleep early because I need eleven hours of sleep a night to be fully rested. I can fall asleep around nine, but I'll wake up a couple times between then and one. After midnight, I'm pretty much guaranteed to go to sleep and stay asleep."

2. PRACTICE "GOOD" SLEEP HYGIENE?

Practicing good sleep hygiene means following the personal practices and before-bed rituals that help us sleep better—and avoiding the ones that make us sleep worse.

But what is that stuff?

That's tricky. While there's enough research to inform general guidelines for good sleep hygiene, what works for each person varies. Plus, because much of the research on sleep hygiene has been done on the general population, there are still a lot of gaps in that knowledge when it comes to the population with ADHD.

Even when we know what good sleep hygiene is, we may struggle to follow it and follow it consistently. Having ADHD means laughing heartily at common sleep hygiene tips because they are so unrealistic for us. "Avoid electronics for two hours before bed?" Are they kidding?

Still, there are a few research-backed sleep hygiene strategies worth trying for most of us.

- **Time your stimulants.** Many of us use stimulant medication, caffeine, and even nicotine to manage our ADHD. Some stimulants naturally last longer than others, and some last longer for certain individuals. For some, caffeine at bedtime can help them "focus" on getting to sleep; for others, any stimulants after noon can make it harder. Try tracking what time you take any stimulants and how you sleep that night. Use this information to figure out the best time for you to take them.

- **Avoid conflict right before bed.** Since sleep happens more easily when you feel safe, give yourself (and your loved ones) enough time to return to your emotional baselines before going to bed. If there's a nonurgent issue, address it well before bedtime or leave it for another day so you have a better chance of being able to sleep. Not only will everyone be less cognitively drained while you're trying to discuss the issue, it also avoids a common ADHD bedtime trap of "I'm bored, and fighting is stimulating!"

- **Keep bedtime and wake times as consistent as possible.** Sleep depends on two factors: 1.) your circadian rhythm, and 2.) your homeostatic regulation, the process that regulates your biological systems, including your need for sleep.* Sleep is most effective when your circadian rhythm

---

* It works like hunger and thirst—the longer we go without eating, the hungrier we get. The longer we go without sleeping, the more tired we get.

and homeostatic regulation are working together. This is why your best bet for good sleep is to keep your bedtimes and wake times as consistent as you can. This way, your body has a chance to build up the need for sleep as your body *clock* starts nudging you toward bed. If you do need to adjust your bedtime, Dr. Becker recommends doing it incrementally, moving it no more than fifteen minutes at a time.

- **Associate your bed with sleep.** The more time we spend in bed staring at the ceiling or completing a task such as answering emails, the more we associate our bed with wakefulness. This can weaken the brain's cue to sleep when you settle into bed. Experts suggest that if you have been lying awake for twenty minutes, get out of bed, do something boring, and come back when you're ready to sleep. If you *do* need to use your bed for other tasks, create a cue that only happens at bedtime to help you differentiate between work bed and sleep bed. For example, you might keep your pillows off the bed until it's time to sleep.

A Note on Electronics

There is conflicting research about electronics at bedtime. The standard advice says to limit screen time and keep devices out of the bedroom. However, there isn't strong evidence that avoiding electronics in the hours *before* bedtime is necessary. (Thank the screen time gods!)

If watching reality TV or wikiwalking on your tablet before bed makes you sleepy, by all means go for it. No matter what you choose to do, keep in mind that there is strong support in the scientific literature for leaving electronics out of the bedroom as a way to promote healthy sleep—and healthy relationships (wink)!

 Shawn P., 46, Michigan

"For the bulk of my life, I've slept poorly, regardless of the time. Last year, my doctor asked if caffeine helped me sleep. Trying such a thing never occurred to me. Now a cup of caffeinated tea right before bed helps me fall asleep, and I sleep better now than ever in my life."

 Rumena N., 34, North Macedonia

"I sleep the best when I do everything opposite of what is recommended: I sleep from two a.m. to ten a.m., drink caffeine before bed, and fall asleep with the TV droning on."

Raven M., 27, Tennessee

"One of the side effects of getting medicated for my anxiety and CPTSD (complex post-traumatic stress disorder) has been the ability to regulate my sleep schedule. But I still follow a nightly routine to the best of my ability. It includes relaxing with hobbies, aromatherapy, a really good eye mask, and listening to *The Great British Baking Show* with a sleep timer on the TV."

3. MOTIVATE YOURSELF TO SLEEP

Knowing that we *should* sleep and that it's important often isn't enough to convince an ADHD brain to shut down for the night. We are attracted to things that are exciting, urgent, and new. Sleep is pretty much the opposite of all that. The societal and social pressures to skip it don't help either.

Here are some strategies you might consider to make bedtime a better time:

- **Get your needs met during the day.** We might assume prioritizing the full amount of sleep our brains need means giving up hobby time, alone time, or social time. But those activities are important, too. If we give ourselves guilt-free time for them during the day, we'll be less likely to do them while we're *supposed* to be sleeping—and more motivated to actually sleep.*

---

*   And getting sleep can make us faster at getting our other stuff done, so we're more likely to have time for both!

- **Create wind-down rituals you enjoy.** Our brains and bodies need time to wind down before bed. The key for those with ADHD is to choose wind-down rituals that are interesting enough for you to want to do them, but not so engaging that you can't stop doing them. Think: putting together puzzles, reading, trading massages, or watching reruns of old TV shows.

- **Consider your sensory needs.** A lot of ADHDers are sensitive to rough blankets, weird tasting toothpaste, the fit of their clothes, or tags on their PJs. On the flip side, we can be drawn to "sensory good" experiences. To make bedtime more appealing, it can be helpful to seek out soft cozy blankets, silk pillowcases, weighted comforters, essential oil diffusers, different flavors of toothpaste, or various states of undress. If your body feels good, it will be easier to relax, mentally and physically.

Marie S., 32, New Jersey

"The more I can do to wind down before I sleep, the better. Dimming the lights in the bathroom, using lavender shower gel, changing into clean PJs—I do all that at least forty-five minutes before bed."

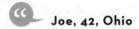 **Joe, 42, Ohio**

> "I have listened to the same *Lord of the Rings* audiobook recordings for over a decade. Now I associate it with sleep. It's Pavlovian when I hear it."

Anne Bettina P., 44, Denmark

> "About six months ago, doing sudoku on my phone helped me sleep. Then it was crossword puzzles, and now it's some TV series. The main thing is to distract my brain."

Andrew F., 37, Washington

> "Since elementary school, I've always drifted off to sleep listening to someone talking. It was talk radio, a baseball game, or 'old-time' radio replays when I was younger, and since college, it's been podcasts. For the last fifteen years or so, I also have a ritual around Sunday nights where I *always* listen to *Wait Wait...Don't Tell Me!* as I fall asleep. That's how I mentally prepare for Mondays."

4. WORK WITH YOUR CHRONOTYPE

Those with ADHD tend to have night owl chronotypes, which can make it hard to get enough sleep in a world that expects us to wake up early.

Still, even though late-to-bed may be the most common chrono-type for ADHD brains, it's not the only scenario, especially when chronotypes can shift over time.*

Understanding and working with our current chronotype can help us plan our day around the times when we'll be most alert—and when we'll get our best sleep.

- **Figure out your chronotype.** For a couple weeks (maybe over the summer or on vacation), try going to bed when you feel sleepy and waking up without an alarm clock. This can give you a clue as to what your current chronotype might be. If you don't have the ability to do this or don't want to wait, you can find a link to the morningness-eveningness questionnaire, which asks questions about your sleeping and waking habits, by scanning the QR code in the "Support Organizations" section (page 432).

- **Plan to tackle focus-heavy work when you're most alert.** Try signing up for later classes if you're a night owl or re-questing earlier work shifts if you're a morning lark. Even a traditional nine-to-five job might offer a more flexible schedule as an accommodation for your ADHD. Even if you can't shift your work hours, it's often possible to choose

---

* Fun fact: Chronotype shifts earlier—and fairly dramatically—with pregnancy.

when you complete tasks that require more focus. Your chronotype doesn't just affect when you get sleepy, but also when you're most alert. Planning work around this can boost your overall productivity.

- **Prep for mornings.** If you need to wake up earlier than your natural chronotype would prefer, prepare what you can the night before. Lay out your clothes, put the things you need for work on a "launchpad" by the door, throw together some overnight oats—you get the idea. This prep work lets you spend as much time as possible in your chronotypical sleep zone and makes good use of the time when you're still wide awake.

- **Create light cues.** Circadian rhythms are sensitive to environmental cues, specifically light. Set smart lightbulbs to gradually dim at night when it's time to go to bed. This will cue your brain to produce melatonin naturally, readying you for sleep. You can also use smart lights to simulate sunrise. And just going outside first thing in the morning and absorbing the sun like a heckin' houseplant can help calibrate your body's circadian rhythm. The sunlight communicates to your brain and body that it's daytime—and that you should be awake!

Olivia L., 34, Texas

"I normally don't get ready for bed on weekdays until after eleven p.m., because I'm more productive in the evenings. My brain does not function at its finest until *at least* one p.m. My mom has always said that I'm like a bat in the morning (moving slowly, don't like lights, would rather not talk). I wish I could be a morning person. I really have tried! Going to bed early and getting up early does *not* work [for me] sadly."

 Shanea, 49, Michigan

"I have to start my evening unwinding with a hot bath; I have a physically demanding job, and I have to relax my muscles. The challenge is I'm a night owl, so my cutoff is eleven p.m. I make a point as an early riser Monday through Friday to take vitamin supplements every morning. I allow myself to sleep in on weekends because of the demands of my job during the week."

A Note on Melatonin

If you have a later chronotype and you don't produce melatonin when it's supposed to be sleepytime, store-bought is fine. In fact, many ADHDers fall asleep with the help of melatonin supplements. Melatonin is the most commonly used treatment for disrupted sleep caused by ADHD, and it can significantly improve our ability to fall asleep earlier. That said, over-the-counter melatonin is not regulated, and there is controversy over who should be using it, at what dosage, and for how long, as well as how it may impact our other sleep challenges, such as restless leg syndrome. Before trying it, talk to your doctor. (I am not a doctor.)

5. HAVE A BACKUP PLAN

Sometimes you do everything "right" and *still* have trouble sleeping. Anxiety about getting to sleep can make it harder to fall asleep, so have a backup plan. Not only will this help you survive the aftermath of a restless night and get through the next day, it might also help you sleep better because you know you've got options in case you can't.*

---

*   That said, if you find yourself relying on backup plans more than usual, check in with yourself. (Are you okay??) More sleep disturbances than usual (for you) can be a sign of other issues with your mental or physical health, relationships, or work life. When in doubt, ask a professional.

- **Sleep somewhere else.** Sometimes, switching locations can help you fall asleep because you don't associate a different spot with the frustration of trying to doze off. At the very least, you can relax better knowing you won't be disturbing anyone else if you don't. You can also switch sleeping positions—I often flip around so my feet are where my pillow should be.

- **Rest.** If you really can't sleep, you can get some of its benefits by simply resting. Getting rest can include meditating, practicing restorative yoga, or even just lying in bed with your eyes closed.

- **Make a wake-up plan.** While those with ADHD have trouble falling asleep, by morning the struggle is typically waking up. Set backup alarms, have someone call or check on you to make sure you're awake, or have whatever helps you wake up at the ready (cats are helpful). Flexible start times at work can help here, too (as can coffee!).

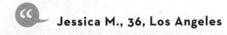 **Jessica M., 36, Los Angeles**

"When I was taking meditation classes, the teacher explained how meditation can be deeply restful and restore energy in a way that's similar to sleep—just not at first. First, it kicks out all the stress-props that have been holding us up, so we may actually be more tired. Now when I can't sleep, I spend more time meditating to try and recharge my body and brain batteries."

Raffael B., 41, Seattle

"When I can't fall asleep, I leave the bedroom and read something that's just interesting enough to keep my focus but not interesting enough to stimulate me. Often, that's factoids on Wikipedia."

 Theresa W., 43, Michigan

"Some nights, my AuDHD teenager can only sleep on 'hard mode.' Instead of resting in their too-quiet bedroom, I'll find them on the couch, fully clothed, occasionally with the lights on."

OWLS AND LARKS

For most of my life, I considered going to bed "on time" to be "early enough to wake up at five or six a.m., so I can do my sun salutations at sunrise." Anything past that time was clearly *late*.*

When I did manage to go to bed "on time," I often felt proud of myself, as if doing so somehow transformed me into a morally superior human being, even just for that day. There are a lot of sayings that reinforce this message: "Early to bed and early to rise makes a man healthy, wealthy, and wise," "The early bird gets the worm,"

---

*   Needless to say, I went to bed "late" a lot.

"Success comes to those who have the will-power to win over their snooze buttons."

When I was researching this chapter, I stumbled across an article in *The New Yorker* with a title that immediately caught my eye: "No, Mornings Don't Make You Moral."

Journalist Maria Konnikova explains there is some research to suggest that people behave more ethically during the day than they do at night—what the re-searchers called the morning morality effect. But there's a caveat: this effect is only observed if it aligns with your chronotype.

> This made me wonder if I'd be a better boss, partner, and pal if I accepted the bedtime appropriate for me based on my chronotype, not someone else's.

"Some people did cheat less in the morning," Konnikova found, "but only if they were early birds to begin with. The opposite was also true: night owls cheated less in the evening. Time of day had less effect on honesty, the group concluded, than did the *synchronicity between person and environment* [emphasis mine]."

Even if being morally superior isn't a priority, I still feel the pres-sure to wake up early because it helps me be productive. If I wake up early, I can get more done during the day because that's when busi-nesses are *open*.

So can we *change* our chronotype and become the kind of people who do yoga every day at six a.m.?

"Good question," said Dr. Becker when I asked him. He explained that while chronotypes do shift naturally over the course of our life-time, intentionally shifting them is another story.

Other researchers agree. For her article, Konnikova spoke with behavioral scientist Sunita Sah, who found that "it's incredibly difficult, if not impossible, to overcome your predisposition and train yourself to function better at times that don't match up with your inner clock."

This made me wonder if I'd be a better boss, partner, or pal if I accepted the bedtime appropriate for me based on *my* chronotype, not someone else's. As the morningness-eveningness questionnaire and plenty of past experience suggests, mine is twelve-thirty a.m. What would happen if and when I made this bedtime work—and got enough sleep—and felt proud of myself for doing so?

The article also got me thinking about how we judge people based on their sleep patterns. It's common to assume someone is "lazy" because they sleep longer than other people, more dedicated if they're awake by six a.m., or no fun because they skip the nightclub.

Now that we understand that people need different amounts of sleep and have significant natural variations in *when* they need to sleep, maybe we can start to let go of these moral judgments. The truth is, there are incredibly productive people who sleep until noon, and social butterflies who get tired by eight p.m.

> The truth is, there are incredibly productive people who sleep until noon, and social butterflies who get tired by eight p.m.

We can also try building a world that accounts for the diversity in chronotypes. Technology has made flexible hours and work-from-home options more common.

The internet has allowed us to connect with others beyond our own time zone. Online options for everyday tasks, such as corresponding with loved ones and depositing checks, make post office and bank hours practically obsolete. You can even find an online notary who's available 24/7. Maybe late-night bookstores and dance party brunches will be next!

And hey, if you happen to hear of (and/or start) any businesses that operate outside of standard business hours, let me know. I know some night owls and morning larks who would love to drop by.

Chapter 6

How to See Time

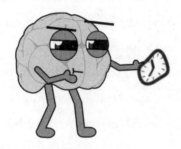

People assume that time is a strict progression from cause to effect,
but actually, from a non-linear, non-subjective viewpoint,
it's more like a big ball of wibbly-wobbly, timey-wimey . . . stuff.

—DOCTOR WHO (THE TENTH DOCTOR)

THE MACHINATIONS OF TIME

Time folds and unfolds itself all the time in my world.

Sometimes, it feels as if it's folding in on me, crushing me with the weight of all the things that need to be done now, tomorrow, last year, and five minutes ago.

Inevitably, whatever amount of time I give myself to do a task, travel to a place, or get ready to meet a friend is not the *right* amount of time. The task takes longer than predicted, or I forget to account for traffic, or I hop out of my five-minute shower to find that a half hour has passed. (*How?*)

Whereas focus feels like something solid, something that is either there or isn't (and it is very clear when it isn't!), time is not a shape-shifter, exactly, but a *state*-shifter. Right before a deadline (or when I'm booked back to back), I can feel the cold, crushing press of unyielding time. When I'm immersed in a hobby or daydreaming, it passes by in an unnoticed cloud. When I'm bored or anxiously waiting for something (or someone), it's a tedious, maddening drip.

As a kid, homework assignments that were supposed to take fifteen minutes often took an hour, which often *felt* like five.

Middle School Me: This is so long and forever-taking!
The Clock: Tick (*infinite silence*) Tock.

Hyperfocus, on the other hand, was like a time Slip 'N Slide. I'd set out to spend half an hour on a school project only to look up and see it was already dark outside.

Middle School Me: (*absorbed*) Let's see, if I glue the Popsicle sticks like this, I bet they could support the structure *here* . . .
The Clock: (*hands whirling cartoonishly behind me*) TickTockTickTockTickTockTick.

By the time I was a teenager, it was clear that I was terrible at managing my time. This did not stop people from expecting me to do so.

"Don't forget to do this next week!"

"Remember, this is due in a month. Plan accordingly."

"Can you start dinner in fifteen minutes?"

I'd nod and pretend I could.

As I got older and became more responsible for managing my time, minutes late turned into weeks, months, or even *years* late. And the effects on my life were profound.

I missed deadlines for college applications, parking tickets, credit card bills, and taxes. I was fired for being perpetually late. I was constantly playing catch-up. I was always running behind.

I tried to plan my time better, but for most of my life, my relationship with schedules has looked like this:

1. Set up a schedule.

2. Fail to follow the schedule.

3. Repeat steps 1 and 2.

For years, I was able to neatly sidestep my time management issues by having a job that didn't require it—waiting tables. Yes, time was critical, but everything that I needed to do had to happen *now*. Besides getting to work, I didn't need to be anywhere at a specific time. I didn't have to plan how long anything was going to take. I just had to complete my tasks, as quickly as possible, and in the right order: offer drinks, take the order, put it in the computer . . .

For anything that needed to be done outside of work, I did it when I remembered to. Or when I felt like it. Or when I was close enough to a deadline that my brain kicked into gear. Planning and replanning took so much time, it felt as if I were wasting it.

Forget about getting things done at a certain time, I'd decide. *I just need to get stuff done.*

So, when I had a lot to do, I would do everything I remembered to do, as I remembered to do it, which sometimes meant all at once, until I lost consciousness. Then I would wake up and do it again.

This was my life in college, and it became my life again when I was working on the channel and waiting tables. As the channel grew, it presented a whole new smorgasbord of responsibilities, deadlines, and expectations. I was already researching, writing, shooting, editing, and responding to comments seven days a week (on top of my actual job) because, again, what is time? And now there were exponentially more comments, I was reading dense research papers on PubMed, and I had perks to deliver on Patreon, podcast interviews to prep for, and conferences to attend. Before, I'd been doing more and more to make up for past failures; now, I was doing more and more because of my success. It was becoming harder and harder to keep up.

It was exhausting. There were times it was clear, often when I was shooting an episode at two a.m., that this schedule (or lack thereof) wasn't working for me. I really didn't know what else to do, though. I felt ashamed. Time management was such a basic requirement for every pursuit in life, and everyone else seemed to have it on lock. I felt ridiculous for being a grown-ass adult who still hadn't figured it out.

WHAT I LEARNED

I thought how I experienced time was how everyone experienced time, only other people were better at wrestling it into submission.

Nope.

Turns out, those with ADHD are at a serious disadvantage when it comes to time management, for reasons ranging from how we experience it to the fact that we forget things so often (see "How to Remember Stuff," page 186).

According to Dr. Barkley, 8 percent of the general population has difficulties with time management.

And those with ADHD? *Ninety*-eight percent.

I'm gonna say that again so you know it wasn't a typo. Ninety-eight percent of people with ADHD self-reported time management difficulties—and their partners agreed.

Ninety-eight percent of people don't self-report liking ice cream.*

Just know, if you related to what I've shared here, you can stop kicking yourself now (although you should probably check what time it is, in case you're running late).

WE EXPERIENCE TIME DIFFERENTLY

Dr. Barkley explains in lectures, books, and research papers that those with ADHD are actually "time blind"—or, more accurately,

---

* I looked up some ice cream stats and found this: "According to new data from YouGov Omnibus, 96 percent of Americans eat ice cream. The most popular flavor is chocolate (14 percent), followed by vanilla (13 percent) and butter pecan (11 percent)."

time *nearsighted*. A significant body of research (and lived experi-ence from the ADHD community) backs this up.

---

time blindness/nearsightedness (n.)
Inability (or exceptional difficulty) recognizing how much time has passed and/or estimating how long something will take.

We Have Differences in Temporal Processing

Some people have a "sharp" sense of time. They know exactly how long they've been chatting with a friend or when it's time to turn off the bath.* They can sense how much time has passed relatively ac-curately. This may be due to their circadian rhythms (or "internal clocks") combined with environmental cues such as light, sound, and temperature changes.

Those with ADHD tend to have a "soft" sense of time. Unless we're intentionally tracking it, we can't tell how much time has passed or *sense* time passing the way others can. Even without slipping into hyperfocus, we may not realize it's time to move on to something

---

*   I didn't know not everyone lacks this sense, because my family doesn't have it. I would be at my aunt's house editing this right now, but, uh, her house isn't guest friendly at the moment. She flooded her main bathroom . . . and bedroom.

else without the help of alarms and reminders. And in hyperfocus, we may completely miss them.

My fellow YouTuber and friend Jesse J. Anderson describes it this way: "It's like a sense I don't have. If I couldn't feel pain, I would use clues to guess how much pain I should be in—'my skin is red from impact,' 'the pot is boiling,' 'oh, I'm bleeding'—but I'm still just guessing. It's the same with time. I can use clues but never sense it myself."

We Have Shorter Time Horizons

Time horizons—the point at which events are close enough to begin to feel real—tend to be *much* shorter for those with ADHD. For many of us, projects, tasks, and events exist either "now" or "not now"—and anything "not now" can feel as if it doesn't exist at all. We often live in the moment, responding only to what's in front of our face and needs to be done now*—and have trouble planning for events later than the next day, unless they're particularly exciting. This makes it difficult for us to learn from our mistakes (we've already forgotten them!) or plan for the future (it doesn't feel real!).

Our shorter time horizons are one reason why we might start studying for a test the night before. The point at which things land on our mental "plate" is typically much closer to the deadline for us. We might know intellectually that we have something coming up, but unlike our neurotypical peers, we haven't had it land on our "I

---

*   Which, in the words of Eddie, one of our producers, is based on "whichever client is screaming the loudest."

should get started on this" radar yet. And the switch won't be flipped from "not now" to "now" until it does.

Time Flies—or Drags—More for Us

"Time flies when you're having fun." While this is true for everyone to some extent, those with ADHD experience a more extreme version of this. Boring tasks can seem to stretch on forever, while activities that are engaging to our brains can easily make us lose track of hours or even days. When estimating how long things take, we often underestimate the time needed for tasks we're looking forward to* and overestimate the time needed for tasks we're dreading.

WE FORGET TO ACCOUNT FOR (MORE) THINGS

An ADHD coach once pointed out that play has three parts: setup, the play itself, and cleanup. The same is true for pretty much everything we do, from making dinner to attending a meeting.† But those of us with ADHD often forget about the "setup" and "cleanup" part, and only account for the time we think it'll take us to do the thing.

When it comes to driving somewhere, for example, we might

---

*   I still forget sometimes that just because something sounds fun to me doesn't mean it won't take a significant amount of time to do it.

†   Right? *I didn't know that either!* But yeah, we have to get there, get our materials or notes ready, attend the meeting, then capture the follow-up tasks, update people on information we learned, and process what we learned.

leave ourselves fifteen minutes (because my map app says it'll take fifteen minutes to get there!) and don't account for the time it takes to get to the car, get gas if necessary, and find parking. Because we tend to forget that we need to plan, prep, put things back, and follow up, we're often already running late before we even get started.

Other factors we often forget to account for:

- **Things going wrong:** We often plan for the version of events where everything goes perfectly. Unfortunately, things don't always go perfectly.

- **Biological needs:** As humans, we need to eat, drink water, move, use the restroom, and sleep. When predicting how long something will take us, we often don't build in time for bathroom breaks or rest.

- **Transition time:** If one activity ends at one p.m. and the next starts at the same time, you're probably going to be late, even if it's just a video meeting. Transitions take time—and our brains need time to switch between two things, too.

- **Contingencies:** Sometimes, we can't do something before we've done something else first. For instance, it's hard to wrap presents if they haven't arrived yet—or if we don't have wrapping paper.

- **Our energy levels:** A lot of time management is actually energy management. We might technically have the time for something but not the energy to actually do it.

- **Ideation time:** If the work we're doing is creative, we can't just create; we also need time to consume content that can spark new ideas, brainstorm, and let ideas percolate.

- **Mistakes:** Mistakes are doubly problematic to forget to account for. We're not just more likely to make them and possibly need to fix them. We're also more likely to need extra time to double- (or triple-) check our work.

WE PLAN FOR A VERSION OF OURSELVES THAT DOESN'T HAVE ADHD

While time nearsightedness is independent of executive function challenges, these EF challenges can play an enormous role in our difficulties with time management.

- **Working memory impairments** make it more likely we'll forget what we're doing or have to run back for something we left behind. Our need to self-accommodate these impairments makes certain tasks, especially admin ones, take longer than they otherwise would.

- **Organizational challenges** mean we're more likely to misplace what we need, have trouble finding it, or struggle to put it back where it needs to be (if we even know where that is). We often have trouble organizing our thoughts and our speech, too; as divergent thinkers, we might be wonderfully imaginative writers, but narrowing down what we want to say (which relies on convergent thinking) and wrestling the brain chaos into some sort of structure is hard.*

- **Difficulty regulating our attention** means there are vast differences in our productivity levels. Some days, we might end up in hyperfocus and get a lot done; other days, we'll be distracted by everything and we won't accomplish much at all.

- **Deficits in response inhibition** make it more likely we'll impulsively start—or have trouble stopping—a task we didn't even intend to do. Those with ADHD can get a lot done; it's just often not what we set out to do.

Unfortunately, we often plan our time (or are expected to plan our time) as if these differences don't exist. We expect ourselves to be

---

* I've personally rewritten entire keynote speeches because it was faster than looking for and adapting the one I'd already written.

able to get things done in the same time frame (and with the same consistency) as someone without ADHD, despite all evidence to the contrary. We expect ourselves to do things when we planned to do them, so rather than giving ourselves the flexibility of hopping around, we drag our feet starting on (or full-on avoid) the task we're "supposed" to do.

The result? Work often spills over into nights and weekends, or we fall behind. We cancel plans with friends, eat into sleep, and don't have time to move, relax, or have fun. We spend excessive amounts of time on things that others ask of us at the expense of things we need to feel fulfilled, or even to be okay. We burn out. Or we give up on trying to manage our time at all.

 Nathan F., 44, Australia

"I am both fifteen and forty-four. Everything in the last thirty years happened in the last month. The future is all happening both tomorrow and at some point I don't need to think about yet. I have no constructive way of coping with this."

 Dan M., 40, Ireland

"For me, there are only three different time experiences:
1. Now vs. not now
2. Why is everything taking so long?
3. Wait? How is it X time already?"

— **Justin D., 29, Kentucky**

"[Time] stretches and compresses, it changes day to day, and has since I was a kid. I would always check the time a lot and had multiple clocks around my room and a watch. Regularly checking the time was just how I dealt with it. Knowing the time was such a habit that the first thing that I asked after waking up from my wisdom teeth removal was the current time. I couldn't open my eyes or speak, so I had to gesture that I wanted something to write with and wrote the question down!"

 — **Angie T., 42, Missouri**

"My unique ADHD experience is being time-nearsighted while also having precise chronoception (sense of time). For example, I'm really good at knowing how much time has passed, but my sense of estimating the reasonable time to complete a task is flawed; so I'm still late basically all the time. To correct it, I have to grossly overestimate and run the risk of being bored when I'm early."

THE TOOLBOX

A lot of generic "time management" strategies do not work for those with ADHD because they don't account for our specific challenges. Here, I've compiled targeted strategies that do. Does that mean they'll make us good at time management? Not necessarily—and definitely not at first. The time-related challenges those with ADHD face aren't magically fixable by "using a calendar."* But over time, we can begin to gain more control over our days, weeks, months, and years, so we can choose how we want to spend our time, rather than time choosing how it spends us.

1. BUILD UP YOUR "TIME WISDOM"

Time wisdom is understanding how long things take (read: how long they take *you* under specific circumstances) and knowing what to do with that information. Building your time wisdom can help compensate for a softer innate sense of how much has passed.

- **When you plan, work backward.** Start with what you want to accomplish (and by when), and go backward from there. What step needs to happen right before you do The Thing, and how long do you think it will take? What's the step before that?† When deadlines are so far in the future that they don't feel "real," this strategy can help us see how our

---

* Trying to stick to a schedule we made with the same brain that has no concept of how long things take is an exercise in immediate failure, as many of us have long ago discovered. Interestingly, we're usually better at making a schedule for someone *else*, maybe because it taps into cool executive function; we're not being influenced by how fun or horrible the task sounds because we aren't the ones who have to do it.

† This one worked (fairly) well for me even before I learned how to manage my time effectively as someone with ADHD. If I knew I needed to post a video for my channel on Tuesday, this meant that I needed to edit the video on Monday, which meant that I needed to shoot it on Sunday, which meant I needed to have a script written by then.

efforts now affect an outcome later. It also makes it easier to see *all* the steps involved in getting something done, which also gives us a better gauge of how long everything will take.

- **Track your time.** Guess how long a task will take and then track how long you *actually* spend doing it. Those of us with ADHD tend to be time optimists, and we often discover that certain tasks tend to take twice or even three times longer than expected. Knowing how long you typically need for those activities will help you schedule the right amount of time for them in the future, making it much less frustrating to try to stick to a schedule.

- **Notice where you're "stealing" time.** "Making up for lost time" is not a thing—it's gone forever. The next time you're trying to play catch-up, notice if you're "stealing" time from another area of your life to do it. Then consider whether it's worth taking time away from that area—or whether you want to make a new plan. This way, you don't accidentally neglect something else that matters to you—and end up having to play catch-up there, too.

Taryn G., 29, Illinois

"I use my smartwatch to remind me to stand every hour. This helps me realize when I've done something (or nothing) for an hour."

 Laura P., 41, New York

"One of my more expensive solutions for sensing time is my under-the-desk treadmill. It's easier for me to 'feel' time passing when I combine my office work with physical movement."

2. MAKE TIME REAL

If you don't have a sharp sense of time, it's important to put systems in place that help you understand when it's passing. This can make time feel less fuzzy and abstract, and more visible and concrete. Clocks are an obvious (and often recommended) example of this, but you can also try the following:

- **Get specific.** If you decide to do something later, decide when later is and add it to your calendar. You can schedule "later" to happen at a specific time or tie it to another activity you typically perform. For example, Saturday at ten a.m., or tomorrow night after dinner, before you sit down to watch TV. The point is to make "later" exist.

- **Use "time pillars" to prop up your day.** Time can quickly become meaningless if you don't have anything to do or anywhere to be at a certain time. Time pillars are regular time-based events and rituals that add structure to your day and make it easier to use your time effectively.* Even if you don't like planning out your day, a few recurring activities like lunchtime, winding down for bed, or even just a few alarms can give your day structure. At the vacation rental where I was writing this book, there was a "TREAT YO' SELF" sign that lit up automatically at 5 p.m. We decided this would be the pillar that told us when to stop working and start winding down.

- **Create some "time buckets."** "Time buckets" are areas of your day, week, or month dedicated to certain types of activities, such as hobbies, admin stuff, or deep work. Time buckets can help us reserve space and time for the things we care about, while giving us the flexibility within that time to do what we feel like doing. If hobby night happens on Tuesdays, you don't need to know which hobby you'll feel like doing beforehand, but because you've set aside this time, it will feel "real" and make it less likely for you to plan to do something else.

---

*   A lot of people think they'll be way more productive when they quit their day jobs; the opposite is often true. Without regular time-based events to plan around, there's less pressure to get anything done at a certain time.

Ryan S., 47, USA

"I have to use an analog watch with a face. Twelve o'clock to twelve-fifteen on a digital clock means nothing to me. But the minute hand moving one quarter of the face of the watch? I understand that."

Matt G., 45, Ohio

"My calendar has blocks of time scheduled to work on specific tasks as well as scheduled time to take breaks, to eat lunch, and to take a walk. I find a lot of comfort in structure, so I create simple structures in my life that I can manage to maintain in order to reduce any anxiety."

3. COMMUNICATE ABOUT TIME

While it's not great to be late, what often upsets people most about tardiness is that their time has been wasted and *you don't care*. As terrifying as it can be to admit you're running behind or having trouble managing your time, communicating your difficulties with others can help them understand that it's really not about them. It might even give the people around you opportunities to offer support, making it less likely that *anyone's* time will be wasted—yours or theirs. A natural place to start practicing this type of communicating is to let people know when you're running late; but there are a few other scenarios where this can be very helpful.

- **Ask for help prioritizing.** If you realize there isn't time to do to all the things, you don't have to figure out what's important and what's not on your own. Getting input from someone else is a win-win, especially at work or with your relationships; you don't have to stress yourself out by trying to get it all done, and they can ask you to prioritize the tasks most important to them.

- **Share your plan with others and get a reality check.** If you share your plan with someone who doesn't have challenges with time management, they might be able to recognize immediately—yeah, that's not how time works. Even sharing it with someone with similar challenges can help because they can offer a perspective that is more objective and logical. (Remember the cool executive function system, page 81?)

- **Before committing to something, ask what it entails.** This can help you understand all the steps involved in a task and what exactly is expected of you. You might realize that a "quick" favor will actually take you fourteen to thirty-eight hours.

- **Ask for time-related accommodations, if needed.** A lot of ADHD accommodations, such as more frequent check-ins, a later (or more flexible) start time, or extra time (or time away) on a test or a project are meant to accommodate, in part, our time nearsightedness. Use them.

Henriikka H., 42, Finland

"When working on my thesis, I asked my supervisor to give me 'hard' deadlines. So instead of just meeting him regularly to show what I had, he gave me specific goals (like you need to show me a full outline by this date, have this chapter finished, etc.). I didn't even have my diagnosis then, just knew by then very well that deadlines set by someone else were a must."

Lisa G., 48, Australia

"My boss knows about my issues with hyperfocus and my lack of time perception, and I've asked for (and received) permission to use timers and alarms in a small office setting. I use alarms to remind me to take a lunch break, medication, to remember when to ring home to remind my kids of things they have to do and when it's time to pack up to go home. Visual timers that count down with a disappearing wedge of color are more useful for shorter deadlines."

Tony S., 53, Australia

"My wife knows to put everything in the shared calendar. If it's not there, I don't know about it, no matter how often she mentions it."

 A Note on Extra Time

When planning workflows, ADHDers are often advised to estimate how long we think a task will take and then double—or even triple—it to make sure we give ourselves enough time to do it. This can backfire sometimes. Having more time to do something might mean that we make *less* progress than we otherwise would have because *now we have time!*

Having extra time doesn't make us any better at managing it. And oftentimes, it can take away the sense of urgency we need to get started and stay focused.

To find the right balance, it helps to play around with the amount of time that you dedicate to a task. You can also try these alternatives to simply giving yourself extra time:

Create buffer time. Only give yourself the amount of time you think you need, while making sure the next activity is something you can cut into if needed. (Bonus points if it's something you don't want to infringe on, like video game time!)

Schedule it twice. Only give yourself the amount of time you think you need, but schedule a "safety" block for the same amount of time on another day, in case you run into issues.

Take time away. Only give yourself the amount of time you think you need to work, but set a timer; allow yourself to hit pause on the timer to that time and step away to stretch, do some push-ups, or think; and resume the timer again when you're ready to come back to the task. This gives you the urgency of having a limited amount of time, while also offering a chance to reset your focus, unstick from a problem, or get a quick dopamine boost to help push through without eating into the time you've allotted.*

4. HAVE TIMES WHEN TIME DOESN'T MATTER

Worrying about time and doing things on a schedule is unnatural and stressful for a lot of ADHD brains. While time management can be necessary (especially when you are, you know, living in a society), it's not *always* essential.

Having time to wander can be wonderful (and highly restorative) for our brains. It gives us a chance to focus on what we're doing, not

---

*   Dr. Barkley argues that taking "time away" from a task for those with ADHD is a better way of accommodating time management issues on assignments—because extra time alone is meaningless for those with no sense of time.

on the clock. This can help us work (or play!) at a deeper level. In fact, losing track of time helps us enter flow states—the experience of being so immersed and absorbed by an engaging activity that we can effortlessly focus on it (also known as being "in the zone"). If you know there's somewhere you need to be, you can't let yourself go too deep. For those who can't control how deep they go, that often means not doing anything *at all*. I hear lots of stories from Brains who are afraid to start any task because they have to go to the dentist in five hours.

There are a few strategies you can use to let your brain off leash without running into traffic:

- **Sequence instead of schedule.** Doing things in a particular order is far easier on our brains than doing them at a particular time. This is why checklists are popular in our community. We can get from A to Z in a way that's a lot less stressful than doing C, E, and F at a certain time.

- **Keep some days meeting free.** A lot of ADHD brains benefit from keeping at least one workday free of scheduled meetings and appointments so that they can find their flow without interruptions. At the very least, set aside some longer time blocks for deep work.

- **Set aside "flexible" days.** If you can, decide on a couple of days when it doesn't matter if you start working or come home late. This gives you built-in buffer time to catch up on stuff you missed, which can make it easier to stick to your schedule the rest of the week.

- **Take a time vacation.** Sometimes, it's good to commit to a day where nothing needs to get done at any particular time or even in any particular order. Brains need rest!

 Lyndall C., 30, Canada

"I learned that ancient Greek has two different words for time: kairos and chronos. Chronos is where we get the word 'chronological,' and it refers to specific amounts of time like hours, days, months. Kairos is about an 'opportune' time, like seasons, timing, and moments.

"An example of chronos time is 'I go grocery shopping on Monday afternoon.' An example of kairos time is 'I go grocery shopping when I run out of bananas.'

"Both happen regularly, but one is about an arbitrary date and time, and the other is about the conditions being right.

"As ADHDers, we struggle with chronos time. However, not all cultures actually use or care about precise chronos time, and many operate more off kairos-style time. Knowing this really helped me lessen the guilt and anxiety around time management. If I'm on my own, I don't worry about chronos time. I live my life in kairos time mostly. That gives me more energy for time management when I need to be in line with the broader North American culture of chronos time."

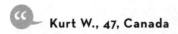
Kirsten C., 49, Michigan

"As a teacher, I reserved one day a week where I told my family not to expect me home. Instead, I stayed at school until all the planning, paperwork, and other nagging tasks were *done*. Whether I was done at five or worked until security kicked me out, I always knew I had that time available."

Kurt W., 47, Canada

"For the past three years, I've actually been leaning into the fuzziness of time. 'Things' are easier if I don't know how long it's been or I don't feel the passage of time."

SCHEDULE JENGA

A year or so into my channel, my wake-to-crash schedule had me a little wound up. I felt like a feral cat, wild-eyed and clinging on to the ceiling by my claws. What was meant to be an interview with ADHD coach Eric Tivers became more of an intervention, with him coaxing me down with tasty nuggets of wisdom and reassuring pets.

"What comes to mind when you think of a schedule?" he asked.

"I don't know. A prison?"

The only times I'd ever been able to stick to a schedule were when I was *rigid* about following it. No matter what else was happening in my life, I would grit my teeth and obey the Schedule. *Life? There is no*

Life. Only Schedule! It didn't make me super fun to be around, because I was constantly anxious about making it to my next appointment. It wasn't super fun for me, either.

He explained that schedules weren't *supposed* to be rigid. A schedule should work for you; you shouldn't be working for the Schedule. As for my "failures"? Turns out, it's really hard to stick to a schedule when it's based on completely unrealistic time estimates. No wonder I was anxious.

Because of that conversation, I braved Google Calendar again. I learned to "time block"—put blocks in my schedule for my tasks and projects—and not worry about sticking to them perfectly. Time blocks weren't marching orders; they only existed to reserve time for that activity. They could be moved! I timed my regular tasks, and I was shocked to discover how long things took me had not much to do with how long it seemed like they should.

The strategies I learned, from him, from others, and on my own—all of which I shared in the toolbox above—worked! I was no longer shooting episodes at two a.m. (most of the time), and I was able to take Sundays off and still get everything done!

I "optimized" my time to the point where my entire week was scheduled down to the hour. Knowing that work-life balance is important, I ended my workdays at six p.m. so I could walk my dog and spend time with my boyfriend, but there was always *more to do.*

If an extra task popped up, it spilled over into the weekend. Where else would I put it? Because extra tasks popped up all the time, I delegated anything that took time but wasn't "productive," like engaging with my community, brainstorming new ideas, and chatting with my team.

I kept optimizing, and soon my calendar turned into the rigid prison I had been so afraid it would be. I didn't feel there was space for *me* in all these blocks and buckets. If I missed one time block, it would mess up my entire schedule for the next three months, which meant I had to block some time to redo the schedule, which would bump more blocks out of place.

I started rebelling. I worked on Project C when I was supposed to be working on Task A, then I would wake up at four a.m. to work on Thing Q and fully sleep through Endeavor X. I ignored some blocks, shifted others, yanked a few. I was playing Schedule Jenga, and the tower was getting *really* wobbly. Chaos crept back in, followed by a familiar friend: anxiety-fueled depression. Who cared if I missed a day now? It would all fall apart anyway. I started hiding from my calendar.

In that fog, I realized time management isn't some magical solution that lets us do *all* of the things. In fact, overscheduling myself had cost me things I cared most about, like visiting the dog park, allowing my brain and body to wander, losing myself in video games, or going down random Wikipedia rabbit holes. There's a limit to how much we can optimize every minute, every hour, every day, and still be okay. We are humans, not computers. We aren't supposed to live that way.

> One off day shouldn't ruin your week, let alone throw off the next three months.

Since then, I've recognized that time management, like many things in life, is a balancing act: you want to manage your time well enough to be productive without feeling that your time is about producing rather than living.

One off day shouldn't ruin your week, let alone throw off the next three months. Time management shouldn't take the spontaneity out of your life or the joy out of your work. The truth is, if you have to optimize to that extent, you have too much on your plate. You're going to burn out. Or, like me, rebel.

Even neurotypical people leave space in their day and give themselves buffer time to breathe or pee or to work on tasks that take longer than expected. And because I have ADHD, I need a little more of that space.

I need *time to wander.* Time when time doesn't matter. If I don't give that to myself, I have learned my brain will take it anyway.

Chapter 7

How to Motivate Your Brain

If we have our own why of life,
we shall get along with almost any how.
—FRIEDRICH NIETZSCHE

I do what I feel like.
—BART SIMPSON

ME vs. BRAIN

Most of my life has been a battle between me, who knows this thing is important, and my brain, which doesn't want to do it.

Me: I'm going to do the thing!

My brain: . . . No.

Me: But I really need to get it done to stay on track with this important life goal.

My brain: What life goals? *wipes life goals from hard drive, overwrites with cat videos*

On the flip side, I've often found myself randomly motivated to do things I don't even care about.

Me: *watches a video showing you how to make cake out of melted ice cream*

My brain: YES, THAT'S AMAZING. LET'S DO IT RIGHT NOW.

Me: Right. So I guess we aren't answering emails today. *grabs pint of Cherry Garcia, leaves laptop in freezer*

I usually understand *why* I should do (or avoid doing) a thing, but that understanding in and of itself doesn't translate into usable motivational fuel. It doesn't matter if the task is critical to something I care deeply about, or entirely irrelevant and a giant waste of my time. What matters is whether or not my brain *feels like doing it.*

> Sometimes I really can't do something unless my brain cooperates.

Sometimes I really can't do something unless my brain cooperates. It feels like a hostage negotiation.

Sometimes I can push through a task with my brain kicking and screaming "I don't wanna!" and actually get the thing done. But there's a trade-off: it takes three times as long, I'm less effective, and there's a good chance it'll be harder to complete the task the next time around.

Sometimes I can excite and engage my brain, only for it to completely lose interest, forget what I was doing, or get stuck at the first confusing obstacle. (I have a lot of half-knitted blankets and half-finished degrees.)

No matter how much I cared about getting a role, graduating college, having a clean home, or landing a "real job," I'd find myself avoiding or procrastinating the tasks needed to stick with and accomplish these goals.*

I often spent so much energy trying to convince myself to do the thing (or figuring out *how* to do the thing) that I didn't have enough left to actually complete it.

> I often spent so much energy trying to convince myself to do the thing (or figuring out *how* to do the thing) that I didn't have enough left to actually complete it.

If something became urgent enough, I'd kick into gear. Everything else fell away while I finished a paper, or scrambled to get to class on time, or apologetically rolled into Jiffy Lube six months overdue for an oil change because I was about to go on a road trip.

The things that were important to me

---

*   Fun fact: While reviewing the copyedits for this chapter, I went down a rabbit hole about why my copy editor changed "procrastinating on" to simply "procrastinating" and WOW he was right! It's correct to use "procrastinate" intransitively when we're speaking about acting on a task and—yeah, this is how this happens. Not only are we more motivated by the new shiny things, we're more distracted by them, too. (See "How to (Hyper)focus," page 47.)

but never became urgent? Like finishing my novel, learning to meal prep, or hosting a murder mystery dinner party? I just never got to them.

It made no sense to me or the people around me. There were "explanations," of course. I must be lazy. I had no willpower. Maybe I didn't actually care about this.

Occasionally, I was convinced I was self-sabotaging. Why else would I spend an entire summer getting an A in statistics but not bother to register for the class? On some level, I must have wanted to fail.

It was frustrating and exhausting. Most things in life require you not only to do things but also do them *consistently*—and motivation, for me, was anything but consistent, so my efforts rarely paid off. I wanted to know why.

WHAT I LEARNED

ADHD brains aren't motivated by what's important. In fact, many of our most important tasks are ones that ADHD brains find viscerally painful to do: the ones that are lengthy, repetitive, or boring. Even if we have the motivation to accomplish a goal, we might still have trouble working toward it. Goals frequently come with multiple tasks, and many of these tasks involve these characteristics, which our brains *can't sustainably tolerate.*

In fact, there's even a term for our tendency to escape and avoid the distress that a delay causes us: *delay aversion.*

ADHD brains often turn to the more immediate reward of doing something fun now—or escaping the distress of facing something tedious—even when we deeply care about the goal.

So, what *does* motivate an ADHD brain? Things that are:

- urgent
- new or novel
- (the right level of) challenging
- of personal interest

In other words, *stimulating*. This is due to fundamental differences in the reward system of ADHD brains.

WE'RE DOPA-DIFFERENT

Dopamine is a neurotransmitter that motivates and reinforces behavior. When something is pleasurable, dopamine, along with other feel-good neurotransmitters, is released and makes its way to its respective receptors in the brain. This signals our brain to remember what led to feeling good: *that felt good; do it again!* The brain might even start to release "anticipatory" dopamine to reinforce behaviors that will eventually lead to something pleasurable, such as filling out tax forms that will result in a refund.

Evidence suggests that ADHD brains don't release anticipatory dopamine the same way neurotypical brains do. Reuptake—the reabsorption of the dopamine—may also happen before it makes it to a receptor.

When this happens, our brains don't "learn" that a behavior like filling out tax forms will lead to anything good. And if nothing good comes from a behavior, what's the point of doing it? This is why it feels as though activities that are more immediately rewarding hijack our brains. When we abandon tax forms and start playing video games, we feel good, and dopamine gets released. If there's enough dopamine to hit at least some receptors, our brain learns to prioritize video games, making it more likely that we will end up firing up the game console the next time we need to do something similarly tedious.

Dopamine levels also shape our perception of life, our emotions, and how capable we perceive ourselves to be. When dopamine levels are low, we feel unmotivated, derive less pleasure from everyday tasks, and feel physically tired. Our brains are understimulated. This is why we wait until right before the deadline to get started on a project. It's why we might make "simple" tasks overly complicated. It's why we switch up our writing style or the color pens we're using, or doodle while taking notes. It's why we do serious things in silly ways. We're instinctively stimulating and motivating our brains by adding a sense of urgency, challenge, novelty, and interest.

REWARDS ARE OFTEN TOO FAR AWAY

There are two types of motivation: intrinsic and extrinsic.

Intrinsic motivation happens when you do something because it is enjoyable and satisfying in and of itself. Intrinsically rewarding activities don't require any external incentives for you to want to do them. For example, eating cookies is intrinsically motivating. No one needs to pay you to do it; they just taste good. You want to eat cookies because you enjoy eating cookies. And the reward of doing so is immediate. For me, tasks that tap into intrinsic motivation include learning something new, spending time with animals, setting up new organizational systems, and cuddling up with a blanket and my Nintendo Switch. These are all activities I enjoy doing for the sake of doing them.

Extrinsic motivation happens when you do something because of the external consequences of doing (or not doing) it. For example, you might work hard on your talk because someone (or a lot of people) will know if you didn't. You might deal with the icky stickiness of making bread because you'll have fresh bread once you're done, or file your taxes (an enjoyable experience for absolutely no one I know) because you'll face financial penalties if you don't.

Many important life goals, such as getting good grades or getting a raise, are motivating because of the extrinsic reward involved. Of course we'd like to get into a good school and graduate; of course we'd like to make more money. And we're willing to do what it takes to make that happen—in theory.

In practice, those extrinsic consequences—both positive and negative ones—often feel too far away to be motivating, especially when they're competing with the more immediate rewards of playing video games or partying now.

This is due to *temporal discounting,* where we perceive a desired result in the future as less valuable than one we could have *now.* Temporal discounting happens for everyone, which is why you might often hear suggestions to reward yourself for a successful week rather than a successful semester. But along with temporal discounting, those with ADHD also have shorter time horizons. A reward that will come next week isn't going to be motivating in the same way because, to us, next week doesn't even exist (more on how we experience time in "How to See Time," page 128). ADHD brains are highly sensitive to rewards, but if the rewards aren't particularly salient (read: alluring), they need to happen more immediately to have any relevance in our decision making.

If a task is intrinsically rewarding—enjoyable enough that we don't need extrinsic rewards to do it—temporal discounting has less impact. It doesn't matter as much that a reward is far off in the distance. In fact, there's arguably a benefit to *not* relying on extrinsic motivation; research has shown that adding extrinsic rewards can actually *decrease* intrinsic motivation.

For situations where we're *not* intrinsically motivated enough to act, we rely on the sense of urgency that kicks in once an extrinsic consequence does appear on the horizon, which is later for us than for others. As a result, we end up in crisis after crisis trying to get things done at the last minute. And this behavior is reinforced: when we pull off getting something done at the last minute, our brains release a ton of dopamine, which tells our brains, "That felt good. Do it again."

To break out of this cycle, it's crucial to add extrinsic rewards that are immediate (or exciting!) enough that they're actually, you know, motivating. Like, eating cookies *while* you work.

What we often forget to consider when talking about motivation is that there is always motivation *not* to do The Thing, too—and that this motivation can be stronger than the motivation encouraging us to do it. Filling out a decisional balance worksheet (see page 417) can help you understand what is motivating you to head in one direction or the other.

THE EMOTIONS WE ASSOCIATE WITH A TASK MATTER

When we do a "simple" task—say, making a phone call—we're not just dealing with that task. We're also dealing with an emotional barrier that has been built from past failures with the task. Brendan Mahan, ADHD coach and founder of *ADHD Essentials,* calls this barrier a "Wall of Awful." The more we've struggled with a task in the past, the more failure, disappointment, rejection, and worry we've experienced as a result. The more of these negative experiences we have endured, the higher that wall.

We don't just need enough motivation to complete the task. We also need enough motivation—and often time—to climb the emotional wall in front of it.

Everyone has Walls of Awful around tasks they've failed at. But according to Brendan, those with ADHD have a lot of them—and they tend to be higher than most. We experience far more failure, criticism, and rejection than our neurotypical peers. Some of the most common emotions that come up for those with ADHD include overwhelm, discouragement, hopelessness, fear, and confusion.

To make matters even more complicated, ADHDers typically have relatively weak working memory (see page 193 to learn more). This means we might not have enough mental bandwidth to remember *why* we're doing something, or how it might feel to finish doing it. Instead, all our working memory "slots" may be taken up by trying to figure out (or remember) what we need to do and how we feel about it right now. As a result, all we see is that Wall of Awful. We can't peer over it. We don't get any windows to show us what might be on the other side.

According to Brendan, there are different ways we deal with this wall. We might get angry enough that we can Hulk-smash through it to get a task done. Unfortunately, that often hurts our relationships, because we're not always nice about what we say to ourselves (or to others) when we bust through the wall.

Sometimes, we can put a door in the wall. We might change our mood with music, turn on a favorite TV show in the background, or work somewhere new to distract ourselves long enough to get the task done.

But often, we need to climb the wall. Before we can face the task and effectively engage with it, both now and in the future, we need to do the emotional work of gearing up for it, facing our anxiety, and preparing ourselves to *do The Thing*.

My friend and colleague Dani Donovan, creator of *The Anti-Planner,* a workbook that includes activities, games, and strategies she designed specifically to address the feelings that get in the way of our tasks, puts it well: "Learning how to identify what's *causing* your mental resistance makes it easier to find or create a tailored solution that addresses those specific feelings."

BEHAVIORS PRECEDE MOTIVATION

When I was an actor, I used to wait until I had enough motivation to spend two hours memorizing my lines. This almost never happened, so I inevitably found myself trying to cram the day of an audition.

What I didn't know then but understand now is that we don't need motivation to take action. In fact, it often happens in reverse: action can *generate* motivation. Here are some examples:

- Picking up our phone often motivates us to check our email, text messages, or social media.

- Sitting on the couch motivates us to pick up the remote.

- Planning a road trip motivates us to make music playlists.

This is the idea behind what psychologists call behavioral activation. You don't have to feel like going for a bike (or motor scooter!) ride to go for a ride. You just put on your gear. You check the air in the tires. You get on the dang thing. And *then* see how you feel.*

Is it possible you still don't want to go at this point? Sure.

You're also more likely to be motivated to do it anyway once you're already ready to go. As a bonus, this activation can also interrupt negative thought spirals, shifting your thinking from "It's too much of a hassle to go for a ride, I don't know if there's even air in the tires, I never have *time* anymore to go riding" to "Hang on, I am literally riding."

Whatever it is we want to be motivated enough to do, it helps to know our behavior—the actions we take—can increase (or decrease) that motivation. Behavior *precedes* motivation.

IT'S NOT ENTIRELY ABOUT MOTIVATION

According to psychologist Dr. Ari Tuckman, motivation is often the first lever we pull when we want to get ourselves or someone we love to do a thing, but it's not always the *right* lever to pull.

Motivation is just one part of a bigger "get stuff done" system—and it might not be where the problem is. Consider these possibilities:

- **A skill gap:** You don't entirely know (or remember) how to do The Thing or the steps involved.

---

* This example is a nod to the family bike rides my family and I went on when I was a kid. My mom, who couldn't ride a bike due to her physical disability, rode a scooter along with us. These rides are some of my favorite memories and . . . I think I just convinced myself to go ride my bike. BRB. (You can keep reading!)

- **A lack of resources:** You don't have what you need to get The Thing done. For example, you might not have enough time, supplies, or energy.

- **Perfectionism:** Perfectionism, and the anxiety that goes hand in hand with it, can keep you from getting started or keep you stuck in mental loops.

- **Overly optimistic thinking:** You might assume that you can get to something tomorrow without checking to see if you're giving yourself enough time to do it. (This is known as positive illusory bias.)

- **Forgetfulness:** Thanks to ADHD-related memory challenges (see "How to Remember Stuff," page 187), you might not remember what your goals even are.

- **An unrealistic goal:** The goal you chose isn't attainable—or sustainable.

" **Melissa H., 38, USA**

"I find that if I do something faster than my brain can realize I'm doing it, then it's like a cartoon. I might be missing motivation slats in my bridge, but I'm just walking on air and not looking down. #cartoongravity."

Kyle T., 27, Malta

"The main way I get things done is by having structure forced on me from an outside source, like a job for instance, where the potential shame of failure is compelling enough to pull me through the wall. With anything else, though, I just don't do it until I literally have no choice (all of my dishes are piled up in the sink so I can't eat) or the deadline is so close that I can ride the panic-induced adrenaline rush of, for example, having to write an entire essay in one night."

 Daniel C., 36, Kansas

"My biggest struggle is starting big and boring projects. As a professor, this means grading. I have no particularly useful strategy for accomplishing this task. It's not regular enough for a timer or other scheduled alert. And it's not something that is part of a daily routine. So, my typical systems all fail."

THE TOOLBOX

ADHDers instinctively do many things to motivate their brains; some are healthier for us than others. It is a very unfortunate truth that many of us internalize the "motivational techniques" others have tried on us, due to a misunderstanding of how our brains work—including berating and punishing ourselves. This can get us through our Wall of Awful. It also makes it *taller*. While it can take time to undo the damage and learn to motivate ourselves more effectively, I promise there are better ways.

1. FILL IN THE MOTIVATIONAL PLANKS

Think of motivation as a bridge that helps us go from wanting to do a thing to actually getting it done. Those with ADHD often don't have as many "motivational planks" to get across. You can hop over little gaps with willpower, but if half the bridge is missing, you'll need to add some planks. Medication can help; there are also other strategies you can turn to:

- **Add urgency.** Invite a guest over if you want to get yourself to clean. Sign up for a class with a friend if you want to get started exercising. Set up a "get stuff done" meeting with a co-worker. Turn a marathon project into a series of mini sprints so you can get started *before* it's almost due. Adding a sense of urgency to tasks now can keep them from becoming a crisis later.

- **Find the right level of challenging.** If something is too easy, it might be too boring; if it's too difficult, it can be too frustrating and discouraging to keep going. If it's something you've already mastered and you're having trouble doing it, add some challenging elements to it. If it's daunting, take it down a notch—and if you're having a bad brain day, take it down a couple more notches. Lowering the bar can help with perfectionism, too!*

- **Tie a task to a personal interest.** When you're doing something you don't want to do but need to do, ask yourself this: Is there *anything* interesting about this? You can also incorporate your personal interests into a task. You might have to make the final draft of your paper sound professional, but who says you can't exclusively use Dungeons & Dragons metaphors to get the first draft done? If your interest is in turtles, maybe you check off items on your to-do list with turtle stickers instead of check marks. You can't always choose *what* you need to do, but you have some control over *how* you do it.

- **Add novelty.** Doing boring or repetitive tasks in a new location, with different people, or with a new tool can make them interesting enough for us to complete them. This works for systems we've gotten bored of, too. There's a term coined by Barbara Luther that ADHD coaches use a lot: resparklize. When the system that's been working great for three weeks suddenly stops working "for no apparent

---

* My favorite example of this type of goal (and one I used while I worked on this book) comes from *Bird by Bird* by Anne Lamott: write shitty first drafts.

reason"—and it's something you would like to continue—resparklize it! Find a way to make it shiny (read: interesting) again.

— Natasha L., 25, Florida

"You always gotta start small. Don't hang up the whole clothing pile. Fold one shirt."

Caitlin D., 37, Ohio

"I have soundtracks for each type of task. I have a 'getting dressed' song so I mentally get myself to listen to the song (and get dressed). I have a 'doing dishes' song to remind myself that the task doesn't take as long as I think it does. I always imagined I would have a soundtrack to my life, but I never thought I would actually use it as an adaptive self-support strategy."

— Sarah G., 39, South Carolina

"It's helpful to find something I like about what I have to do. When I meal prep, I focus on making pretty bento-style lunches or using new ingredients. I put on a show I like to get on the treadmill. I use a new cleaning spray. (No, really—sometimes the 'newness' helps!)"

2. REDUCE FRICTION AND GREASE THE WHEELS

The more barriers between you and a task you can remove, the less motivation you'll need to get started—and stay started. Eliminating obstacles reduces the friction and makes a task more accessible. Greasing the wheels means doing anything that makes it more likely we'll want to do it (including adding rewards—more on page 179).

- **Do what you can ahead of time.** Sleep in your gym clothes, book classes in advance, or make yourself a checklist. Doing what you can ahead of time means there is less to do—or get stuck on—when you need to get going.

- **Remove physical obstacles and other barriers.** If something is in the way of the piano, it's going to make it harder for you to play the piano. If a task is overwhelming for sensory reasons—for example, there's something about it that is too bright, too noisy, or too icky—find a tool that helps you avoid the unpleasant experience. Use gloves while washing dishes, earplugs for noisy trips, or sunglasses for running errands outside.*

---

*   We don't always notice the barriers if we aren't looking for them. Keeping a "barrier log" for tasks you're routinely having trouble with can help you figure out where exactly you're getting stuck—so you can remove the removable barriers for future you, too! This is one of the most powerful things I've ever done, and it is why I'm able to (generally speaking) get videos out on time: I was able to recognize patterns in the barriers I was facing.

- **Invest in tools you enjoy using.** Many of us have negative associations with tasks partly due to the tools we associate with the task. Choosing ones that feel good and look nice is a great way to "grease the wheels" toward doing The Thing. Plus, it can make or save us money in the long run. For example, how much have we spent on takeout because the "nice pans" or tools that might make cooking easier are "too expensive"?

- **Tap into your "why."** There's a reason you're doing The Thing. What's the reason? It might not be about the task itself. There's a sweet example of this in an episode of *The Simpsons*. When Homer went back to work after Maggie was born, he papered pictures of her over a foreboding sign from his boss that read "Don't forget. You're here forever." The baby pictures covered enough letters so the sign now read "Do it for her."

- **Ride the wave.** If you feel like tackling an important task that you usually don't like doing, take care of it now. Strike while the iron is hot—or, more accurately, while the friction is low.

- **Eat the ice cream first.** This one came from Jesse J. Anderson, a friend and author of *Extra Focus:* rather than trying to eat the frog first, it can help to eat the ice cream first. Doing something we enjoy rather than trying to tackle the hardest thing on our list is much more likely to keep us in a productive mode.

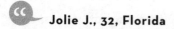 **Jolie J., 32, Florida**

"I set up a system to make a task easier and more fun. I customize everything, I use stickers and paint to make things more attractive to me. As soon as something is pretty, fun, and super easy for me to access, I can do it. Remove all obstacles!"

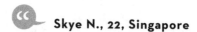 **Skye N., 22, Singapore**

"I've been trying to change my thinking about tasks—rather than forcing myself to study, I 'invite myself to learn.' The positive connotations make it easier to overcome the Wall of Awful."

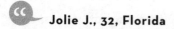 **Spider, 39, Florida**

"After I take my Adderall in the morning, I reserve about an hour to deliberately 'rev it up' by sitting idle. I play very chill video games, watch walk-around videos of gardens or parks until my meds have long kicked in and I'm literally seething at myself to get to work."

3. ADD (OR INCREASE) ACCOUNTABILITY

Accountability helps shorten the distance between the action we need to take and the consequences of taking (or not taking) it.

Accountability alone isn't enough, because, again, motivation isn't always the issue; in these cases, adding accountability can make things *worse*.* But if we do have the resources and skills to do what we need to do, added accountability can spur us to action; because if we don't do the thing, people will *know*. And if we *do* do the thing, people will know!

- **Decide on what you're doing—and not doing.** Sometimes, all we need in terms of accountability is to get clear on what we're doing and what can wait. If you need support with figuring this out, coaches, therapists, and even a friend or co-worker can help you make (and adjust) a plan to ensure progress on things that are important to you.

- **Find productivity partners.** There are a lot of groups designed to help people connect and support each other toward specific goals; you can also ask someone to "body double" with you—sit quietly in a room with you while you work. This can include going to public places where others are working or studying, because there's low-key social pressure for you to do the same.

- **Shorten the feedback loop.** Sometimes we have trouble finishing a project because we get stuck on one part of it; sometimes it's because the deadline is too far away to kick

---

* Read: increased anxiety, panic attacks, and dissociation.

our brains into gear. Either way, asking for shorter dead-lines and/or more frequent check-ins can help. Those check-ins can be with your boss, colleagues, or random friends: "Hey, this Friday, can I show you what I've got on my project so far?"

- **Make it a competition!** There are apps, programs, and competitions that gamify productivity, but you can also keep it simple. Challenge a friend to work with you on building a habit (like making your bed in the morning): the first person to text the other a picture of their beauti-fully made bed wins.

 Solstice H., 33, USA

"I have a really good online support group that has nor-malized 'executive function trades.' One person goes, 'Uuuuugh, I need to do laundry,' and another responds with something like 'If you put in a load of laundry, I'll go microwave something for dinner.'"

 Amy H., 49, South Carolina

"I have pretended that I'm one of those YouTube chan-nels that are just a person's life, and I narrate what I'm doing for the pretend camera. Sometimes it works—I still want to please the pretend audience."

Katherine E., 30, Virginia

"The best motivation for me is to attach a tangible hand-off point for the task. At work, who needs the baton from my work to do their own work? Does my partner need clean dishes to make dinner tonight?"

A Note on Procrastination

Procrastinating is common for those with ADHD—and for good reason. The sense of urgency we feel as a deadline approaches kicks our brain into gear. Starting closer to a deadline instead of well ahead of time, as many of us have learned, can save us a lot of time and mental energy.

But *how* you procrastinate matters.

Research suggests that those who engage in what is called active procrastination—the "wait until your brain kicks into gear" or "put off homework until the night before it's due" form of procrastination—experience similar performance and outcomes as non-procrastinators. On the other hand, those who engage in passive procrastination—the "head in the sand" form where you avoid even thinking about The Thing—are more likely to experience negative outcomes such as poor grades, missed opportunities, and—I don't remember what else. Ironically, I keep procrastinating on revisiting the research.

Even so, active procrastination has its costs. You might

still have to blow off something important as you try to get the more urgent task done. Your efforts might affect how well your brain will function the next day. Sometimes these costs are worth it; sometimes they're not.

The takeaway? It's unrealistic to expect anyone, especially someone with ADHD, not to procrastinate at all. But if you're going to procrastinate, procrastinate mindfully.

4. MAKE REWARDS MORE SALIENT

Make sure rewards are motivating to the person you're trying to motivate (who is *you*). For tasks that aren't intrinsically motivating, adding extrinsic rewards that are can be a great way to generate immediate interest, especially when the goal (and prize!) you're working toward feels so far away.

- **Pick a reward that is meaningful to you.** Different people respond differently to different rewards. Maybe the best reward for you is something you don't often let yourself have or something that's related to the steps you're taking to reach a goal. I like to buy myself fitness gear as I keep working out, and soft cozy sweaters to write in as I make progress. If a reward is personally meaningful, it's more likely to motivate you.

- **Scale a reward strategically.** Think economics. If a reward is too big, it floods the reward market and inflation happens.

If you reward yourself with sushi for emptying the dishwasher, that is now what emptying the dishwasher costs. Good luck trying to convince your brain to do the same task tomorrow for less. At the same time, if it's not big enough, it won't be motivating enough: "Okay, I am *not* emptying the dishwasher for five minutes of video game time. Emptying the dishwasher takes me longer than that!"

- **Make the reward more immediate.** A reward that happens right away is one that is more salient. Immediate positive feedback is a great example. You can also try rewarding yourself as you go, or pairing something rewarding with the activity itself. If a reward is "stuck" in the future—like an upcoming trip you have planned—make your progress more tangible by posting a picture of your destination and marking off days on your calendar. Tap into your excitement!

- **Give yourself the reward for doing The Thing.** Rewards don't work as motivational fuel if you give them to yourself regardless of your efforts—or don't give them to yourself at all. Make sure you can enjoy your reward soon after you've finished (or made progress on!) a task, but put barriers in place until you reach a certain point.*

---

* A fellow writer friend gave me a care package when I was editing this book. It had several mini gifts and cards, along with instructions. I could open one gift immediately. I could open another when I was a quarter of the way done, half done, three-quarters done, and finished. This was super cute—and super motivating!

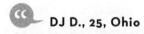 **DJ D., 25, Ohio**

"When I need to get work done, I start with the hardest thing, then I plan a fun thing to do when it's all done. Making a list and checking off boxes gives my brain a dopamine rush because it feels like I've accomplished something as I move from one thing to the next."

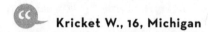 **Kricket W., 16, Michigan**

"My mom used to try to get me to do my math homework using M&M's. At first, she would offer me a small bag when I finished my worksheet. That didn't work. Then, one night, she opened the bag and put a single M&M next to each problem. That worked. Instant reward, and an incentive to keep going."

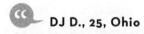 **Lucila S., 30, Mexico**

"To motivate myself to work out, I bought myself the most bougie, delicious body foam for my showers after swimming. I can only use it in that context, and it makes me feel like I'm in a spa."

5. DON'T EXPECT YOURSELF TO STICK WITH THINGS

Hang with me here. A lot of the time, we start a new venture without an end date. We might assume this new habit, job, hobby is *the one,* and we're going to do it forever. We understandably get frustrated and disappointed when it doesn't turn out that way. Instead of expecting we'll magically be able to stick to things despite all past evidence to the contrary, it's often more helpful to *plan for* the variability in interest and motivation inherent to ADHD.

- **Cycle through hobbies, jobs, and interests.** When the novelty of one thing wears off, it's fine to switch to something else. Stepping away from something gives it the opportunity to feel new again.

- **Be a bumblebee.** Carry what you learned from one experience and use it to "pollinate" your next venture. Those with ADHD are often referred to as a "jack of all trades, master of none," but have you heard the expanded version of that quote? It says, "A jack of all trades is a master of none, but oftentimes *better* than master of one." There's value in building a diverse skill set.

- **Set a date to reevaluate.** Agree to stick to something for a set amount of time, whatever feels reasonable for you to commit to. When you reach your end date, see if it's worth continuing with what you're doing. That way, we don't keep putting time and energy into something that isn't working for us. This strategy also helps with the ADHD tendency to give up on a project, system, or task at the first sign of failure.

Cashel R., 45, Louisiana

"Well, I can say that in the theater, having ADHD is a major boost. I've got short-lived projects that vary enough from show to show to keep my interest piqued. It's also let me slide into whatever position needs filling for that show. Need an actor? I've got you covered! Scene designer, set builder, set dresser, director, prop mistress, costumer? I'm your gal. I've achieved just enough mastery of each to do the job well. Then, it's on to something new, keeping my ever-racing mind engaged."

 Jeffry C., 47, Alaska

"Sometimes I just don't get motivated, and that can be okay. It's important for us not to always have to be motivated. Sometimes we can exist and enjoy the world without getting stuff done."

Coach A vs. Coach B

While I was writing this book, Dr. Patrick LaCount, a psychologist and How to ADHD's research consultant, told me a story that he shares with his clients.

Imagine an eight-year-old kid who is the goalie of her soccer team.

It's almost the end of the game, and a player from the other team is about to take a shot at the goal. Our goalie guesses which way the ball will go, dives in that direction, and misses it completely. The ball flies in the other direction and into the goal. The game is over—and her team loses.

Coach A calls her over. He starts yelling. "What's wrong with you? You cost us the game. We went over this in practice. You knew what to do!"

The kid feels terrible and goes home, defeated. The next time there's practice, or even a game, she says she has a stomachache and stays home.

Now imagine that same scenario—only this time, Coach B calls her over after the team loses the game.

"Hey, come here. Remember, when you're trying to figure out which way they're gonna kick it, look at where their eyes are looking, and at the position of their foot. You got it? Yeah, you got it."

The kid still feels awful that she cost her team the game, but now she has something to try differently. And the next time she needs to play, she shows up.

After Dr. LaCount tells this story to his clients, he asks them, "Which coach would you want your child to have if you wanted her to have fun?"

Everyone chooses Coach B.

"But who do you choose if you want her to go pro?"

Still, everyone chooses Coach B.

When it comes to motivating ourselves, though, we often speak to ourselves as Coach A. "What's wrong with you! You knew this was important; you should have started sooner." Or "Why did you do it that way? You *know better*." Or even "God, you're such a (fill in your go-to, probably ableist term)—how could you forget/miss/ mess up something so important? So *obvious*? You're a grown adult—*act like one*."

For many of us with ADHD, we grew up hearing messages like these and internalized them. They became our default.

Many people have asked how I, someone with ADHD, was able to write a book, when we often have trouble even *reading* one. To be honest, it's been hard.

This chapter was incredibly challenging. I wrestled with having too much to say. I didn't know where to start. I sat in my car in the parking lot outside my office for an hour and seventeen minutes, freezing my butt off, because I didn't have the energy to go inside and finish writing the chapter but I also didn't want to give up and go home. I've had to use every single strategy in this chapter's toolbox (and a lot from the other chapters) to get it done.

And even still, I missed deadlines. I read what I wrote and hated it. I was embarrassed to show my editor the mess that I'd written, and the Coach A voice crept in. "What's wrong with you! You should have started sooner. This is terrible. Why did anyone let you write a book?"

And when that happens, I use the trick Dr. LaCount teaches all his clients: notice when you're berating yourself and then ask yourself:

"What would Coach B say?"

My Coach B would remind me I've never written a book before. I'm figuring this out as I go.

Instead of telling me what I should have done, Coach B would suggest I adjust my deadlines based on the pace at which I was writing. Ask my editor for guidance. Swallow my pride and hire a writing buddy to help me with parts I struggle with. Text a friend in that freezing parking lot and ask if she wanted to body double.

I also got advice from friends. Dani, who was actually a goalie as a kid, told me, "It can feel like the entire game comes down to you and missing the ball, so it's easy to take all the blame on yourself. But there are a lot of other people on that team who are involved in whether you win or lose. Sometimes the system that you're operating in isn't exactly setting you up for success. Even if it is, it is so unrealistic to expect yourself to save every ball. Come to terms with the fact that you're going to miss some—and that's gotta be okay."

When something I tried didn't work out, I learned from the experience. I reminded myself what I could try differently next time.

> I reminded myself what I could try differently next time.

And the next time I needed to write, I showed up.

Chapter 8

How to Remember Stuff

*The only thing faster than the speed of thought
is the speed of forgetfulness.
Good thing we have other people to help us remember.*

—VERA NAZARIAN

I FORGOT

A year into working on this book, I connected with Pina Varnel, creator of the webcomic *ADHD Alien,* about the challenges we faced writing our respective brain manuals. As we talked, the topic of "forgetting stuff" came up. She asked how I was covering it in my book.

I stared at her.

I had spent a year writing a book about ADHD and had completely forgotten to include a chapter about forgetting stuff.

I figured that alone was proof I needed to include it. Was it too late? The manuscript was due in less than a month, and I was not close to finishing it, even without this new addition.

People deeply concerned for my well-being asked me if there was another way to do it. Could I combine it with another chapter? Cover it quickly in a funny anecdote at the end? Leave it for another book?

I shook my head. I had to make it work. Ninety percent of the ADHD experience is saying two things on loop: "I'm sorry I got distracted" and "I'm sorry I forgot." I knew there was a lot to say on this topic.

I reached out to my research consultant Dr. Patrick LaCount (who also has ADHD):

> Me: Hey, Patrick!
> Are you able to get research for How to Remember Stuff to me by Saturday morning? I'm going to start on that one next week.

> Patrick: Absolutely.

I followed up Monday morning:

> Me: Hey, Patrick! Did you send it? If not, would you have time to touch base on it tomorrow? I'm starting to write How to Remember Stuff on Thursday.

Patrick: F*ck, I knew I was forgetting something! I can do a write-up tomorrow morning and then I have an opening from 3-4 pm Mountain Time.

Then I almost missed the meeting, because *I* forgot he said "Mountain Time."

It's not that I don't remember anything. I can recall the color of the curtains in my childhood home. I'll never forget the first time I danced with a boy—or, more accurately, stood facing a boy—at a school dance, and how long I stayed hiding in the bathroom in shame after I realized I didn't know what to do once the song started playing. I can tell you how many crumpled dollar bills a group of six demanding adults left as a tip when I was working the graveyard shift at Denny's in my twenties. (It was six.)

But remembering what I'm doing while I'm trying to do it? Nope.

Remembering the lines I spent three hours memorizing? Probably not.

Remembering the name of the person standing in front of me? . . . mayyyybe.

On the surface, it doesn't always seem like that big a deal. I can laugh about it. It's part of what makes me me. As my mom often pointed out, I'd forget my head if it wasn't attached.

Under the surface, though, it's not so cute or quirky. ADHDers forget things all the time—and we work ourselves into the ground compensating for the things that slip our minds.

It's cost me self-esteem. When I'd realize I'd forgotten obvious or important stuff, the negative thoughts were immediate and automatic. Judgments starting with "I'm so" and "I'm such a" played in my head and sometimes spilled out of my mouth.

It's cost me financial security. I've lost jobs due to forgotten paperwork and follow-through. I've built up, then completely wrecked, my credit—twice—because of missed payments on bills I had the money to pay. It's cost me housing security, when my credit wasn't good enough to rent an apartment.

It's cost me relationships. Not only have I had friends give up on me for being unreliable, I've also had relationships go south because I can't keep track of how I'm being treated. Is this friend saying something unkind for the first time or the fiftieth? What was that last fight about, anyway? Forgetful people—particularly those of us with low self-esteem (see above)—can be easy to manipulate.

I knew I was capable of remembering stuff. I also knew I couldn't trust my memory to work how and when I needed it to.

A *Very Incomplete* List of Things I've Forgotten

- What you just said

- What I just said

- What I was doing

- Where I put my keys/phone/the thing I was *just holding*

- What happened yesterday

- Why I was mad ten minutes ago

- Whether I've taken my meds

- The life-changing epiphany I had yesterday

- What I agreed to do tomorrow / next week / next month

- The supplies I needed for whatever it is I'm trying to do

- The boundaries you set

- The boundaries *I* set

- Everything I just read

- What I'm supposed to do differently now

- The name of the app I'm trying to open and have used a thousand times

- How to work the remote

- My jacket

- My socks

- The pants I fully intended to put on *before* I answered the door

WHAT I LEARNED

Before I started researching for the channel, I was aware of two types of memory: short-term and long-term. Welp, there are a whole bunch of other types that brain scientists are still debating: sensory memory, implicit memory, explicit memory, haptic memory, procedural memory, and more. There are too many to remember. For me, anyway.

The point is, memory is complicated, but here's what is most important for those of us with ADHD to understand.

OUR LONG-TERM MEMORY IS . . . FINE?

In several studies on long-term memory, participants with ADHD performed just as well as, if not better than, neurotypical participants on tests for certain types of memory.

Case in point: episodic memory, a type of long-term memory that allows us to recall the details about a specific experience—what happened, what was said, how we felt, and so on. A 2008 study found that when discussing a special event in their life, children with ADHD provided lengthier and more descriptive narratives than those without ADHD.

This is true for me. Even as an adult, I can describe entire scenes from my childhood with as much visual and emotional detail as a movie. My writing buddy, who doesn't have ADHD, can't; though she does remember what it is we're supposed to be working on today. ("It's Chapter 8, 'How to Remember Stuff,' babe.")

On the other hand, some studies on ADHDers *have* found deficits in long-term memory. Why?

The ability to remember depends on three processes: encoding information, storing it, and, finally, retrieving it. A meta-analysis of long-term memory in adults with ADHD suggests that our difficulty remembering things long term is actually a *learning* deficit that happens at the stage of *encoding*. In other words, we can't remember what we never actually learned.

Findings like these are really interesting—and also useful, because there's a *lot* we can do to support the encoding process. Being able to provide this support starts with understanding working memory—and how it works (hehe) for ADHD brains.

WORKING MEMORY IS OFTEN IMPAIRED IN ADHD

working memory (n.)
A type of memory that gives us the ability
to hold new information temporarily in our
head while we work with it.

We use working memory for many everyday tasks: Remembering a time and date while we look for a pen to write them down. Knowing what we came into a room to do. Remembering somebody's name and telling them ours, while trying to gauge a new social situation.

Everyone's working memory has a limited number of "slots." When there is information we need to attend to, we hold on to it in these slots. It then disappears quickly, constantly shuffling to make room for new information. (For the information that we need later, we can save it on our brain's hard drive through techniques that encode it like "taking notes" and "studying.")

Working memory is often impaired in ADHD brains. We essentially get fewer slots, especially when it comes to verbal and auditory working memory. This makes it hard to remember something we just read or heard someone say.

Let's say a neurotypical student has a working memory capacity that allows her to temporarily hold on to five pieces of information. And another student with ADHD can only hold on to three.

The teacher asks the students a question, followed by three possible answers.

The neurotypical student might be able to answer the question no problem, while also thinking about the cute boy in the second row. But by the time the teacher shares the third possible answer, the ADHD student has likely forgotten the question, *even if they're completely focused*. They don't have enough slots to store all the information.

Our ADHD student also needs to use more effort to direct their attention and actions. Their difficulty with attention regulation means the information in those slots can get kicked out a lot more easily. We also take up valuable working memory slots to remember that we need to "sit still," "be quiet," and all the other things we are told to do and that don't come naturally to our brains.

WE ALSO HAVE TROUBLE RECALLING INFORMATION

We can't remember what we weren't paying attention to in the first place, and as I explain in "How to (Hyper)focus" (page 47), those of us with ADHD have a hard time regulating our attention. Still, that's not the *only* factor contributing to our difficulties with remembering things long term (and by long term, I mean things that happened, like, yesterday).

We Can't Remember What We Don't Understand

The process of encoding information into long-term storage requires our brains to compare new information with what we already know and then figure out where to file it. For this to happen, we need to rely on our working memory to hold all of this information long enough for it to happen.

If the new information is easy for us to understand and related to a familiar subject, the encoding process can be quick and easy. If, on the other hand, we have no clue what someone is talking about—possibly because we missed or didn't encode the foundational knowledge well enough—we may not have enough time for this process to take place. Before our brains are able to encode it, new information comes in and bumps it out of our working memory.

I learned this the hard way when I was invited to sit in on a college professor's algebra class and offer feedback. He handed out a quiz halfway through the class. Despite knowing, at this point, how to support my working memory and attention, I couldn't answer any of the questions on the quiz about the day's lesson. *None.*

To the professor's credit, he had paused occasionally during his lecture to ask, "Any questions?" But because my working memory couldn't hold on to the information coming in long enough to make sense out of it, I didn't understand enough to even know what questions to ask.

I felt like a bad student, as I had so many times in my actual classes, then remembered—I'm not. I just didn't have enough foundational knowledge about algebra to encode what the professor was saying before it slipped from my working memory.

The professor was teaching the same material to the next class. During the ten-minute break between classes, I gave myself a quick foundation in algebra by doing what I do best—googling it. I scanned through articles about the basics of algebra and learned what some of the terms meant and the "five steps" to solving an equation. (There were steps?! Well, this explained a lot.) During the next class, I understood more of what the professor was saying. And when he handed out the quiz, I remembered some of what he'd taught—and answered several of the questions right.

Because I had a "hook to hang" the lesson on—which, in this case, was the information I googled—I could chunk multiple pieces of data into one working memory "slot." And that, in turn, meant my working memory could hold on to more information—enough that I was able to understand and encode at least some of what the professor was teaching us.

We Can't Remember What We Don't Remember to Remember

In general, the long-term memory issues those with ADHD face are about difficulties with encoding rather than storage or retrieval. There is one notable exception.

While cued recall and serial recall aren't impaired in ADHD brains, studies done on ADHD children and teens suggest that free recall *is*. Free recall, also referred to as uncued recall, is the ability to spontaneously remember something without a cue to prompt us. For example, we know we brought a jacket to school, and maybe even remember where we put it, but we'll probably forget to grab it on our way out the door unless something (or someone) reminds us.

This tendency for things and people to be "out of sight, out of mind" is sometimes mistaken for an issue with object permanence. Object permanence is an important developmental milestone achieved in early childhood, often through games like peekaboo. It's the understanding that when we can no longer see an object or person, they continue to exist.

Understanding that our friend continues to exist when they leave the room is not the issue with ADHD.

But *remembering* that our friend exists when they leave the room—and that we should text them later and make sure they got home okay? That we do have trouble with, because it depends on free recall.

"I'm Sorry I Forgot!"

Our difficulty with free recall also helps to explain why prospective memory—the ability to remember to do something in the future—is impaired in those with ADHD. At least, *time-based* prospective memory.

Time-based prospective memory is what allows us to remember to do an action at a specific time or after a specific time period has elapsed.

Let's say our friend wanted us to check in with them in a few hours. Or perhaps we told them we would call at four p.m. We may have made plans to do this, understood those plans, and stored that information somewhere in our brains. (And we know the plans are in our brains because they often pop back into our consciousness at random times.)

Still, when the time comes, we absolutely forget about those plans. Half the time, we don't even realize what time it is (see Chapter 6, "How to See Time," page 128).

If we forget to call our friend back at four p.m., then how come we remember to ask them about that book they said we could borrow the next time we see them in person?

That's because our intention to borrow that book when we see them again is stored in our *event-based* prospective memory, which doesn't seem to be impaired in ADHD brains. Event-based prospective memory allows us to remember an action in response to an external cue. When there's an external cue involved, our ability to remember to do something isn't impacted by our wonky sense of time—or our difficulties with free recall (though it is entirely possible that we forget the exact wording of what we wanted to say, we will at least remember that we wanted to say it).

But again, just because someone asked us to do something after dinner doesn't mean we actually heard or encoded it. Yes, even if we totally agreed to do it. Again, our brains wander . . . a lot.

 — **Anonymous, 25, USA**

"Remembering appointments, birthdays, and even holidays is generally a disaster. I find myself constantly having to write reminders down."

 — **Koen S., 33, Belgium**

"I can tell myself not to forget things, but even if it's the most important thing in the world, I'll get distracted, and the existence of the earth-shattering realization will just evaporate from my mind. I won't even remember I had such an idea. It's just gone."

Dez C., 47, Washington

"I feel like things either fall out of my head or I never forget them. There is no middle ground."

 Suzanne S., 37, Alaska

"The biggest lie I tell myself is 'I don't need to write that down. I will remember.' Ninety-nine percent of the time that I say that, I forget."

THE TOOLBOX

So, do we just, like, give up on remembering stuff? Nah. Well . . . sort of. It's important to accept that we will forget things, and understanding *why* we'll have a harder time remembering things makes it easier to figure out which strategies can help (when we remember to use them, of course). At this point I have so many ways of supporting my memory challenges, it almost doesn't bother me anymore. *Almost.* Here are my favorites. I use these all the time.

1. USE AN "ASSISTANT"

Executive function is like the CEO of the brain—and what CEO doesn't need an assistant? Calendars, checklists, apps, and planners function as either virtual (digital) or in-person (analog) assistants.

Though it isn't always easy for us to use these tools, they help us reserve our working memory slots for actually doing a task at hand. Don't worry, you're still the boss; your assistant is just there to keep your brain free for more important stuff. Like deciding whether or not you actually *want* to do the thing.

- **Journal:** A journal gives you a place to record your thoughts, feelings, and dreams, somewhere you can look back at interactions and track how things are going. If you'd like it to function as a planner as well, the Bullet Journal and the Hero's Journal are both great for this.

- **To-do list:** Sometimes our overwhelm comes from trying to hold too many "to-dos" in our head. It can be helpful to dump out everything we want to do, and then narrow that down to what we're actually able to do.* Dr. LaCount recommends choosing no more than three to five to-dos per day. Because prioritizing can be a challenge for us, he suggests choosing ones that, if you do them, will make you feel like today was a success. Remember, just because your to-do list is short, it doesn't mean you can't do more. Many people in our community also use "to-did" lists to track all they accomplished!

---

*   Which is often less than we think, because we already have tasks related to our normal "living life" routines, and we also have brains that like to spontaneously do stuff we didn't have planned.

- **Project management software (e.g., Asana, Monday, Trello, and Notion):** These programs can track to-do lists and entire projects. Be careful, though! Their capacity is unlimited. Ours is not.

Annamarijn V., 31, Belgium

"We have a big whiteboard that has our schedule and important notices for the current week in our kitchen. It also has our menu. By writing it down at the start of the week I don't have to remember it during."

Phoenix R., 39, California

"I like to use my hyper-fixations as tools to remember things. Right now, it is on stationery items, so writing down my events in different colors helps me focus on which category that event is for (e.g., purple for family, each family member getting their own color, a separate color for school, etc.)."

Jen M., 40, North Carolina

"Whenever I make a commitment, I immediately add it to my calendar. No 'I'll get to it later,' I do it on the spot. I also have a Bullet Journal app on my phone that keeps my ongoing to-do list. It has been helpful using an app, because I'd misplace a paper list and totally forget about it."

A Note on Notes

Sticky notes aren't great assistants. Sticky notes do, however, make fantastic assistants *to* your assistant. Think of sticky notes like short-term memory. They're great for holding on to important information for a little bit of time, but if you want that information to stick around (hehe) it helps to encode the information into long-term storage (e.g., your calendar).

2. LOWER THE DEMAND ON YOUR WORKING MEMORY

If we have fewer working memory slots, we need to use them more effectively. This is especially important for new tasks, because they place greater demands on working memory; we haven't chunked any of that data yet, so we can't fit as much into one slot. It is also important for stressful tasks; when emotion kicks in, so does our hot executive function system, which shuts down cognition (see page 81). (This is one reason tasks that are "just as simple" aren't necessarily "just as doable.")

- **Empty your working memory slots.** We've all been there: during important conversations or brain-heavy tasks, a thought that is begging for your attention pops into your head. The next time this happens, take a sec to write it down. Off-loading it allows you to use your entire working memory to hear and process what your conversation partner is saying, or to work on the task at hand (not just the part that isn't trying to remember what you wanted to say or what you suddenly remembered you need to do next week). Because this can look like I'm being distracted, I try to let people know, "Hey, this deserves my full brain. Let me jot this thought down so I can give that to you."

- **Use a visual or auditory reference.** Checklists are one type of visual reference that many of us with ADHD use. But that's not the only way to support our working memory. Dual monitors can keep more information in front of your eyes so you don't have to hold it in your brain. Likewise, a notepad or whiteboard surface gives you a place to write on and serves as an at-a-glance reference. You can even pull a tab out from your browser so you can reference the webpage in a separate window (just grab the tab and move it!). If what you're doing requires moving around (like cooking or cleaning), or you have a visual impairment, a podcast, video, or self-recorded tutorial can help!

- **Use an active body double.** While a body double can be someone who simply sits with you while you work, an active body double, like a study partner who can quiz you, or a co-worker who can read information aloud while you enter it, offers additional assistance. Working with an active body double splits up the mental load of a task, which makes doing it easier—and less frustrating—for both people. It also frees your working memory slots for more intense cognitive tasks, like encoding, analysis, or checking your work.

- **Work on one task at a time (aka monotasking!).** While multitasking can help with motivation and (weirdly) focus, we can dedicate more working memory slots to a task when we're monotasking. This is important if one of those tasks needs our full brain. (See "A Note on Multitasking," page 56.)

- **Take one step at a time.** Breaking the task down into individual steps and completing them one at a time can also help. For example, decide what we want to say *before* trying to say it, or gather all the ingredients for a recipe before we start cooking it.

Andrea M., 34, Sweden

"I use dual monitors at work: one for showing the information I need, and the other for writing or doing calculations. Not having to alt+tab means reducing distractions and removing the possibility of opening something I shouldn't."

Lyskari V., 30, California

"I gather what I need beforehand. For baking cookies, it means I take out all of the ingredients that I need and line them up, in order, based on the recipe. Then I make sure all my measuring cups, mixing bowls, and other tools are within easy reach. The less I have to think about trying to grab or find something in the moment, the less stress on my working memory and the more likely I wind up with delicious cookies."

3. IMPROVE YOUR ENCODING

Since our long-term memory issues happen at the encoding stage, it makes sense to focus on supporting the encoding process. Encoding requires multiple steps. Paying attention. Making sense of the new information. And giving our brains time to process. The internet is full of suggestions to help with encoding (aka learning and studying), but here are a few that are brain-friendly:

- **Give yourself a hook to hang new info on.** Those with "great" memory are those who can chunk data together more effectively. Giving yourself a "hook" to hang it on can help. Ask for questions or topics in advance, get an overview of what a meeting will cover, ask what a story is about (so you understand how the details relate), or quickly review new material before trying to intentionally learn it.

- **Use active studying strategies.** Our brains are more likely to wander when we use passive study techniques, such as reading. Doing something with the material engages the part of our brain that makes up the task positive network, which shuts the door on the default mode network (see page 54—it's responsible for our chronic mind-wandering). Write down the information, make and use flash cards, take notes from a textbook.

- **Make it sticky.** We remember things best when they are meaningful to us or when they stand out as odd. Put what you learn into your own form of expression. Turn something you want to remember into a story, acronym, joke, or drawing. Act it out. Use silly voices!

- **Teach it to someone else.** When we explain what we've learned well enough for someone to understand it, we reinforce our own understanding of the material. You can also teach it to yourself—or pretend to teach it to a five-year-old. If you can explain something in a way that makes sense to a five-year-old, you've got it.

- **Give it time.** Space out learning sessions for new material and let your brain rest—meditate, nap, or review what you've already learned. ADHDers often cram the night before a test, but giving our brain time to rest helps us encode information more effectively—and strengthens our ability to remember it.

- **Sleep!** Getting enough sleep makes it easier to stay focused, and—as a bonus—it helps us process and strengthen what we learned that day. Think of sleep as a study session you don't have to be there for.

“ **Anonymous, 20, Florida**

“My dad helped me with my math in elementary school by making flash card studying into a game, complete with funny voices. He noticed that my brain didn't absorb any information if I wasn't interested. This was way before I got diagnosed, so I'm still impressed he figured out how to help me study.”

Laura W., 29, Australia

"I'm a PA (personal assistant) and I always make sure I have my laptop on me so that I can write down any instruction I get. Whenever I'm given a new job, I write down every step explicitly. I create a lot of process documents for exactly this reason, which thankfully are useful for everyone else. If I don't have something to write on, I chant the thing in my head until I get to somewhere I can write it or I can do it. If I'm asked to do two things at once, I'm kind of doomed."

4. USE CUES—BUT WITH CAUTION

Suggesting the use of cues to someone with ADHD is like handing a blowtorch to someone who *really likes fire*. You can end up with a crème brûlée; you can also end up burning the house down. Cues are a powerful and important tool for brains that struggle with free recall. There are also a lot of skills required to use them artfully—and you'll need to learn what to do if something ends up on fire.

- **Put things where you can see them.** Make sure anything you want to interact with is easily visible. Use labels and clear containers. Create a "launchpad" by the door so you can grab anything you need before you head out. Store vegetables on refrigerator shelves, not in drawers. On the flip side, there is a point where it becomes hard to see what we need because there are so *many* things visible. Use this moment as a cue to put some stuff away.*

- **Keep "to-do" cues to times and places where you can follow through on them.** If the reminder to use a language learning app goes off while you're driving to the store, you'll either train yourself to ignore that reminder, or you'll respond to the reminder and risk *l'incidente d'auto*. If you already tend to ignore reminders, make 'em weird: a sock on the doorknob to remind you to change the laundry, a metronome in your snack cupboard to remind you to practice. Unusual cues jolt us out of default mode and increase the likelihood we'll notice them.

- **If you ignore a to-do cue, do it mindfully.** To-do cues always prompt action, even if that action is to ignore the cue. To safeguard your cues, be mindful. Try to pause before choosing your response. If you choose to ignore or snooze the cue, notice why you are making that choice. You can use this valuable information to refine the cue in the future, or to recognize barriers to action you can now remove.

- **Use cues to remind you of your *intentions*.** While we want to be careful with to-do cues and where we introduce

---

* Or get creative with it! My aunt puts her cellphone in her shoe. When she goes on a walk, she might forget her phone, but she won't forget her shoes.

them, we can plaster intention-related cues all over the place. ADHD coach Caroline Maguire suggests we craft cues that remind us of the person we want to be and choose locations where we will find them throughout our day or week. These cues will help us connect our daily tasks to our greater goals and values, helping us remember why we wanted to do them in the first place.

Examples of Intention Cues

Intention cues can take many forms, including:

- **A single evocative word:** This can be great when you want to keep your intentions private.

- **Silly or inspirational posters:** We remember things better when they stand out or spark emotion.

- **Vision boards (analog or virtual!):** These can help strengthen our vision of the person we want to become or the eventual outcome we're hoping to achieve.

- **Questions that hack our brains:** When we ask ourselves a question, such as "Why am I so interested in practicing the piano?" or "Why am I so good at saving money?" our brains are inclined to look for answers: "Oh, because __." This can increase intrinsic motivation.

Holly K., 33, Oregon

"I try not to use cues for anything that will take more than two minutes to complete—the longer the task, the more likely I am to tell myself, 'Oh, I'll remember to come back to this,' when *decades* of experience has irrefutably proven that to be a dirty lie."

 Çağatay A., 26, Turkey

"I try to put cues where they will annoy me. I work with a computer most of the time, so that means sometimes I post a note in the middle of the screen. If I put it on my desk or something I'll just get used to it, but if it being there annoys me I'm actually motivated to do what I'm supposed to and get rid of the Post-it."

 Scott H., 39, Japan

"I leave objects out if I need to do something with them, which is a huge part of why I come across as a 'messy' person. I leave things in places where I can't ignore them; if I put bills away in a file or something, for example, I would one hundred percent forget that they exist. I leave the garbage bag out in the middle of the hallway so I won't forget to take it out for trash day. I leave unfinished tasks out and open so that when my brain starts looking for something new, I might land on an existing project and work on that some more."

THE JOY OF FORGETTING

My working memory is the *most* impaired aspect of my ADHD brain.

I suspected this was the case from the moment I learned what working memory was. It was confirmed later when I had it tested. As the report delightfully understates, my working memory is a "relative area of weakness."

The good news is, not everything is something I *want* to remember.

Sometimes, when a friend asks how I'm doing because of an earlier conversation about a difficult situation I was navigating, I like being able to honestly ask, "What difficult situation?" I'd long since forgotten about it, which means I hadn't been reliving it. I'd already moved on.

Forgetting what my limits are lets me jump into a new project with enthusiasm and ambition. It also gives me the opportunity to test what those limits even are. Sometimes they've changed!

Forgetfulness has given me experiences and an entire career that I wouldn't otherwise have. The differences in my memory have helped me learn useful compensatory skills. Because I have trouble remembering where I put things, I'm now a pro at using search functions on webpages and computer programs. Because I don't assume anyone remembers anything, I've become a good science communicator. I'm motivated to collect and share what I've learned because I know that I will forget if I don't.

I love the joy of rediscovery. I used to leave $20 bills in coat pockets so I could dig through them when I inevitably ran out of cash. ("Thanks, past me!") This week, it's "Oh, right! We bought a new car!" I keep forgetting about this development, because I've been so immersed in trying to finish this book that I haven't seen the car in days. *Out of sight, out of mind.*

> I lose things, yes, but this gives me the joy of finding them again and appreciating what I thought I'd lost.

I get to walk through much of the world with childlike wonder, experiencing moments as if for the first time. I lose things, yes, but this gives me the joy of finding them again and appreciating what I thought I'd lost. After all, we often don't realize how much something means to us until we can't find it.

My most prized possession (at the moment) is a button I got from a wonderful woman who works in the disability services office at the University of Washington Eau Claire. It reads simply: "We all belong here." While I can't recall the name of the woman who gave it to me, I can vividly conjure the way she smiled at my enthusiasm as I dug through the basket of buttons as if I'd found buried treasure.

I remember the courage the button gave me when I was onstage, giving my first in-person keynote in years, when I was scared that I would mess up because of my memory difficulties. My button assured me I'd still belong if I did. *We all belong here.*

I can't remember for the life of me where I put that button after returning home, but when I find it again, I plan to frame and hang it in a shadowbox. If, by then, I remember I had wanted to.

This is how I move through life. And I kind of love it, the way I kind of love how when I take my contacts out at night, all the lights look like snowflakes.

Especially now that learning these tools gave me more choice, I can move through life with a greater ability to choose what to remember and what to let myself forget.

My memory challenges have strengthened my faith, even in things I can't see or feel or touch, because so much in my life is a dream or a memory, fuzzy at the seams, brought into focus only by my imagination. The picture that comes to mind of the earrings I lost as a kid is no clearer to me than the picture of the future I hope for. But I believe in them both. I trust in their existence.

One of my favorite things about my forgetfulness is that when I get excited about a new project, I forget how hard the last one was. I forget about the downsides and potential negative consequences, the long hours and the sitting in my car crying. There's a cost to this forgetfulness, as I learned and will share at the end of this book. But the reason I dream so big and do big things is because I forget about the constraints of reality, for a bit, and I go after what I want without considering what might get in the way.

Many of us do the same. It's one of our strengths.

> My memory challenges have strengthened my faith, even in things I can't see or feel or touch.

Chapter 9

How to Feel

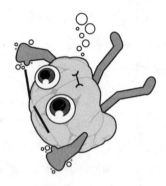

Your emotions make you human.
Even the unpleasant ones have a purpose.

—SABAA TAHIR, *A TORCH AGAINST THE NIGHT*

Heads-up: this chapter discusses drowning, panic attacks, and suicide.

FLOODED

When I was five, my dad took me out to sea on a boogie board that I'd insisted I was big enough to learn how to ride. I remember the excitement of it, my dad tugging me along on that board, holding it in place as a wave began to swell behind us. Then just as it crested, he let go.

I did not know this was part of the ride. The wave pulled me under, the strap connecting me to my board came loose from my wrist, and I plunged, tumbling, disoriented. I knew I should swim, but not which way to go. I knew it wasn't safe to breathe, but I needed to. I inhaled, panicked and overwhelmed, *drowning,* until the wave had run its course and I landed, coughing, back on the shore.

My dad was unaware of the experience I'd had underwater. He didn't know how terrified I'd been, how desperate. *"Fun, huh? Let's do it again!"*

This is how emotions often feel to me. There's a wave behind me building, and just as it crests, I am let go. I lose my tether, and I'm pulled under with an intensity that doesn't make sense to those around me. Overcome, I frequently do and say things that make the situation worse—the equivalent of swallowing water because I'm desperate for air.

Often, I'm unaware of the rising tide of my emotions; when I am, I'm often talked out of my concerns. To everyone else, it's just a day at the beach. I remember so many moments when I tried to tell them about the warning signs:

I am eight years old, and I am upset about my socks. The seam is in the wrong place over my toes, and I can feel it with every step I take. I ask if we can stop so I can fix them. *"No, you're fine, let's go."*

At school, someone teases me, and I tell them my feelings are hurt. They tell me I'm too sensitive. When a teacher sees me cry, they tell me to go wash my face, so I do. I spend the day trying to do what I am expected to do and feel what I am expected to feel.

I fall apart when I get home. I drop my toy and it breaks. *"Stop crying."* I can't. I'm underwater. Dad is angry. *"Stop crying or I'll give you something to cry about."* More waves. I can't breathe. I run to my room and hide under the blankets, my face in a pillow. This makes me feel better. The wave sweeps me back to shore.

> Throughout the day, I hear that I am wrong about what I'm feeling, or that I shouldn't be feeling it.

Later, at dinner, my sister makes me laugh. I make her laugh. We both laugh, uncontrollably, until we are ordered to stop. I can't stop; I'm too swept up. I am sent away from the table.

Throughout the day, I hear that I am wrong about what I'm feeling, or that I shouldn't be feeling it.

"It's nothing!" "Don't be scared." "Calm down." "Don't cry."

At ten, I still cry in class. The messages shift.

"You're too old for this." "Stop being so dramatic." "It's not that big a deal."

At twelve, after my mom is in a car accident, I have to go to a new school. I feel guilt and fear and anger. Change after change becomes too much, and one day, I yell. My aunt scolds me: "You're a bad daughter." I shouldn't be angry with my mom. It's not her fault. I stop speaking up.

My new school sells cinnamon rolls at break. I eat them every day. The sweetness is like a life preserver. I am trying to keep my head above water.

At assembly, I reach my hand for the boy next to me. I'm not allowed to be sad, so I seek out what makes me happy. Not *too* happy, though. Happy enough so that I'm not a problem. Not so happy that I become one.

I'm an adult now, but the messages I grew up with ring through my head.

"Don't be scared." "Calm down." "Don't cry." "It's not that big a deal."

If I feel hurt, I explain to myself why I shouldn't. If I feel lonely, I explain to myself why that's wrong. I talk myself out of my feelings instinctively, the moment they come up. I play Whac-A-Mole. That one's inconvenient. Whack. That one's wrong. Whack. Push past it. Work through it. *You're fine.*

When someone gives me permission to feel something specific *"Aren't you excited?" "You must be so sad."*—I learn to agree.

I have my first panic attack at age thirty-two, and it feels as if I'm unraveling. As though someone found a loose end in the sweater that is my knitted life and pulled. I knit myself back together and keep on. Things will be easier when I get through this day. This week. This month. This project. This miscarriage. This divorce. This pandemic. This—

After my mom dies, the waves come too quickly for me to recover. They create a riptide that pulls me far from shore, farther than I have ever been. No one wants to get too close, because in my flailing, I might pull them under. People don't think straight when they're drowning, and they don't think straight when they're flooded with emotions, either.

I drown for almost a year, clutching at life preservers, never finding shore.

One day, I stop believing I ever will.

I've promised myself *"things will get easier when"* and it hasn't *"gotten easier when"* so many times that I've stopped believing it ever can. If there is no shore, it's easier to just swim down. I can't do this forever. *I'm so tired.*

I realize I can stop. That my fight to find shore can be over, not eventually or maybe or someday but *now.*

It is shocking how quickly it happens, how practical and even *easy* the solution suddenly seems compared to continuing on. In the space of a few minutes, I go from a terrifying plunge into despair to a *plan* and, with it, *relief.*

The mental health expert part of me recognizes the danger and jumps in like an unwelcome lifeguard. This is the part of me that has training and has helped others through similar situations before. It knows what to do for the part of me that has stopped struggling and is now dangerously peaceful and calm: *create time and distance.*

I get myself away from anything I see as a great solution to my problems, and call people who can help me ride out this unexpected tidal wave: suicide hotlines,* a friend a few hours away, and an ex who lives close enough to intervene if needed. He has been trying to distance himself from me emotionally, but that night he comes over and hugs me hard. "Don't go."

By then, it feels bizarre that he is saying these words. "No, of course I won't." I feel guilty for worrying him. There is no danger anymore; I have no desire to hurt myself. But it matters that he says

---

* If you or someone you love is experiencing a mental health crisis, check out the resources in the back of this book.

it. It tells me he cares, and so I admit to my struggle and ask for help. I cry and explain how exhausted I am. I explain the endless ocean of pain.

I asked a therapist once how to get to land. She told me I was good at the ocean. My next therapist tells me something different. The better I can get at my feelings—feeling the swell, riding the wave, even letting myself be pulled under sometimes—the more easily I will be able to feel the land beneath my feet.

> The better I can get at my feelings—feeling the swell, riding the wave, even letting myself be pulled under sometimes—the more easily I will be able to feel the land beneath my feet.

My then ex that night tells me something different still. When I tell him I've stopped believing this ocean of pain will ever end, he says simply, "Oh, it doesn't. There will *always* be pain."

All of them are right. And none of them, entirely. To understand why, let's start with the science.

WHAT I LEARNED

ADHD brains don't regulate emotions very well. Not only do they hit us harder and last longer, we also tend to be more reactive to them than someone who is neurotypical. This intensity and reactivity have an enormous impact on how we interact with the world, as well as how the world reacts to us.

---

emotion dysregulation (n.)*
An impaired ability to control your
emotional response, which can lead to
extreme and/or disproportionate reactions
that are not necessarily appropriate to the
situation.

Unfortunately, like most people with ADHD (and many doctors who *treat* ADHD), I didn't know that emotion dysregulation was part of the deal because the *DSM* doesn't list it as part of the diagnostic criteria for ADHD.

While the emotional component of ADHD has been observed as long as ADHD has, the simple truth is that emotions are harder to measure in a lab than inattention, impulsivity, and hyperactivity—so when the diagnostic criteria were formed in the *DSM-II*, they were based on that research. Emotions were left out.

This is the reason people with ADHD are often misdiagnosed with mood disorders, and why we don't get the support we need even once we're diagnosed correctly: we don't know the extent to which our struggle with emotions isn't normal. Emotions hit us harder and faster, and take us under, in ways most medical providers, teachers, and loved ones don't understand.

---

*   "Emotion dysregulation" and "emotional dysregulation" are often used interchangeably but refer to the same thing.

(Why) Emotion Regulation Is Hard for ADHD Brains

Emotion regulation—the ability to exert control over one's emotional state—is what allows us to calm down and make good choices when something gets us worked up. This sounds simple, but emotion regulation relies on skills the ADHD brain tends to have trouble with, such as:

Inhibition, as in *not* impulsively reacting to an emotion. According to Dr. Russell Barkley, the more generally impulsive we are (and impulsivity *is* in the *DSM* criteria for ADHD), the more emotionally impulsive we are, too.

Self-soothing, which is the ability to calm and comfort ourselves after experiencing an emotion. Most of us do have ways to self-soothe, but they're not always healthy (and our healthy ones aren't always "socially acceptable").

Refocusing our attention, which is the exact problem for which our disorder is named. Fantastic. Moving on . . .

Responding to our emotions in a way that aligns with our goals for the situation. This assumes, of course, that we know what our goals even are. To make matters even more complicated, emotion regulation is a cool executive function—and emotions activate our hot executive function system. Once we're emotionally "in the red," we can no longer executive-function our way out; if we don't have automatic go-tos to de-escalate a situation, there is a tip-ping point at which we're *not going to be able to*. This is true for everyone; cognitive ability declines as emotions rise, and that includes the cognitive ability required to reg-ulate our emotions. But for those of us with brains that impulsively react to an emotion, there are times we don't have any window to recognize our rising emotions and even *try* to regulate them. We skip past yellow and go straight from green to red.

EMOTION DYSREGULATION GETS US IN TROUBLE

As kids, emotion dysregulation can get us labels like "overly sensi-tive," "immature," or (sadly) a "brat." Our emotional meltdowns are sometimes misinterpreted as tantrums, and we're often shamed and even punished for having emotions our brains just don't know how to manage.

Dr. Barkley contends that out of all the challenges adults with ADHD have in the workplace—arriving late, being disorganized, struggling with focus—emotion dysregulation is the one that gets us fired. We're quick to get emotionally "flooded" and to express raw emotions even when it's not appropriate for the situation. To make matters worse, when cycling from one mistake, obstacle, deadline, or oversight to the next, we frequently don't have the time we need to return to our emotional baseline. And the words that come out of our mouths when we're frustrated or furious are tougher to forgive than a late clock-in or a messy desk.

But ADHDers experience emotion dysregulation with other emotions, too. Sadness, fear, desire, or rejection (even perceived rejection) can be unbearably intense (more on rejection sensitivity in "How to People," page 248).

Positive emotions, such as excitement, joy, humor, and even love, can spiral out of control, too. As anyone who's watched *The Notebook* can attest, too much of a good thing can lead to some questionable decisions.

Because our difficulties with emotion dysregulation create very real problems in our lives, we might come to believe that our emotions *themselves* are the problem. Therefore, we do what we can to avoid them.

WE TRY NOT TO FEEL

After years of struggling with the fallout from our too-big, too-loud, too-unregulated feelings, it's common for us to go to great lengths to avoid and/or suppress our emotions:

- We avoid situations that might bring up difficult emotions.

- We distract ourselves from them.

- We "reframe" or intellectualize our emotions.

- We try to make the situation more tolerable, often with food or substances, such as alcohol or drugs.

- We mask our feelings and pretend we're fine.

To be clear, there's nothing wrong with occasionally distracting ourselves from uncomfortable, inconvenient, or outsized emotions or choosing situations that are less likely to bring them up. (Take a look at the sidebar below.) Using these strategies mindfully can be helpful for managing our emotions on a day-to-day basis.

How We Regulate Our Emotions

According to Dr. James Gross's process model for emotion regulation, there are five strategies for managing our emotions:

1. **Situation selection:** the ability to choose situations that are less likely to lead to emotion regulation challenges. ("I *could* have my birthday party at da club, but I think I'd feel less overwhelmed if we go to a restaurant instead.")

2. **Situation modification:** the ability to change or modify a situation known to trigger emotion dysregulation. ("I'll change seats so I *don't* sit next

to my friend during bio lecture. I always end up giggling when I do.")

3. **Cognitive change or reappraisal:** the ability to change the way we view a situation or our emotional reaction to it. We can also change how we think about how we manage our emotions in a particular situation. ("You know what, it's actually *better* that I got fired from that job. I didn't like it anyway! ThIs iS FiNe.")

4. **Attention deployment:** the ability to turn our attention away from the source of hard-to-regulate emotions. ("Ugh, my house is such a mess. Crap, feelings! *Where's the remote?*")

5. **Response modulation:** the attempt to alter our emotional response. ("*AUGHH* performance anxiety *DEEP BREATHS* wait, HOW DOES BREATHING WORK? Oh right, in for four . . .")

Unfortunately, the way—and the extent to which—we use these tools isn't always healthy for us.

Even adaptive coping strategies can become maladaptive, as is the case when an occasional "I'm just gonna escape into this book for a bit" turns into "I have spent my entire year in a book or, more accurately, six hundred books." Research finds that cognitive avoidance—a set of coping mechanisms in which a person uses cognitive techniques like avoidance, suppression, or rumination to escape mental and emotional distress—is particularly common among those with ADHD. When mindful coping crosses the line into unhealthy avoidance, we can end up avoiding or repressing emotions we need to face.

CHRONICALLY AVOIDING EMOTIONS IS PROBLEMATIC

Emotions can't be avoided or suppressed forever, and ignoring them comes with many negative consequences. If our fear of confrontation prevents us from asking for a promotion, we may miss a chance to advance in our career. If we are afraid to be lonely, we might stay too long in an unhealthy relationship. Chronically avoiding our emotions leaves us ill-equipped to handle them when we finally can't run from them anymore.

Suppressed feelings don't stay suppressed. While some emotions can naturally come and go, the ones we push down on a regular basis don't phase out of existence. Often, they intensify, especially if the situation that initially caused them isn't resolved.

Most parents of ADHD children have observed the phenomenon called after-school restraint collapse, where their child comes home from school and melts down. After a long day of trying to hide their symptoms and stifle their emotions, they all erupt to the surface. In adults, psychological symptoms like irritability, mood swings, or even panic attacks can occur. Physical symptoms like sleeplessness, chronic pain, gastrointestinal problems, and even sexual dysfunction can result when you persistently suppress intense emotions.

Not only can avoiding and suppressing our emotions cause damage to our lives, health, and mental wellness, it causes us to miss out on what our feelings are trying to tell us.

Feelings give us information we need. Our emotions are always communicating with us, sending us signals about what works for us—and what doesn't. Think of your emotions like a smoke detector. Sure, it might start blaring when there is not, in fact, a fire; this alarm system can sometimes be hypersensitive. But if there isn't a fire, it is at least sensing some smoke—and that's often worth investigating.

Unfortunately, many people with ADHD experience psychological symptoms that create distance between them and their feelings, including:

- **Dissociation:** The feeling of being disconnected or detached from your surroundings, or even from yourself.

- **Anhedonia:** The impaired ability to experience pleasure, even when doing something you usually enjoy.

- **Alexithymia:** The inability or impaired ability to recognize and describe your feelings. We might know something's wrong but not *what*.

Avoiding our emotions doesn't necessarily cause these symptoms, but it can. No matter the cause, the treatment is the same: learn to feel your feels. Not only does feeling our emotions help us process them, but being able to accurately identify our emotions is critical to being able to manage them effectively.

As psychiatrist Dr. Dan Siegel puts it, you've got to "name it to tame it." Labeling the emotion can diminish the response of the amygdala and limbic system, decreasing our emotional reactivity to negative emotional experiences. And understanding what we're feeling can help us identify which of our needs may not be getting met (we have them, yes; all humans do!).

Many of us weren't taught this stuff, so it can be worth taking some time to learn about emotions—what they are, what they're called, what purpose each one serves. In the resources (scan the QR code on page 432), I include a link to an emotion tracker worksheet, as well as a great resource that has reference cards for common human needs and the feelings we experience when they aren't met.

I also link to a resource to help with finding a therapist. Therapists can help us explore and learn about our emotions, as well as establish healthier ways for us to cope with big feelings, making it safer for us to acknowledge them. This is especially important for those who have a history of abuse or trauma. *Exploring our* emotions opens feelings doors that were closed for a reason—and can bring up feelings we don't yet have the ability to cope with in a healthy way.

Jerica T., 31, Virginia

"It's been difficult figuring out how to deal with my emotions in a healthy way, especially when everyone around me puts me down for having them."

Hendrik M., 28, Germany

"I have a hard time even realizing *what* I'm feeling. During the 'analysis,' I fall into a pit where executive function crawls to a halt. This conditioned me to try to fence my emotions off. But when they inevitably break through, it's even harder to control."

Ellie M., 25, Colorado

"When experiencing intense emotions, I might appear catatonic. Something major could be happening and I'm either super calm or don't have any reaction at all. Sometimes it makes me look like I don't care, but it's the opposite: I care so much that I can only process the major emotion one small piece at a time."

Jay R., 38, Canada

> "I've learned recently that I haven't been dealing with my emotions. Just hiding them, bottling them up. 'Boys don't cry' and all that. That isn't 'dealing with it.' Then I found out last year I have ADHD, and now I have answers. I'm trying to allow my feelings to come out, because Having Big Feelings is just how I am."

THE TOOLBOX

When you have big emotions, it's especially important to learn how to cope with them. Thankfully, there are many ways to do that. I've collected some of my favorites here. If these tools seem a bit daunting, don't worry: according to research, even the act of *noticing* our emotions—without judgment—can make them easier to handle.

1. LABEL YOUR EMOTIONS

Identifying your emotions is key to being able to manage them effectively. This can be easier said than done for those of us who can't always tell what we're feeling. Many of us have a hard time even telling the difference between our feelings and our thoughts.* Here are some ADHD-friendly ways to make it easier:

---

* Feelings are physical or emotional experiences. Thoughts are mental cognitions—our ideas, opinions, and beliefs. One-word journaling can help you distinguish one from the other. Thoughts take many words to describe ("I feel like everyone hates me"). Feelings, on the other hand, only require one ("sad").

- **Label the intensity.** We can often tell how *intense* an emotion is before we can tell *what* the emotion is. There are different ways to do this. You can assign a color (such as green, yellow, or red) or use a one-to-ten rating scale, where one is the least intense and ten is the most. Even if you can't tell what you're feeling yet, identifying its intensity can let you know if it's worth addressing (if it's a ten, probably!)—and if it's a good idea to do that right now (if it's still a ten, probably not).

- **Use external prompts.** Feeling wheels—circular diagrams that help you identify your feelings—can help you put words to your emotional experiences. So can paying attention to what your body is doing. Daniel Jones of The Aspie World YouTube channel, who also has ADHD, points out that emotions are energy in motion. What does the energy in your body make you want to do? Laugh? Cry? Rock? Throw rocks?

- **Create your own labeling system.** For some, describing their emotions isn't as easy as, say, pointing at a color. I have a friend who communicates her feelings in terms of what kind of potato she feels like that day.

- **Look for the emotion behind the emotion.** Emotions that we're less comfortable with having and/or expressing often quickly get masked by other emotions. If you notice you constantly feel angry, there might be a different emotion behind it, such as hurt or even fear. It's important to look for the *first* emotion that you experienced in a situation. If you respond angrily when you actually *felt scared,* you probably won't get the results (and safety!) you need.*

Jen D., 29, Connecticut

"Understanding and properly labeling what I'm feeling is hugely important. Often my body signal feels like the equivalent of a check engine light with no detail. It's tough to process emotions if you don't know what they are in the first place."

Anonymous, 20s, USA

"I try to visualize big emotions—usually as a big rush of air or energy, or a big wave. I'm either something sturdy (like a cliff or a tree) or something very agile (like a bird), and I just wait it out for a moment or two. Or I'm a lightning rod, just guiding it all into the ground."

---

* We can do this with our thoughts, too. If a harsh thought comes up, especially one disguised as a feeling (e.g., "I feel like I'm going to fail, and everyone is going to laugh at me"), we can look for the emotion behind it. In this case, it might be fear, specifically fear of humiliation.

Emelie S., 24, Sweden

"If I get severe anxiety [at home], I say out loud, 'My name is *name*, I'm at home in *city*, I'm anxious about *thing that set it off*, and it's okay to feel bad, this won't last forever.' It keeps me from spiraling or suppressing the thoughts (then they continue all day anyways)."

2. MAKE SPACE FOR YOUR EMOTIONS

We may have been told for years, even decades, that our emotions are wrong or that we're not supposed to feel a certain way. Making space for our emotions can combat these beliefs, help us process our emotions, and validate how we are feeling. It also communicates to yourself (and others) that it's okay to have emotions, so we can acknowledge them more easily when they come up.

- **WAIT before taking action.** Immediately "fixing" (or even "reframing") the situation that made you feel an emotion can reinforce the idea that our emotions aren't allowed to exist. It also increases the likelihood that we'll take a less helpful action because we haven't gotten time to process and understand anything yet. While putting on the brakes when emotions are running high is incredibly difficult, we can learn skills that can help (scan the QR code on page 432 for resources). We can also ask others to give us time to think or take away our means of communicating (for example, our phones) when we're running hot.

- **Sit with your feelings.** As my therapist taught me, even our biggest feelings can't last forever; in most cases, the body can only sustain an intense emotion for about twenty minutes. It can often be less emotionally distressing to sit with your feelings and watch them fade than to dodge them and have them hang around waiting for you to notice them.

- **Take time to explore your emotions.** This can mean drawing, painting, or talking them out—with a journal or a third party who may be able to help us process and figure out what, if anything, we want to do next. Feelings are in their rawest form when they first come up. While this is not the best time to communicate them, it can be a *great* time to write them down. Exploring your feelings on your own while you're feeling them can make it easier to communicate them when you're in a better place to effectively do so.

❝ **Rowan N., 31, Colorado**

"I take time alone and write out my feelings. Sometimes in a doc on the computer, sometimes by hand. It helps me sort things into a semblance of order and figure out not only *what* I'm feeling but *why*. I have CPTSD [complex post-traumatic stress disorder], so the 'why' isn't always obvious."

Sharon G., 34, Massachusetts

"I do my damnedest to avoid making any irrevocable decisions while in the grip of a torrent of emotions. I do anything I can to give myself time—take a nap, listen to an audiobook, hide in the bathroom."

 Juliana N., 24, Pennsylvania

"I let myself feel the emotions. I held back for so many years—and then would have breakdowns every few months—so now I let myself feel whatever it is. After about ten to fifteen minutes, I write them down or talk it out with someone, asking questions like: Did I overreact? If I did, what did I overreact to? If I didn't, is it something I just couldn't control? Analyzing my emotions and realizing that they're often reactions to something I can't control helps me gain more sympathy for myself."

3. USE YOUR EMOTIONS

In our attempt to suppress or avoid our emotions, it's easy to forget how useful they are. Feelings exist for a reason. They're indicators that we might need more of something, less of something, to keep going with something, or to do something different.

- **Use them as (motivational) fuel.** ADHDers often push past challenges and take on projects that no one else would because of the passion driving us. We can also use our strong emotions and passion to motivate others, which can help us be effective leaders. Successful problem-solving relies on emotion and motivation; when extrinsic motivation is lacking, i.e., we're not getting the results we want quickly enough, we can tap into our emotions to get the engine revved back up.

- **Use them as a compass.** Sometimes our gut knows something is off before our brain does. If something comes up on your emotional radar as danger, it might be worth checking out. You might not be in actual danger, but your brain might be picking up on something that reminds it of something unsafe. Our emotions can also let us know if our actions are (or aren't) in line with our values. They can hint at whether something is being received well by another person. They can indicate whether our needs are being met. They point to where our boundaries are (more on boundaries in "How to People," page 248). Paying attention to your emotions can help you navigate a situation more effectively and figure out if you're on the right track.

- **Enjoy them.** Some people (maybe you!) enjoy experiencing emotions. There's a reason we go to the movies, ride roller coasters, listen to sad songs, or fall in love. We want to feel. Feeling deeply reminds us we're alive. Research has found that mindfulness, being fully present, makes us happier—even when what we're experiencing is negative.

- **Foster connection.** Expressing what you think can be divisive, but expressing what you feel is typically connecting. Pixar had it right. Expressing sadness brings people together. Communicating how you feel can help you bond with the people you love, mend rifts, and find common ground. Feelings can also help us connect with the world. Communication—whether it's personal, artistic, or even scientific—moves people more when there's genuine emotion behind it. People connect better with what you say if you make them laugh or if you make them feel.*

 Tanya K., 55, Washington

"I do use my emotions to connect with some people. Excitement, exuberance, delight are of course really good ways of connecting with people (although I've met some who are turned off by these). But sometimes, frustration and anger can connect us with people who are also experiencing these things. When something in the news upsets me, hearing someone else express frustration helps me feel less alone and hopeless."

---

*   For many of these pages, I tried to communicate my experience by intellectualizing it, and it didn't work as well. I had to go back and rewrite—to let myself feel enough to connect with you through the page. Hi!

Sam G., 28, France

"Love is a great motivational fuel. If I don't want to do something but it'll make life better for someone I love, I'm more likely to do it. This works well to motivate myself to do chores or cooking. I do them better if it's for my cat, or for my partner, than if I do them for myself."

 Emily Z., 32, New Jersey

"I used to ignore my gut feelings, but now I'll take a moment after someone asks me to do something to see if there's any physical resistance (like upset stomach or tight chest) when I think about doing the thing. Ideally, I do this check before I agree to do something, but if the sensation is strong enough after I've said yes, I'll go back to the person afterward and tell them 'on second thought...'"

4. FIND YOUR (EMOTIONAL) BALANCE

While there's nothing wrong with having emotions, being emotionally "flooded" can be deeply uncomfortable and diminish our choice in how to respond, often resulting in actions we regret. Emotions might feel as if they have an on/off switch, especially if we've made it a habit to ignore or suppress them until they're screaming at us. In actuality, emotions are more like a mixing board. While we can't directly control our emotions, there *are* many things we can do to impact them. Our thoughts, behavior, and environment all play a role. We can adjust the emotional volume by being proactive about these factors.

- **Practice meditation.** Each stressor we experience increases our adrenaline level. If our adrenaline continues to spike and doesn't get the chance to come back down, which is common with our hectic ADHD lives, at some point its level is high enough that even a small stressor can push us over our metaphorical edge. Practicing meditation is a way to take regular breaks from the constant barrage of input and settle our emotional glitter (aka return to our emotional baseline) so we're less likely to be pushed over the edge when stressors pop up. The busier and more stressed we are, the more important this can become.

- **Seek support before—and take breaks from—emotionally difficult situations.** When possible, go into difficult situations with a plan, especially one you've worked through with a trusted friend or mental health professional. And if you need to, step away. While you don't want to avoid emotions chronically, that doesn't mean you have to constantly force yourself to feel them, either.

- **Put your effort into things you can control.** One of my favorite ways to be okay when things are not okay for an extended period of time is to redirect my efforts to stuff I can directly control. Putting emotional energy into stuff you cannot control is like putting your heart on a kite. It might be fine on a sunny day, but if it's starting to look like tornado season, rein it in.

Neli U., 36, United Kingdom

"When it feels like I'm falling in a deep black hole, then it's super important for me to feel present. I make tea; I can feel the warm mug in my hands. I put cream on my face; it smells nice and feels soft. I walk my dog, and I try to look at the pretty trees and buildings... I might still feel awful, but it's kind of like grabbing on to the boat instead of falling in the ocean and drowning."

Nikki P., 22, Texas

"I take a deep breath in, hold my hands out, and as I exhale through my mouth, I lower my hands at the same time. For some reason having a physical and visual cue really chills me out."

Scott D., 35, Ohio

"I head to the gym or work out if I can. I describe it as my 'reset button': the combination of listening to music, focusing on the exercise, and the resulting endorphins settle me when the emotions surge or get overwhelming."

Samantha B., 37, Alabama

"I was prescribed a mood stabilizer to help. I don't blow up as much as I used to, but it does still happen."

Megan C., 41, Vermont

"When I am overwhelmed, I don't do anything, I undo things. I undo the expectation that the dishes will get done. I cancel meetings and plans. I identify what can come off the to-do list. I decide what is too much for right-now-me, and I give it over to future-me. I have trust that future-me will be able to put things into perspective. So far, she has never let me down."

BUT NOT *THAT* FEELING, RIGHT?

As I began to explore my emotions, I quickly realized my feelings *about* my feelings ranged *widely*.

Sadness, for example, was an emotion I felt I was allowed to have. I was discouraged from experiencing it as a child, but as an actor, I was commended for expressing it. Feeling vulnerable enough to cry on camera was a skill. And the times I'd allowed myself to cry about my own feelings on camera when I was making videos for the channel, the community had been supportive and even grateful for making it seem okay for them to feel their feels, too.

By the time I went to a therapist after my mom died, sadness was an emotion that, while not *fun*, felt at least socially acceptable.

Especially in this situation. People are *supposed* to be sad if someone close to them dies.

When my therapist asked me to imagine my grief in my body, I immediately could. I imagined colored glass tubes that ran throughout my body and wrapped around my heart. I explained to her that sometimes they lay dormant and benign. But then a reminder of my mom, or someone's offhand comment, lit up the whole system. These grief-and-trauma tubes squeezed my heart and it hurt.

Later, when something triggered my grief, I imagined picking one of these tubes up and holding it above me. I followed my therapist's advice about sitting with my feelings: I held it and looked at it with curiosity, until the intense sadness started to fade, and the colorful glass tube burst into glass glitter. It showered around me, disappearing like snowflakes when it hit the ground. I finally understood how to sit with my sadness in a way that could make it fade.

When my therapist asked me to draw a picture of my anger, I drew it in my mind, too—a harsh children's scrawl of red and black crayon. She suggested I hang it on the wall, and I imagined it on the wall.

"Maybe see how it feels inside you," she suggested.

I revolted. "*Why* would I want that?" Anger isn't okay, I told her. Anger is bad. Why would I let it *in*? It's not good to feel anger.

When she asked why not, I patiently explained. "Anger makes people do bad things. Anger is *abusive*." My introduction to anger had come from my dad flying into a rage and spanking my siblings and me to make us behave.

She asked me what level of anger I was comfortable with. I blinked.

She explained. "If on a scale of one to ten, abusive anger is a ten, what level are you allowed to have? Like, if frustrated is a four, and irritated is a—"

"Frustration," I said. I was allowed to be frustrated. Later, I recognized that was a bit of a cop-out. Because of course I was allowed to be frustrated; I was typically frustrated at myself. So I chose a form of anger that I was allowed to feel about other people's actions: "irritated." I decided I was allowed to feel irritated, but even this was scary.

A few months later, as those of us with ADHD often do, I doubted whether I'd made any real strides in therapy. My therapist told me, "You've spent the last few sessions talking about how angry you are. When you first came to me, you never let yourself express anger at all. You're making progress."

Huh.

It's *progress* to be able to feel and express your emotions. Even the ones we've come to believe are "bad." Because if we can't do that—if we can't manage our emotions effectively—our emotions manage us. If we don't know how to respond to them, we can only react to them.

Now when I'm angry, I'm able to acknowledge my anger, and this allows me to communicate it and set boundaries based on it. It doesn't build up and then explode out of me the way that it used to, confirming my fear that anger is bad, it makes people hurt people. I'm able to tame it, sit with it, and express it in healthier ways.

There might be less helpful ways to respond to feelings, but there aren't any "bad" feelings. Feelings are signals. It's important that we allow those signals to come through and know how to interpret what those signals mean. We can *maybe* exclude a behavior, like yelling, from our repertoire, but we're more likely to be able to do so if we have a handle on the emotions that lead to it.

I still have ADHD and all the big feelings that come with it. It was *after* learning this stuff that I went from intense distress to passive suicidal ideation to active suicidal ideation to a self-interrupted suicide attempt in the span of a few minutes, the speed of which was likely due to my issues with response inhibition and emotion dysregulation. I think that's important to know. Sometimes our emotions will swallow us regardless of how many coping skills we have because life is hard and ADHD makes it harder. Grief happens. So does trauma. And opening up these doors to big feelings can let in an absolute flood.

I'm grateful I opened them, though. Understanding the sheer vastness of the pain and that there is no magical point at which it goes away made me decide not to add to the ocean I and others drown in. It helped me realize I needed a *boat*. Someplace safe and warm I could mentally escape to when I needed a break.

> It's progress to be able to feel and express your emotions. Even the ones we've come to believe are "bad."

When the water levels are more manageable, my therapist was right—being better at recognizing and experiencing my emotions helped me feel the land beneath my feet. Sometimes when I feel like I'm drowning, I'm really face down in a puddle and just need to stand up.

Learning to manage, not outrun, my emotions has helped me be still enough to be rescued, too. Not just by others, but by myself. I'm a better lifeguard for myself because I am an easier person to rescue. I am easier to pull from the water.

Understanding my own emotions and having the ability to be present with them has made me better at sitting with others' emotions, too—as well as stepping in to support when their water levels rise.

Chapter 10

How to People

The only way to have a friend is to be one.
—RALPH WALDO EMERSON

I HATE THAT QUOTE

I mean, Ralph Waldo Emerson isn't wrong.

Reciprocity *is* key to friendship. Give and take, take and give. Friend texts me, I text friend back. Emerson makes it sound easy.

As with many areas in my life, I tend to underdo or overdo it when it comes to social stuff. And difficulty regulating my *social* efforts is often more of a problem. Projects don't care if you ignore them for a month and then tackle them all in one day. People *do*.

I've felt socially awkward as long as I can remember.

Eighth-grader: Hi, my name is Amanda.

Me: Oh . . . hi.

(Long pause, as twelve-year-old-me-at-a-new-school waits for this yay-new-friend to continue.)

Amanda: What's *your* name?

Me: Oh, right! Jessica. *dies in shame*

Once I was medicated, I was more confident and outgoing, but just as bad at socially self-regulating:

Fellow sophomore: *Hi!* I'm—

Me: HI—HERE'S MY ENTIRE LIFE STORY!

Like many people with ADHD, I didn't have many close friends growing up. I generally *understood* the social rules, but I had trouble applying them. I could pretend to belong for a little while, but soon I'd be too loud, too weird, too *me,* and the others would edge away.

Eventually, I learned to edge away, to escape to a place where I did belong.

I spent a lot of time in the water, in the pool in my grandparents' backyard, then on the swim team.* On land, I brought a book with me everywhere. Books were a portal into another world. I understood how to interact with books. I knew what

> I generally understood the social rules, but I had trouble applying them.

---

*   At five years old, I decided I wanted to be a fish when I grew up. Tellingly, I never imagined myself in a school of fish. In these fantasies, it was just Fishie-Jessie swimming around, happy and free.

the characters were thinking, what they wanted, because it was all laid out on the page.

The first time I found a sense of belonging with my peers happened when I got a boyfriend. When he broke up with me, my world caved in. It hurt so badly, to be expelled from the one place I had felt valued, accepted, and seen by someone my age. I decided to never let that happen again.

From then on, I became an expert in the care and keeping of romantic relationships. I only dated guys who I knew *for sure* were more interested in me than I was in them. I learned what they liked and how to make them happy. I became a people-pleaser. Well, a *person*-pleaser—I did not have the executive function required to please a crowd.

When I started How to ADHD, though, I began to develop deep, meaningful connections with people—*peers*—from all over the world. I'd never thought to seek community online before, but here I was *building* one. I found my people! I *could* have friends! They just happened to be online.

Finding these friendships started to undo some of my long-held beliefs: that I'd never fit in, that there was no place for me outside of whatever job or romantic relationship I had. They gave me purpose, hope, and connection.

After my mom died in August 2020, though, I found the limits of online friendships. You can't hug someone through Discord. My long-distance friends couldn't sit with me through the grief.

Leaning on a romantic relationship to meet my in-person needs had been my go-to before—but now, my needs were too great for one person to handle. I had moved to a new city to be with a new partner, but between my grief and pandemic isolation, that relationship fell apart.

Single again, I used my inheritance to put a down payment on my first home. The day I got the keys, I wound up sitting on the floor of my empty house, crying. This was a huge moment for me, but I had absolutely no one to share it with. I had friends all over the world, but there was no one to sit with me, eat pizza, and talk about where the furniture should go.

After that experience, I realized no one relationship, no online community, no long-distance friendship could truly meet all my social needs. Humans are social creatures, even those of us who have trouble socializing. We need *people*—to share things with, to hug or sit with us when we're sad, to give us somewhere we can go and feel like we belong. I couldn't get out of the "in person" part of friendships without missing out on an important part of *life*.

Which brings me to where I am now: a busy professional adult, trying to make friends in a city I'm just beginning to explore. By the time this book comes out, I will hopefully be farther along on this journey—especially with the insights and tools I learned while writing this chapter.

> Humans are social creatures, even those of us who have trouble socializing.

WHAT I LEARNED

While some ADHDers may have no trouble making and keeping friends, that isn't the typical ADHD experience. Those of us who struggle socially are not alone . . . in being alone. (Oh, the irony.) When I learned this for the first time, I read the research papers on it with tears streaming down my cheeks. *This explains so much.*

WE STRUGGLE TO DEVELOP OUR FRIEND CIRCLES

Disability advocate Judith Snow is one of my new heroes thanks to her work on how those with disabilities can develop strong social support networks. She created a concept known as "circle of support," and according to this framework, the people in our lives exist in one of four circles:

- **The circle of intimacy (circle one):** This includes the people closest to us, who know us on a deep level, and who we can't imagine our lives without, such as immediate family members, our partner, our best friend.

- **The circle of friendship (circle two):** This includes our good friends and allies, the people we call when we have good news, vent to when we fight with a family member, laugh with, and invite to our birthday parties.*

---

* If you're thinking, "What? But that's what my best friend and/or partner are for!" you probably see where I'm going with this. *Apparently*, humans need other people for these moments in life, too, if we want to be fulfilled.

- **The circle of participation (circle three):** This includes the people we participate in shared interests with, the people with whom we interact in our community, work, classes, and clubs.

- **The circle of exchange (circle four):** This includes people we pay, or who pay us, including doctors, rideshare drivers, therapists, housekeepers, hairstylists, and bosses.

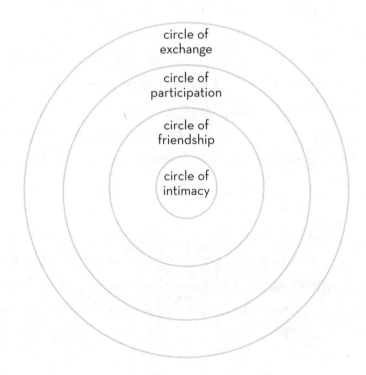

According to Judith Snow, those with disabilities tend to have about the same number of people as non-disabled people do in their inner circle, but far fewer in circles two and three, and a much *higher* number in circle four. This means all of our needs tend to fall disproportionately on our innermost circle or on paid transactions, aka people who go home at the end of the day and aren't going to answer a phone call at two a.m.

This happens because, simply put, it's more difficult for us to make and keep friends.

While we have a lot to offer, our noticeable ADHD symptoms can make it harder for us to socialize in a world that stigmatizes them. We're fidgety and impulsive. We have trouble waiting our turn and staying focused on activities that don't interest us. We keep forgetting everybody's name. And because ADHD is a neurodevelopmental disorder, most of us grew up out of step with our peers. We might have gotten along okay with kids two to three years younger than us or those older than us, but we seemed "immature" and lacked the self-regulation skills to stick to the social rules our peers were already able to follow.

As a result, we were left out. We didn't have as many opportunities to practice socializing compared to our peers. As adults, our social skills are often (understandably) underdeveloped. And because we have busy, often chaotic, lives, we also have trouble executive functioning well enough to keep up with friends.

WE MISS A LOT OF STUFF

We miss people's birthdays.

We miss the fact that we did not in fact hit send.

We miss social cues.

We miss the impact our behaviors are having on those around us.

According to the research, children with ADHD have trouble monitoring their social behavior and adjusting it when needed. They also have a harder time integrating and organizing social cues coherently, and are more likely to interpret social situations based on "the most recently supplied social information."

As an adult with ADHD, I can tell you that this is true from experience. There's a reason we return home from a social event and mentally review everything we could have possibly done wrong. From past experience, we know that there are things we may have done "wrong" socially that *we missed*. And because we also "base our interpretations on the most recently supplied social information"—if the current *message* we're getting is negative (like, they haven't responded to our text messages saying we had a good time) we assume the status of the *relationship* is negative.

EMPATHY CAN GET IN THE WAY

The idea that empathy (or the lack thereof) contributes to our social struggles seriously surprised me, because we feel the feels *hard* (see Chapter 9, "How to Feel," page 216).

However, there's a difference between sensitivity and empathy.

While those with ADHD tend to be sensitive and may even pick up on others' emotions thanks to our higher likelihood to be hypervigilant, we might *misunderstand* other people's perspectives and emotions. These misunderstandings can happen either because we miss crucial details about a situation, or because we're so caught up in our own stories and emotions that we can't see past them.*

Even those who are highly empathic can have a difficult time applying their empathy effectively. Feeling overly sad or distressed when someone else is suffering can make it hard to give them effective support. We might have a hard time regulating our empathy, just like we have a hard time regulating our emotions and our attention.

A Note on Small Talk

Those with ADHD tend to *loathe* small talk because it feels fake and can be boring. (Unless the weather is of particular interest to us, *who cares*? Why are we talking about this?) We'd prefer to get right into big talk—deep, meaningful conversation. We are interest-based creatures and have difficulty focusing on things that feel meaningless.

---

*   There are two types of empathy: cognitive empathy, which relies on the ability to take someone else's perspective, and affective empathy, which relies on the ability to understand and identify emotions. It's possible to be great at one type of empathy while struggling with the other.

However, there is a reason small talk exists and why it involves talking about inconsequential things. In fact, there are many of them:

- Some people use small talk to see if they have chemistry with another person, which helps us decide if a deeper relationship is possible.

- Small talk is a less risky way to connect. Sharing details about ourselves can put us at emotional and physical risk. It's *safer* to stick to small talk until we get a sense of who someone is.

- Small talk allows you to see which conversational topics might be welcome. If someone's small talk is all about adorable kittens, they might not be in the mood for a more intense conversation.

- Small talk is expected in many situations. When we start with big talk, others might feel it's jarring or coming out of left field. (Think of small talk like a social lubricant.)

While small talk may be challenging for our ADHD brains, the benefits are (at least sometimes) worth the effort.

MINDSET IS A PART OF THE PUZZLE

Much of the research that exists on ADHD and social difficulties focuses on our behaviors and our trouble noticing the impact of those behaviors. However, being awkward in a social situation isn't typically what damages our relationships as adults. After all, everyone behaves awkwardly sometimes.

According to Caroline Maguire, author of *Why Will No One Play with Me* and an ADHD coach who is pioneering this field of understanding—how those who are neurodivergent make friends—it's not the ADHD behaviors themselves that flag us as needy, too much, or weird. It's the fifteen anxious text messages we send when we get home apologizing, explaining, and seeking reassurance. And what drives us to send those texts is the *mindset* with which we view and approach social situations.

Our mindsets are part of what leads to the anxious overcorrection, rumination, and thought spirals that many in our community experience when we navigate social settings. We get stuck trying to understand what went wrong, or why something happened, or how we can fix it. We slip into emotional reasoning: I feel this way, so therefore it must be true. We might even expect a relationship to fail, and this can become a self-fulfilling prophecy.

There are factors affecting our mindset that we may not even be aware of:

- **Having unrealistic expectations of others:** We sometimes expect someone to be there every time we need them and that they'll have unlimited capacity to do what we ask them to. We think they can do something just because we need them to or because they've done it before. The social expectations we place on others require a *lot* of hypervigilance, and that's not something they can always maintain. We can forget that they have their own goals, needs, emotions, and *lives* to tend to.

- **Having unrealistic expectations of ourselves:** We sometimes expect *ourselves* to be there every time someone needs us and to have unlimited capacity to do what others ask or need. We think *we* can do something just because someone needs us to, or because we *sometimes can*. The social expectations we place on ourselves require a *lot* of hypervigilance, and that's not something we can always maintain. We forget that we have *our own* goals, needs, emotions, and lives to tend to.

- **Operating with a scarcity mindset:** We often have this "I'll take anyone" or "I'll do anything" approach to relationships. We underestimate our worth to the point that we feel we're lucky to have anyone in our lives. As a result, we spend a lot of time and energy trying to maintain relationships with people who are a bad fit.

- **Thinking we're unlovable:** Because we have fewer people to lean on, we can seem "high maintenance." Those closest to us sometimes get frustrated or need a break from our need for support, which can trigger our rejection sensitivity (see sidebar below) and reinforce the idea that we're too much, not worth it, or even unlovable.

- **Thinking we need to "fit in" to belong:** Fitting in has its place (like when you're moving through airport security), but it does not lead to belonging. As Brené Brown puts it, "When we sacrifice who we are, we not only feel separate from others, but we even feel disconnected from ourselves."

 Rejection Sensitivity and Mindset

Rejection sensitivity is the tendency to find rejection—or even perceived rejection—profoundly painful. Rejection sensitivity isn't unique to ADHD, but it is a *very* common experience for those who have it thanks to difficulties with emotion regulation combined with a lifetime of experiences of actual rejection.

Learning how to cope with emotion dysregulation (see page 222) can help us manage rejection sensitivity. But I'm including a sidebar about it here because our mindsets and behaviors affect how we experience rejection sensitivity (and vice versa). While we can't control our emotions, we can influence them through our thoughts and behaviors.

When it comes to rejection sensitivity, we quite naturally adjust our *behavior* to avoid it: we people-please; we suppress our ADHD and cut off pieces of ourselves trying to fit in; we avoid risky social situations entirely. We've been experiencing rejection since before we had metacognition—the ability to think about our thoughts. By the time we're adults, we've learned that we're often rejected for *our behavior,* so it makes sense that our go-to strategy for avoiding the pain of rejection is adjusting our behavior.

But as I mentioned in the motivation chapter, the lever we instinctively pull is not always the right lever to pull. Those with ADHD often have significantly skewed mindsets when it comes to social situations, including the mindset that we need to *be someone else entirely* to belong (or its other extreme—this is who I am and people just need to deal), and adjusting those *mindsets*—not our individual behaviors (which often stem from them)—is often what is needed most.

For me, the most important mindset that I needed to shift was this:

Making friends is a ~~one-~~*multi*step process that relies on ~~other people liking me~~ *connection* ~~today~~ *over time.*

MAKING FRIENDS IS A MULTISTEP PROCESS THAT RELIES ON CONNECTION OVER TIME

Making friends is a *process,* and like any process that occurs between two or more people, it carries with it an element of uncertainty. Many with ADHD (including me until *checks watch* last month) try to skip past this uncertainty.

When we like someone and are excited about the possibility of a new friendship, that feeling (like all our feelings) can be very intense. Sometimes we respond to that feeling by acting *as if* a secure connection already exists: we share intimate details about our lives, make elaborate future plans, hyperfocus on them to the detriment of other relationships and obligations, or blow up their phone or social media to a cringe-inducing extent.

Sometimes this behavior scares people off. Other times the person responds well but is disappointed later when we can't keep up that level of intensity. In the worst cases, we find ourselves deeply attached to people who take advantage of us or treat us poorly. In the best cases, these relationships settle into a more balanced rhythm, ultimately becoming the kind of friendship we so badly wanted to already have.

When these friendships do work out, it's not because of how intensely they started, but because of how they *continued.* Friendship generally isn't made (or lost) in a moment. It requires a level of intimacy and mutual trust that is earned with time and experience.

The more moments of connection you have with someone, the

harder it is to break your bond with them. If you think back to the circles of support diagram on page 253, the way you reach the circle of friendship is by going through the circle of participation and working your way in over time. You can't get to real friendship unless you spend time in the participation circle, over and over again. Trying to have "close friendship" levels of intimacy with someone before doing this is kind of like writing a bunch of checks we can't always cash.

Mike, who manages our Discord community, points out one reason why:

> Most folks will assume they're one of the few people who know the big details of your life, and thus expect to be kept up to date. When you suddenly drop someone from this intimate role, it can damage the relationship. Either they find out they're not unique or special because you talk intimately with everyone, or they feel rejected because you've suddenly cut them off.

Friendship takes time to build and to maintain. The quality of the time you spend together is important, but so is the amount of time you put into it *over time*.

Friendships are held together with many individual threads of connection, and there is no magic formula for how long it takes to create them. Some people become friends because you spend a lot of time with them. Other people become friends because the time you spend together is always amazing. What matters isn't strictly how much time you spend with them or whether every minute you spend is incredible, but rather, is the time you spend together enough to stitch you together?

Disappointingly (particularly for those of us who are averse to uncertainty), that's not always something we can control, rush, or even predict. Lots of hurdles can get in the way of a budding friendship: time constraints, stress from life events, scheduling logistics. Life is complicated. All we can really control is whether we engage in that circle of participation often enough to give a potential friend a chance to become an actual friend.*

"But all this takes too long, and I just want people to do stuff with!"

Good news, buddy. *You don't need to make friends in order to have people to hang out with.* That was how I thought it worked, too, but no, I had it backward.

It's not friend, then participation. It's participation, then (maybe) friend.

You can't pick your friends. You can only pick who to do stuff with that you find meaningful. And then see what kind of relationship evolves over time.

---

*   If even this sounds daunting, you're not alone. For many of us who have a limited number of activities we can participate in or have difficulties inviting people into our circle of participation, we may need support to build connections. In *From Behind the Piano*, you can learn about how Judith Snow, who was physically disabled, built her unique circle of friends.

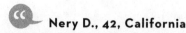 **Nery D., 42, California**

"I am friendly with many people, but I have few friends and I dream of someday having a best friend. I can't manage a good balance between being too aloof and too overinvolved, and I think that may turn others off."

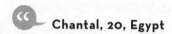 **Chantal, 20, Egypt**

"I realized I have always loved people so much. So much! But I always let people down one way or another. I wanted to call but I forgot. I wanted to answer your texts, but I'm kind of dreading the task. I wanted to wish you a happy birthday, but I got caught up in a million things. And it looks to them as if I don't care about them, which is completely false. I just was never good at showing the love I have."

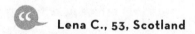 **Chris P., 39, Wyoming**

"I didn't necessarily make friends. I have a few people that just picked me out of a group and said, 'I like you.' I don't know why they picked me, but I'm forever grateful."

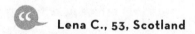 **Lena C., 53, Scotland**

"I don't think I ever really believe that people like me. It's like I constantly have to prove why they should be friends with me and as if I owe them something for being kind enough to be my friend."

THE TOOLBOX

At this point, I hope it's clear that friends are not something we *find*. This is good news! Really—it takes a lot of pressure off ourselves. If we can't just *make* friends, we can start to focus on something more approachable and low stakes: doing activities we find meaningful with people who agree. I have collected some tools to help me on my friendship journey that I hope will be useful on yours.

1. FIGURE OUT WHAT YOU HAVE TO OFFER

We tend to attract people who treat us in a way that aligns with our view of ourselves. It's helpful to spend time considering what's great about you and what you have (and *want*) to offer. This also helps us show up as ourselves, not as a version of ourselves we think others want us to be—which increases our sense of belonging in our relationships with others.

- **Notice the qualities you appreciate in others** that you yourself have. It's often easier to appreciate characteristics that others have than to value them in yourself. This is one of the reasons I love hanging out with others with ADHD. Spending time with people who have interesting things to say and start sharing enthusiastically when they arrive has made me realize others may feel the same about me!

- **Listen to what others say they appreciate about you.** Notice when you're about to auto-reject a compliment and consider writing it down instead. Say thank you. Take it in. You know, *they might be right.* If you're confused about the compliment, ask for specifics.*

- **Figure out what you're looking for.** If I know I'm looking for people I can go hiking with, that means "being a hiking buddy" is something I have to offer, too!

- **Reassess!** What we have to offer (and *want to*) can—and will—change over time. Maybe we have more, fewer, or different things to offer now. Maybe we're a pretty cool YouTuber now with a book out, IDK.

 **Anonymous, 23, Oregon**

> "Make a list of your positive qualities. 'I'm funny. I'm creative. I'm empathetic. I'm a good listener. I'm insightful. I'm kind. I try hard. I am good at giving compliments.' And on and on! Fake your belief you're a friend worth having until you realize that you are. Not everyone will want to be friends with you and *that's okay.* You won't be everybody's cup of tea just like some other people aren't yours. Your people are out there."

---

* While general compliments can be hard to accept ("What do you mean I did a good job? I was late and this went wrong and . . ."), specifics make the compliment harder to argue against. Because it is a fact that the person did enjoy this one specific aspect of what we contributed, it can be easier to accept it.

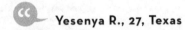

Yesenya R., 27, Texas

"I had such bad social anxiety due to my ADHD. Going through CBT helped a lot, especially learning to point out logical fallacies I'd use to convince myself that an interaction went badly. People will naturally gravitate toward you when you are learning to accept yourself."

Michael K., 43, Ontario, Canada

"There will always be someone who does not see the unique gifts of my mind; that person will not be me."

2. MEET NEW PEOPLE

We're not going to click with everyone, but meeting new people is the best way to find the ones with whom we will. This can keep us from getting stuck trying to be friends with people who aren't a great fit or who treat us badly. It can also help us avoid overrelying on any one person for support, making our relationships more sustainable.

- **Go where people meet people.** There are online dating apps that have a "friend" mode and websites for people with common interests to meet (like Bumble BFF or Meetup.org). There's an immediate advantage to meeting people through channels like these. They're probably there for the same reason: to find potential friends.

- **Go where your strengths will shine.** If your conversation is better than your dance moves, hang out where people can hear you talk. If your dance moves are killer but you get awkward when talking, hang out where you can dance. There are many ways to connect socially—when you can, choose ones that are in line with your strengths.

- **Prep some conversation topics in advance.** Remember cool executive function (page 81)? Planning what to talk about is much easier *before* you're on the spot (or when your foot is already firmly in your mouth). Caroline suggests having three topics ready to go. (The topics are ideally noncontroversial . . . and ones that people actually talk about.) Come up with some "get to know you" questions, too! People love talking about themselves.

- **Look for shared values.** While shared interests are great for short-term connection, shared values help relationships stand the test of time. Examples of shared values include kindness, honesty, humor, and playfulness.

Siona L., 32, Nevada

"How to Make Friends:
    Step 1: Practice D&D with your family for years.
    Step 2: Find nerdy, queer, neurodiverse people on-
        line.
    Step 3: Beg them to play D&D with you.
    Step 4: Stay friends for years."

 Max V., 32, Oregon

"To make friends, I started by just finding a place I felt I belonged that also required other people to be there regularly. For me, that place was theater. When I got there, I found a lot of people who were like me, which was ideal!"

 Lindsey J., 37, Maryland

"I find people who have similar weird niche interests as me, then basically say 'Hi, I have no idea how to make friends as an adult. Want to grab coffee?' Sometimes it actually works."

3. LEVEL UP YOUR SOCIAL SKILLS

When I was learning about social skills for the channel, I realized the reason I thought I was bad at making friends was because, in video game terms, I was playing levels I wasn't ready for. Thanks to my neurodevelopmental delay, I've spent much of my life playing on levels that required skills I hadn't yet developed. This left me frustrated and not wanting to play. And not playing left me further behind. The truth is, no one is born with social skills. We learn and acquire them, even as adults.

- **Observe others.** Caroline calls this being a social spy. Watching what others typically do (and don't do) in social situations can help us calibrate our understanding and expectations. You can also study how those with your brain type interact with one another. Social norms are often different in neurodivergent communities, and it's good to be fluent in your own language, too. Otherwise, how will you connect with others who speak it?

- **Ask for stronger social cues.** Social feedback loops help people get good at socializing. Unfortunately for us, these feedback loops typically depend on subtle social cues. If you know you tend to miss or misread those cues, it's totally fine to ask for them to be more overt. When my friend Alex realized I wasn't getting a chance to jump into the conversation, she said, "Hey, I know I can talk over people when I get excited. If I do that, say 'Pongo!' And I'll know to let you talk."

- **Try a tutorial.** If you're anxious about not knowing how to navigate a social situation, it can help to know what to expect. Ask someone you trust if there are any pitfalls to look out for. Call the place you're going and ask what the vibe is like. You can also look up tutorials about how to navigate specific social situations online. (WikiHow is *amazing.*)

- **"Play" on levels you enjoy.** If you get frustrated or incredibly anxious while socializing, it might mean that you're playing a level you're not ready for. If Level Three: Going to Yoga Together is enough of a challenge, it may not make sense to struggle through Level Ten: Going on a Yoga Trip Together. Spend most of your time on levels you're comfortable with, and you'll probably have a lot more fun. You'll also play more, which helps with leveling up.*

---

*   But also, expose yourself to new levels once in a while. It's good to limit-test. We might not enjoy something the first time because of the stress from not knowing what to expect. We might have more fun the next time now that we do!

A Note on Masking

Leveling up your social skills does not mean "learning how to mask your neurodivergence 24/7." Masking for long periods of time is damaging to our emotional and mental well-being because it requires suppressing behaviors that help us cope with a world not built with our needs in mind. While masking can help us fit in, it does not lend itself to deep meaningful relationships long term. Masking our neurodivergence so much that we can't find each other leaves us lonely and disconnected. What we want to aim for here is interfacing effectively with others—or as Brené Brown puts it, "learn how to be present with people without sacrificing who we are."

 Sebastian L., 29, Guatemala

"Bring your friends into whatever really interests you in the moment. Really into baking right now? Bring cupcakes to the next party. Really into why the sky is so dark? Find some articles so you can talk about it or invite someone to a museum with a space exhibit. You'll be surprised how interesting you become to others."

Sarah N., 52, USA

"I like gravitating toward folks who like to low-key collect and connect people. You probably know the sort. They're not the obvious social superstars, but they make friends easily and delight in mixing them gently. Their need to be social helps with ADHD-related inertia."

Rachael, 28, Washington, DC

"Being a social spy is a skill that makes such a difference in social and professional settings alike. Taking the time to be a social spy and relate to people on their level is vital to being successful in any relationship."

4. MAKE SOCIALIZING ROUTINE

We aren't great at free recall (more on page 198). When you build socialization into your routine, this means you don't have to rely on free recall to remember to do it. It also makes connection a regular part of your life, which, according to a ton of studies, is *critical* to our happiness and well-being. Like sleep, *friends* are not a side quest. They're part of the main storyline. Weave them in.

- **Set aside a regular day or time to check in with people.** This can take the form of a weekly class / club meeting / game or short blocks of times in your schedule set aside for socializing. If you're like me and get overwhelmed, it can help to prioritize by circles: e.g., respond to circle one peeps on breaks or after work, reach out to circle two on set days, get in touch with circle three people only on weekends. When I need to cocoon, I take it down a circle.*

- **Have go-to people for certain activities.** When you want to go bowling, maybe you text a certain friend. Errand buddies are a great way to build friendship into everyday life and make tedious tasks less mundane. Going to a friend's house to wrap Christmas presents together is way more fun than doing it alone!

- **Reach out when you remember to.** I used to be afraid to start a conversation when I thought of someone because I didn't want to get distracted. Now, I know that it's fine to send a message that says, "Hey! Still working, but saw this and thought of you. Catch up later?" and leave it at that.

---

*   When I need to cocoon, my first instinct is to stop responding to *everybody*. But then, as soon as I come out, I'm overwhelmed because now I have to respond to everybody. I'm learning to recognize when I'm getting socially overwhelmed and take it down a circle, so I still get more alone time without neglecting all of my relationships at once.

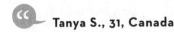 **Tanya S., 31, Canada**

"I have daily calls with my besties where we play a video game or do a video chat during our lunch hours. The regular schedule means we hop in and out as needed."

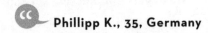 **Phillipp K., 35, Germany**

"Be proactive. Be the one who organizes meetings and don't only wait for invitations. Today is the best day to plan."

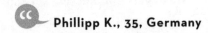 **Gwenyth T., 30, Michigan**

"I have weird little things I do to make sure I'm keeping in touch with my friends. I use the Sweepy app for house-work, but I've added a 'social' section. It helps me see how long it's been since I've texted someone and makes it a part of my to-do list. It helps me remember that the social part of my life is just as vital to my life as cleaning a toilet, and it gives me a little boost from checking something important off my list."

5. COMMUNICATE YOUR BOUNDARIES

People can't read one another's minds. It isn't obvious to others why we're interrupting, if we're overwhelmed or overstimulated, or if we've hit our limit on sitting still for the evening. It also isn't obvious to them that we're really hoping they'll invite us to go to the event they just told us about. This means we might have to, like, *tell* them. Not only does communicating this stuff make it more likely that we'll get our needs met, it makes it safe for them to do the same.

- **Differentiate between "want to" and "willing to."** We often say "I'd love to!" when what we really mean is "I'm willing to do this thing you clearly want because I value your friendship." Both are good. Both are important. Doing some "want tos" and some "willing tos" means the friendship is *reciprocal.*

- **Talk about expectations.** This can be an elaborate and emotional conversation. It can also be as simple as "Hey, dude. Gym tonight?" You do you.

- **Ask for what you want, but respect their limits.** As Betty Martin and Robyn Dalzen share in *The Art of Giving and Receiving:* when receiving, it's your job to ask for what you want, communicate expectations, and respect the limits of the giver.

- **When you're the one giving, respect your limits.** In the excitement of "*I have something to offer! That somebody wants!*" we can forget to ask ourselves if this is okay for us.

- **Set your own policies.** Creating policies that aren't about a specific person or situation makes it easier for you to remember them and others to hear them. Here are some examples of my own: "I don't loan money to friends," "I'm currently looking for in-person friendships," and "I'm going to take a lunch break every day from one to two p.m."

Claudia S., 32, Mexico

"I used to be shy and self-conscious about my character 'flaws' when meeting new people. Now I always try to be my loud, chaotic, silly self when I meet someone new because I want them to know who I am from the beginning."

Merlin S., 32, Maryland

"It helps to have some plain discussions about expectations at the start. Knowing if someone sucks at texting or prefers phone calls helps me to adjust accordingly."

Sebastian L., 29, Guatemala

"Be honest about your limits and challenges in a way that is respectful to yourself. 'Hey, Becky! Could you text me later this week to remind me about our hangout?' 'Could we share a ride? I want to make sure I get there on time.' 'Could we stay one night instead of two?' 'Come with me to find X's birthday gift or I might forget to get them one.'"

WHAT'S THE POINT?

One day in frustration I asked my therapist, "What's the point of friends?"

Friends felt like something I was supposed to have just because I was supposed to have them. "Like, I have to stop what I'm doing to message somebody back, or go hang out with them, and usually it's not as fun or productive as what I could have been doing instead. So . . . what's the point of having them?"

My therapist's response: "Good question. What *is* the point of friends? Get curious about that. The next time you spend time with someone, ask yourself, what are you getting out of it?"

I had never in my life asked myself this question. I mean, wasn't the point of friendship to have friends? So I wasn't alone? So I could check off some arbitrary box that meant I was doing life right?

Until this point, I'd learned to find all of the benefits that friends could provide through other avenues. Entertainment? Video games. Connection or attention? My partner. Connection or attention when my partner isn't around? I had a dog.

Going without friends is easier now than ever. As Caroline pointed out to me, apps now provide a lot of everyday support that we used to turn to other people for. Need a ride to the airport? Feel sick and need soup? Need someone to pick up groceries for you? There are apps—in some cases, *many* apps—for all this.*

---

*   Apps improve accessibility, which is important (especially for those of us with disabilities), but when they completely replace people in your life, it can get lonely.

They say friends help you build your life. Since I didn't have many of them, I'd learned to build it myself. In fact, the life I'd built didn't even have room for them. If I was going to weave friendship into my main storyline, I needed to know why it was worth the effort, the potential rejection, and the uncertainty.

And it couldn't just be "so you won't be lonely." Because, honestly, my attempts to make friends often made me feel far lonelier than I would if I'd stayed home alone.

So I started getting curious. What was the point of friends? Maybe I didn't turn to friends to meet specific needs, but I could pay attention to what I was getting out of it when I did spend time with them.

At first, the answer was disappointing: not a whole lot. I realized how often I went along with activities that weren't really for me. I wasn't getting much out of a hangout, especially compared to how much it was costing me. Because the friendship was about making them happy and serving their needs; it wasn't making me happy or serving any of mine.

My original goal was just to have friends, so I tried to keep them happy.

But now I had a new goal—to have friendships that benefited me, too. This changed the game.

I realized I could invite people to do activities I wanted to do. I changed my BFF profile on Bumble from one that said "Pick me! Look at what I have to offer!" to

> If I was going to weave friendship into my main storyline, I needed to know why it was worth the effort, the potential rejection, and the uncertainty.

one that said, "Here's what I'm looking for and here's what I need in a friend." And I found people who fit with me. Who I could be myself around. Several had ADHD. When I came home in tears one night because I thought I had gotten too excited about the activity we were doing and that's why they looked annoyed at the end of the night, this time I was wrong. They were just *tired*. Things were fine. I wasn't too much. Not for them.

> What I wanted to get out of in-person friends, I realized, was the same thing I had found in my online community: a sense of belonging.

What I wanted to get out of in-person friends, I realized, was the same thing I had found in my online community: a sense of belonging.

And I'm slowly finding that. As I write this chapter, I'm half thinking about what I want to do at the D&D game I'm going to tonight. Even though I was behind schedule on finishing the edits for this book, I took a day off to explore my city with a long-distance friend who was in town.

I know now that I can't completely avoid the pain—or the work—inherent to the process of making friends. But I can pursue friendships that are worth it to me.

Instead of trying to fit, I can select for fit. I can look for places I might belong. I can look for potential friends who have qualities I value, who value what I want to give. Who value me not for the persona I effortfully present to others, but for the person I actually am.

Chapter 11

How to Make ADHD Harder

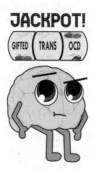

There's no limit to how complicated things can get, on account of one thing always leading to another.

—E. B. WHITE

ADHD AND . . . ?

For most of the book, I've talked about the experiences those of us with ADHD tend to have in common: difficulties with attention, executive function, time management, sleep, and more. I can't tell you how many times I've posted about my specific ADHD struggles, only to be quote tweeted a dozen times by Brains across the globe who are all saying: "This! This right here! This explains my whole personality!"*

---

* Apparently, a lot of us have at least five different drinks on our desks at any given time. Who knew?

In this chapter, though, I want to talk about the ways our experiences differ.

There are many biological, psychological, and socioenvironmental factors that impact the lived experience of any human on Earth; there will always be factors that differentiate our lived experience. This is part of why a tool that works for one person with ADHD may not for another with the exact same support needs. To use an innocuous example, let's consider a big whiteboard. Maybe it works great for one person; for the other, maybe the smell of the markers is distracting. Maybe the walls in their workplace don't have space for one.

This difference in lived experience would exist in our community even if we all had the same access to resources, faced the same level of discrimination, had the same impairments, and experienced the same demand on our executive function; we would have differences even if our ADHD symptoms and impairments remained constant over time. But we do not and they do not.

While ADHD impacts brain development and cognition in much the same ways across gender, race, class, and nationality, those aspects of our social identity—also called intersectionalities because they, you know . . . intersect—significantly affect the way we live our lives. They can determine the level of disadvantage and discrimination we may face.* They can influence how our ADHD-related behaviors are perceived by those around us, how we get diagnosed, *if* we get diagnosed, and what kind of treatment we receive.

---

* The concept of intersectionality was developed by Kimberlé Crenshaw, an American lawyer, scholar, and activist, who wanted to make it clear that different forms of oppression aren't separate; they're linked.

I was just beginning to understand this when I learned that ADHD is also a biopsychosocial disorder. While ADHD is highly genetic, there are many, many genes involved, and many factors can influence how our ADHD presents, the severity of our symptoms, and the extent to which our cognitive impairments actually *impair* us. Our social identities and the level of discrimination we face as a result quite naturally play a role in this, too, though they're not the only factors. I was about to dive deeper into understanding and untangling the interplay when my mom died suddenly, and I learned it the hard way.

I heard the news in a phone call from a coroner's office. This happened on the same day I found out my divorce was final. In 2020.

I was not okay.

The grief I experienced was so big, so all-encompassing, that it overwhelmed my mental resources and coping strategies. I often couldn't function well enough to use my tools, and many of them no longer worked. My grieving brain functioned completely differently when it functioned at all.

At the insistence of a friend, and with her support, I enrolled in a peer support program to begin processing my grief. I learned I had experienced a "traumatic loss," and that, like so many adult children from complicated backgrounds, the loss of my last living parent had triggered the reemergence of significant childhood trauma that needed to be processed. I started trauma therapy as well.

As I made progress toward healing, I began noticing that my ADHD was beginning to impact me differently. Turns out, symptoms I had for years attributed solely to my ADHD were influenced by other factors. I began thinking of my life not just in terms of my ADHD, but in terms of my "ADHD *and*."

Take ADHD and trauma. Emotion dysregulation is a common experience for ADHD brains, but even before my mom died, the trauma I'd experienced as a child and the trauma patterns I'd repeated throughout my life had exacerbated the way I personally experienced it.

My ADHD impulsivity? In therapy, I learned that a lot of my impulsive actions resulted from my intolerance for uncertainty. This, it turns out, is common among those who, like me, also have *anxiety disorders*. The impulsive choices I made as a young adult with ADHD *and* anxiety may have cost me opportunities and friendships, but making those choices eased the anxiety of not knowing how those things would have turned out.*

I realized years of damage to my self-esteem hadn't been about the ADHD alone, but from constantly running up against both neurotypical and *gendered* expectations that my ADHD made it difficult to meet. I felt ashamed and discouraged when my body, home, and relationships didn't look like they were "supposed" to, never realizing that my idea of what things were "supposed" to look like had a lot to do with being ADHD *and* a white, middle-class, cisgender woman in the United States.

Over time, I learned to see the nuance involved in my challenges. ADHD wasn't the *only* factor. In a way, this was good news. I would

---

* Would the opportunity have led to failure? Would that friend ultimately hurt me? Would it be easier to impulsively blow it all up rather than living with that uncertainty? Yes, yes it would.

always have ADHD; I would always experience emotion dysregulation. Just as there are other factors I can't control that sometimes impair me, like, being short. But . . . I didn't have to rely on just managing my impairments with literal and figurative step stools.

I could start to heal my trauma in therapy.

I could recognize my anxiety, practice sitting mindfully with my uncertainty, and work on setting healthy boundaries.

I could strengthen my self-esteem by expanding my vision of womanhood beyond the "shoulds" and "supposed tos" I grew up with.

There were aspects of my experience I could shift, and aspects I couldn't, but they all played a role in my experience of ADHD.

As I began to emerge from the fog with this new perspective, I was learning how it applied to the people in my community, too. We have ADHD to connect us, but there are so many other factors that make our experiences unique and complicated. Members of my community are ADHD and so many other things: Autistic, Australian, gifted, queer, unhoused, immigrants, physically disabled, Southeast Asian, dealing with chronic pain; the list could go on for pages.

As I learned about the impact these coexisting conditions, social identities, and other biopsychosocial factors have on their individual experiences with ADHD, I also began to understand how bias against ADHD and other disabilities intersects with bias against other social identities to compound the discrimination we face (more on page 300). As I began intentionally listening for the complexities of my community's experience, I felt that I was seeing a lot of my community, really seeing them, for the first time.

I'll never forget a comment a Black member of the How to ADHD community left on an episode called "What It's Like to Be ADHD and Black," which was the project I did right before my mom died. It said, "We've been here. You didn't see us?"

It broke my heart, because the answer was no. I hadn't considered the individual differences in lived experience, because I'd been so focused on ADHD to the exclusion of everything else. Doctors, specialists, and ADHD experts (including me) tend to zero in on their area of specialty and often miss the bigger picture. We—I—can do better. We owe it to those who look to us for resources to see them as whole, complex, inimitable human persons.

WHAT I LEARNED

With ADHD, coexisting conditions are more often the rule than the exception. There are also biological and socioeconomic factors that impact our lived experience. While I am just beginning to understand the complexities of this interplay, I felt it was important to try to tackle it, because all of the factors in this chapter can impact not only our lived experience and access to care as people with ADHD, but how our ADHD even shows up.

It's impossible to give each factor the space it deserves, or to cover it comprehensively here. Each one could be its own book, but I did my best to include the most common or most impactful factors and include experiences from the community in their own words.

PSYCHOLOGICAL FACTORS

An estimated 60 to 80 percent of adults with ADHD have *at least* one condition listed below. These conditions are complex alone, but I've listed at least one common way they can interplay with ADHD. If you have one of the conditions below, or if you treat them, hopefully you will be inspired to dig deeper.

Neurodevelopmental Coexisting Conditions Common with ADHD

Neurodevelopmental conditions involve differences in the development and function of the nervous system. These conditions affect how our brains work on a fundamental, structural level. Think of these as our brain's "operating system"* or even firmware. Our functional impairments can be lessened, but the core differences in how our brains work don't go away. The symptoms of those differences can only be managed or masked.

ADHD is a neurodevelopmental condition (see Chapter 2, "How to ~~ADD~~ ADHD," page 21), but having one neurodevelopmental condition doesn't preclude you from having another, including:

---

*   A tech-savvy community member has pointed out that this metaphor is flawed, since operating systems are installed rather than built into the computer, and that a better metaphor would be "firmware," since firmware is what is in there before any other software can be installed. Use the metaphor that resonates most with you.

Autism

In brains with autism and ADHD (or AuDHD, if you like a portmanteau), restricted, repetitive interests + ADHD-related difficulty focusing on things that don't interest you = great difficulty focusing outside a narrow range of interests.* Those with ADHD miss and misunderstand social cues for a variety of reasons, but when they are also Autistic, they may also have significant difficulty recognizing (or "reading") them in the first place, which can make social connection *very* confusing.

Tic Disorders

Hard-to-control verbal or motor impulses can worsen social difficulties due to ADHD and increase the pressure to mask one's neurodivergence. Tic disorders occur in less than 10 percent of the ADHD population; however, 60 to 80 percent of those with Tourette Syndrome also have ADHD.

Learning Disabilities

The prevalence rate for learning disabilities among ADHD brains is 43 to 55 percent, compared with 5 to 15 percent in the general population. Common learning disabilities include:

---

* An AuDHD friend joked to me that when AuDHD people first meet, they might as well just see if they have any special interests in common right away. If not, cool, nice to meet you, moving on.

- **Dyslexia:** a learning disability that affects reading and related skills. ADHD brains often have trouble regulating their attention while reading; when the reading process itself is a struggle, academic difficulties are compounded.

- **Dyscalculia:** a learning disability that affects math-related skills. This disability affects life well beyond school. Money management is already a challenge for those with ADHD; dyscalculia can make it overwhelming.

- **Dysgraphia:** a learning and fine-motor disability that affects handwriting. Students with dysgraphia have difficulty writing quickly and legibly, which, combined with ADHD difficulties related to organization and note-taking, can make traditional study practices all but impossible without accommodations.

Giftedness

Intellectually gifted students with ADHD may struggle to access support for either or both of these neurodifferences. Attention and executive function challenges related to ADHD may prevent the "twice exceptional" student from having their intelligence recognized and challenged. Likewise, rapidly acquired skills in a 2E student may impress teachers who then miss the opportunities to identify and support challenges in other areas.

The conditions described above are the result of brains that develop in a way that *diverges* from (neuro)typical development. This is why the term "neurodivergent" has come to be a preferred way to describe brains like ours.* These differences in development mean that the symptoms of our conditions are written into the very structure of our brains.

Non-neurodevelopmental Coexisting Conditions Common with ADHD

Conversely, non-neurodevelopmental conditions are not a result of differences in brain development. Think of them as "software"—or malware. They can change an individual's perceptions and thought processes, which can interact with our ADHD in profound and challenging ways.

Unlike the symptoms of neurodevelopmental conditions, the symptoms of these conditions can change with treatment, situation, or time. In some brains, conditions like the ones below may develop as secondary to the ADHD. In others, they would occur regardless of whether the person has ADHD.

---

* Although not everyone likes using this term, since it centers neurotypicality as the norm, it helps people in our community find one another. Personally, I like the incidental nod to the fact that we are often good at divergent thinking. It's one of our strengths.

Depression

One of the most common symptoms of depression is anhedonia, which is defined as "markedly diminished interest or pleasure." When ADHD motivation relies on interest, and on us being able to reward ourselves for doing things that *aren't* interesting, anhedonia can be significantly disabling.

Depression can worsen the self-esteem issues that many ADHDers have. Depression tells us we are useless, a failure, a burden. Intrusive, judgmental thoughts like these make it easier to believe the negative labels and assessments we too often receive from the outside world.

Anxiety Disorders

Anxious rumination—basically, thoughts cycling like a broken record of badness—is a common result of anxiety and ADHD. Anxious thoughts keep us stuck in our heads, making it paradoxically *more* likely that we'll miss important information, which can lead to more errors, which leads to more anxiety.

Sometimes anxiety can lead to hypervigilance. Because anxiety is convinced that it's helping us survive, anxious watchfulness is reinforced when it catches something we might otherwise have missed due to our ADHD.

Also, ADHD brains are motivated by urgency, and anxiety is *great* at creating a sense of urgency. This can cause issues in ADHD brains who are treated for anxiety but not ADHD: they often find themselves struggling to be productive without the anxiety to propel them.

Oppositional Defiant Disorder (ODD)

In a clinic sample of adults with ADHD, 47 percent had been diagnosed with ODD, significantly higher than in the general population where 4 percent received the diagnosis.

Many experts challenge the validity of ODD as a distinct disorder, particularly in people who also have ADHD. Some see it as a collection of *symptoms* resulting from years of being compelled to do things in ways that don't work for their brain.

According to Dr. Sharon Saline, it's important to recognize that those who are oppositional aren't oppositional with everyone or every task. Oppositional behavior is a relationship issue, and it is relationship dependent. Sometimes the relationship issue is with the person; sometimes the issue is related to our relationship with the task.

Trauma-Related Disorders

Ten percent of adults with ADHD have post-traumatic stress disorder (PTSD). The incidence of PTSD in the general population is only one percent. Some research implies that ADHD may put male veterans at a higher risk of developing PTSD than those without ADHD.

With both ADHD and trauma, people have intense reactions to specific triggers that can cause emotional flooding, which tanks our executive function. The presence of trauma triggers worsens emotional dysregulation, and ADHD impulsivity can make us more likely to react to those triggers when they occur.

Substance Use Disorders

Self-medicating is common with ADHD, particularly untreated ADHD. Current alcohol and drug dependence is much greater in adults with ADHD than in neurotypical adults (25 percent versus 13 percent according to one study).

One common concern with prescribing stimulant medication is the potential for misuse and abuse. Those with a history of substance use may not be given the option of stimulant medication at all. The unfortunate irony is treatment with stimulant medication can actually decrease the risk for substance abuse in those with ADHD.*

---

*   For the record—as prescribed, stimulant medication is not addictive. As my community often jokes, if our meds are so addictive, why do we keep forgetting to take them? When stimulant medication is abused, however, and taken at much higher doses, as it often is by those who don't need it and/or are using it recreationally, it can be.

Let's Talk about Eating Issues

According to Dr. Carolyn Lentzsch-Parcells, a board-certified pediatrician who works with adolescents with ADHD and eating disorders, there are some food issues that tend to be more common in ADHD:

Bulimia and binge-eating disorders: Bingeing and purging behaviors increase dopamine release in the brain. For some people, this can help them cope maladaptively with their ADHD. In addition to bingeing and purging behaviors, those who restrict and/or exercise excessively may also be using the resulting dopamine boosts to cope with underlying, untreated ADHD.

Avoidant restrictive food intake disorder, or ARFID: With this disorder, a person severely restricts the amount of nutrition they're taking in due to fear of either the food itself or of what will happen as a result of eating the food. ADHD-related sensory issues and negative experiences around food can lead to the kind of anxious restricting typical of ARFID.

Disordered eating: While a minority of our community develop eating disorders, a lot of us will experience disordered eating—eating or thinking about food in a way that negatively impacts our lives but does not meet the criteria for an eating disorder. Disordered eating can be influenced by body image issues, but it can also be due to sensory issues, interoception issues, and/or executive function deficits, which make it difficult for us to meal plan, shop, and prep.

Why do we want to eat so much when we go off our meds?

Dr. Lentzsch-Parcells also answered this question that many people in our community ask. Stimulant medication may suppress our appetite during the day, so we might not eat enough to keep our functions functioning. When the meds wear off, our brain might say to us, "Dude, we need more calories! Go get some!"

Conversely, if we are eating sufficiently but then go off our meds and nom our way through the fridge like Ms. Pac-Man, there could be a couple of reasons why, including:

- Your ADHD impulsivity is no longer being treated, so when you see food you eat food.

- Your brain might not be getting adequate levels of dopamine after your meds have worn off, so it is not happy that it's back on the struggle bus. "I NEED DOPAMINE, DUDE. I KNOW WHAT GIVES ME DOPAMINE. WHERE ARE THE COOKIES?"

BIOLOGICAL FACTORS

Sometimes with all our talk about brains, it's easy to forget that, yo, *we also have bodies*. Even our brains themselves are just one part of a whole nervous system that affects every part of us. Let's talk about how our brains and bodies cooperate with each other (or don't).

- **Hormones:** ADHD is often detected during or right after puberty due to the rapid hormonal changes involved. Higher levels of testosterone, which increases sevenfold during male puberty, have been linked to more impulsive decisions and greater hyperactivity. Estrogen, on the other hand, is associated with dopamine production. When estrogen levels rise, dopamine levels rise, too. Estrogen levels fluctuate throughout the menstrual cycle, which can worsen ADHD symptoms during the premenstrual phase (the days or week leading up to our periods). And they drop significantly post-pregnancy and during menopause.

- **Biological sex:** Cisgender boys tend to display more of the hyperactive traits of ADHD, while cisgender girls tend to have more of the inattentive ones. According to research, girls are less likely to be referred for diagnosis, less likely to be diagnosed with ADHD if they are referred, and less likely to be treated for ADHD if they are diagnosed. However, ADHD can also be missed in boys and men who have a more internalized presentation, too.

- **Age:** ADHD presentation changes with age. As we get
  older, our likelihood to present inattentively goes up. Similarly, impulsivity and hyperactivity symptoms evolve over
  time, especially as demands change. While an impulsive
  child might run into the street, an impulsive adult might
  quit a job or say yes to an extra project (or five). Executive
  function develops more with age, and we learn coping
  skills (both adaptive and maladaptive) as we go.

- **Pregnancy:** Existing research on the impact of stimulant
  medications taken during pregnancy suggests the risk of
  complications is minimal to none. However, the limited
  nature of this research means that some doctors are not
  comfortable allowing their patients to continue those
  medications once they become pregnant. Meanwhile, as
  my own psychiatrist explained to me, ADHD significantly
  impacts our ability to handle stress, which we know negatively affects a growing fetus. And recent research has
  highlighted the negative impact of discontinuing meds
  due to pregnancy on parents-to-be.

- **Migraines:** Migraine disorders are common in the ADHD
  community. In one study, men with ADHD were twice as
  likely to experience migraines compared to non-ADHD
  men. Migraines don't always involve pain, as I discovered
  when I began experiencing "migraines with aura." I could

have an amazing brain day but be unable to write because I couldn't see the screen.

- **Chronic pain:** Those with chronic pain deal with having good, moderate, or bad pain days, which get more complicated when combined with good, moderate, or bad *brain* days. Pain at any level is distracting, and ADHD brains aren't great at filtering out sensory distractions. Chronic pain can also make us avoid activities that support our mental and physical health. Doing things we love increases dopamine, which boosts our mood and decreases our experience of pain. Avoidance of activities that boost our dopamine due to bad pain days can lead to more bad brain days because we aren't getting the dopamine needed for us to focus.

It's important to note that any chronic condition can be more serious and difficult to treat in the presence of ADHD, because it may require extensive follow-up or complicated medication management. "Treatment compliance" is difficult when we have trouble complying with . . . life. Rather than denying treatment to those who struggle with compliance, providers should collaborate with patients to find treatment plans that work with their patients' brains as well as their bodies.

Similarly, ADHD brains struggle with regular preventative healthcare. For many of us, this involves navigating a minefield of executive function traps: complicated healthcare systems, scheduling, and insurance issues. That doesn't even cover the everyday challenges of showing up to appointments on time and filling out the correct paperwork—*correctly.* Plus, since the nature of preventative health-care is that it's *not* urgent, it's much harder for us to follow through on annual exams, screenings, dental cleanings, and so on.

Stigma, Biases, and Discrimination

There is significant stigma around ADHD; misconceptions and stereotypes about those who have it are rampant. The resulting biases lead to prejudice and discrimination— more specifically, *ableism*. Abelism is discrimination and social prejudice against people with disabilities, including ADHD, based on the belief that (neuro)typical abilities or those with (neuro)typical abilities are inherently better or more valuable.

You can find examples of ableism on display in many environments—even a kindergarten classroom. Posters often outline the following (or similar) "rules for good lis-tening": "eyes are watching, ears are listening, lips are closed, hands are still, feet are quiet." We're not only ex-pected to follow these rules, some of which can hurt our ability to focus, but we're often punished when we can't. (See Chapter 3, "How to (Hyper)focus," page 47.)

Those with ADHD receive regular messages through-out our lives that it is socially unacceptable and even unsafe to exhibit ADHD or other neurodivergent traits. Or to engage in many of the coping mechanisms we use to navigate social situations and meet expectations.

We experience overt and covert discrimination on a routine basis. The bias that leads to discrimination against those with ADHD often intersects with the bias against other marginalized identities, amplifying the discrimination. For instance, bias against the LGBTQIA+ population can result in homophobia and transphobia, which can compound the ableism those with ADHD experience. In the United States, Black children who are disruptive in class are more likely to be punished than similarly disruptive white children due to "the role of racial bias in painting school adults' views of African American youth as less innocent, older, and more aggressive than their white peers."

In pretty much any society, people face discrimination for many possible reasons: gender, religion, national origin, ethnicity, sexual orientation, medical or disability status, and more. Each one of these intersectionalities can affect any and all of the factors we'll talk about in the socioenvironmental section below. All of this is rooted in stigma—the belief that some identities or ways of being aren't acceptable and don't belong.

SOCIOENVIRONMENTAL FACTORS

We have our brains, which are integrated into our bodies. These bodies are also integrated into complex cultural, economic, and environmental systems that span the whole globe and possibly space. The way we interact with these systems (and the way these systems interact with us) can deeply affect our lived experience as ADHDers.

- **Culture:** ADHD exists in the same presentations across cultures, but not every culture acknowledges, views, and supports it in the same way. Some cultures are more accepting and supportive of mental health challenges than others, and there are cultural differences in treatment approaches as well.*

  In addition, values differ among cultures, and some may align more with our brains' tendencies than others. For example, some cultures are more relaxed about time, which makes it easier for ADHD brains with time nearsightedness to function.

- **Socialization / societal expectations:** Those with ADHD often find themselves out of step with societal expectations.

---

* While studies have found significant differences in reported worldwide prevalence of ADHD, a systematic review of those studies found that these differences could be attributed to cultural differences in the diagnostic criteria used as well as in how impairment is evaluated. In other words, cultural context seems to be what is driving these differences, not variability in the existence of ADHD.

ADHDers are more often gender-nonconforming. There are many reasons for this, one of them being that we commonly have difficulties meeting (often gender-based) societal expectations. Societal expectations vary depending on the culture you come from and exist within, and we often contend with multiple subcultures that each demand different things from us. However, meeting any expectations— from work, friends, family, society, and our political or ideological communities—requires executive function, and trying to meet all of these expectations often overloads our capacity to cope with competing demands.

- **Religion:** Many people, including those with ADHD, turn to religion to experience a sense of hope, comfort, belonging, and tangible social support. Unfortunately, ADHD-related cognitive impairments can be perceived as a moral issue in some traditions, and those struggling may be expected to turn toward religious tenets or their higher power(s) for support, providence, or even to "pray it away." While religion offers many forms of support, it can't always provide the kind of support we need. In some cases, those with ADHD can feel like a "bad Catholic/Christian/Muslim/etc." because their impairments make it difficult to do things "right"—which alienates them from their religion.

- **Ethnicity and race:** We know that diagnosis and treatment rates for ADHD vary widely by race, as a result of many factors. For example, one recent study in the US found that Black adults were 77 percent less likely to receive an ADHD diagnosis than white adults, but Black youths were 24 percent more likely to receive a diagnosis compared to white youths. Another study found that Black and Latinx children have lower odds of being diagnosed with ADHD and of taking ADHD medication compared to white children when controlling for socioeconomic status. Compared to white children, Asian children had the highest odds of receiving no treatment. These numbers highlight a clear racial disparity in how ADHD is diagnosed and treated—which also impacts outcome.

- **Socioeconomic status:** ADHD is much less impairing when you can afford to replace the stuff you've lost or broken, take a day off without impacting your ability to pay the bills, order takeout when you can't figure out what to cook, and hire help for day-to-day tasks. Most people with ADHD don't have room in their budgets for these accommodations.

- **Access to care:** Accessing appropriate care and treatment is not a universal given for ADHD brains around the world. The obstacles are many: as I write this, the United States is dealing with a stimulant medication shortage. The NHS in the UK has a years-long waiting list for evaluation.

In other countries, such as Russia, stimulant medications are straight-up illegal. While there are wonderful therapists who specialize in adult ADHD, there are not nearly enough, and when you add other conditions and identities (especially marginalized identities) into the mix, it becomes exponentially harder to find a good provider fit.

- **Changing demands:** Certain life events—moving, marriage, starting a family, changing careers, taking care of aging parents—come with significantly increased demands on executive function. Someone who starts college, for example, may experience what researchers call a "double deficit." They may struggle simultaneously with increased demands on their executive function from tasks (such as registering for classes, navigating a new campus, accessing accommodations, feeding themselves), as well as the new social context and additional social pressures that come with making new friends, living with roommates, dating, and attending parties.

Many people don't seek a diagnosis and treatment for their ADHD until the demands on their executive function overwhelm their ability to cope. Unfortunately, this means we're often already drowning by the time we seek help. We are now faced with understanding and managing our ADHD for the first time despite being overwhelmed already. Too often, those in a position to offer support and treatment fail to realize that their newly diagnosed patients aren't always in a place to implement many new strategies due to these excessive demands.

There's Interplay Among All These Factors, Too

Some factors can improve access to treatment and support. Some factors can be simultaneously positive and detrimental. Others are undeniably negative. Regardless, it's important to understand that there is an interplay not just between these factors and our ADHD, but between all of these factors as well.

For example, some people may have a higher genetic predisposition to anxiety, but the genes don't get "switched on" and trigger the development of an anxiety disorder until the effects of certain socioenvironmental factors combine with the effects of living with ADHD.* Cultural differences, medical discrimination, and lack of access to care may lead to that anxiety being untreated, and untreated anxiety can lead to depression, all of which can make the ADHD more difficult to manage.

The pressure on students to excel academically and

---

* Our DNA is like a library full of books—and only the genes that get "read" are expressed. Epigenetics, the study of how genes switch on and off based on environmental factors—is super cool. Seriously, google it.

the pressure on parents to support their children's performance in certain cultures can be beneficial for students with ADHD. For example, the parents of a student struggling in school may engage a tutor that works with their learning style, which can lead to a positive outcome. However, that same cultural emphasis on academic achievement can cause parents to feel stress and shame about their child's difficulties. It may incentivize the parents to stay up until two a.m. every night to help their children with homework. It may also discourage them from seeking mental health or learning support for their child because they think they just aren't "doing enough."

In my case, my mom's death pushed me to face and process my childhood trauma, which improved my mental health overall. But this was possible only because I had a support system that helped me find a trauma therapist, as well as a flexible schedule and supportive team that allowed me to schedule three p.m. sessions. Differences in outcome can't be reduced to effort, virtue, or even the specific diagnoses that someone has. There is interplay between many other factors, and they all impact our lived experience of ADHD. Attempting to pick apart the interplay of various factors can be overwhelming, but acknowledging them is critical to effectively supporting someone with ADHD—especially if that person is yourself.

IT'S NOT ADHD ALONE. IT'S ADHD *AND* . . .

I asked my community to share how the interplay between ADHD and other factors, including their intersectionalities, affects their everyday life. I read story after story, days on end, and was left with a greater understanding of how webbed, wonderful, and often woeful our individual experiences are; I want to share a bit of that with you. *Heads-up: some of these stories include frank discussions of topics like medical conditions, racism, transphobia, homophobia, and disordered eating.*

 Tiger T., 47, Maryland

"Autism and ADHD often ends up in an interesting dichotomy in my head. Routines are good, but then boring. We need to be stimulated, but *not too* stimulated. Burnout comes from *both* sides of the equation. And many systems that are really ADHD defense mechanisms were created by the autistic side of me."

 Lee D., 39, Massachusetts

"Being gay and having ADHD is a double coming out process for me. I worry I'll be judged for these factors that are beyond my control, and I am always at least a little bit afraid of the consequences of telling someone who isn't understanding."

Seren S., 35, Canada

"If you have ADHD, you are much more likely than the non-ADHD population to also have hypermobility or EDS [Ehlers-Danlos Syndrome] and dysautonomia. If you do, some behaviors or struggles that might have been attributed to your ADHD may be adaptive strategies for your body. For example: always moving to mitigate joint pain, fidgeting, or sitting strangely to manage orthostatic intolerance. I've also found that my executive functioning is significantly worsened by pain from my joint issues."

 Traci L., 38, California

"ADHD and fatphobia can both lead you to overcompensate to prove you are not 'lazy.' Rejection sensitivity is also worse in a world that is not built to accommodate your body and constantly tells you that these feelings of exclusion are your fault or something you can control by being more 'disciplined.'"

 N.C.M., 37, United Kingdom

"When you're born into a poor family with uneducated parents, finding out what's wrong with you is much harder. There was no one to keep me accountable at home, and teachers just assumed I didn't want to do any schoolwork because I was poor. This never gets talked about—you only hear middle-class perspectives."

Mark J., 63, California

"I lived with undiagnosed ADHD until my 40s. I'm also a third-culture kid, who grew up outside the culture of my passport. I was always wrong. It got to the point in Scottish Catholic school where I would take the blame because the leather strap didn't hurt my hands anymore."

Ying D., 26, Virginia

"Just because I might look organized from the outside, it doesn't mean that's the case in my brain. Being overly on top of paperwork is necessary masking for my Asian first-generation immigrant ADHD brain."

Rex M., 34, North Carolina

"I'm trans and ADHD. I'm not comfortable leaving the house without a binder, but I'm also not comfortable wearing a binder because of sensory issues with clothing. This means I'm just not comfortable leaving the house."

Cecilia C., 37, Mexico

"Having ADHD and hypothyroidism makes you extra forgetful and extra depressive (even when in treatment). Hypothyroidism also drains your energy in the already difficult circumstances of not getting enough dopamine to start a task."

Emrys H., 32, California

"My disordered eating started because I was bad at managing money. (Hello, ADHD.) I still remember the first time I completely ran out of food. It's difficult to fully describe the nightmare of starving for days, not by any choice, but because I'd entirely run out of food. When I got my hands on food, I quickly learned that if I ate it all, I would have nothing left and would be just as tortured as I had been before. If I only ate a little, I would still have food later and wouldn't suffer from having nothing at all. In this way, restricting became associated with safety, and ironically, with the *avoidance* of total starvation. It became ingrained and instinctive. Even now, during periods of stress (like finals), I have to actively override the instinct to restrict my intake."

Geneva L., 34, Michigan

"I have congenital nystagmus, and because my eyes are of different strengths, I developed a head tilt when looking at things. This along with my ADHD 'ditziness' were dismissed as 'cute little girl things' until I reached an age when they were more annoying than endearing to those around me.

"It took me reaching sixth grade for my visual impairment to be diagnosed and to receive an IEP [individualized education plan] for classroom accommodations. My teachers largely proceeded to ignore them unless I fought for them."

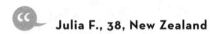

Julia F., 38, New Zealand

"The intersection between ADHD and socioeconomic status is rough. So many strategies that would help my executive dysfunction require money.

"Getting assessed in the first place is so expensive that it's a barrier for many people. It's common knowledge in the ADHD community here that there's no point going on the waiting list to be seen under the public system because they won't diagnose you unless your life is literally falling apart. I was lucky enough to have the money to get assessed privately, but you need a follow-up every two years to renew the special authority to get stimulants. That appointment is expensive, too. There is also a prescription fee every month (not every three months as usual) because they are controlled drugs. If you don't have money, you run into so many barriers along the way to get the help you need."

Ike A., 23, Illinois

"Part of the reason it's so difficult for Black people to get treatment is because of medical racism and the distrust our community has for the medical system. This means even if we are diagnosed, we're still not likely to get help."

Khiry S., 32, California

> "I inadvertently masked my symptoms because I had to be 'twice as good' as a young Black guy. Many ADHD traits overlap with stereotypes. Acting impulsively would have had a higher chance of being seen as deviant rather than 'oh, maybe he should get tested for ADHD.'"

THE TOOLBOX

I read through hundreds of quotes like those above, in awe of others' resilience, hopeful at the occasional protective factors, but more often sobbing at how we have to fight so hard to navigate such complex struggles largely on our own. It would be impossible to offer targeted strategies for every interplay of factors, but there are some general principles that seem to hold true for many of us.

1. LEARN WHAT YOU'RE DEALING WITH

For many, especially those of us with limited access to care, their journey toward seeking help starts with self-suspecting or even self-diagnosing. If that's true for you, it can help to seek a professional diagnosis *if and when you can* to see what else may be going on. There is an opportunity cost involved in not understanding all the factors you are dealing with as soon as possible, because there may be more effective ways to address them. An accurate diagnosis (or diagnoses) can save years of wasted time and effort addressing a condition you don't have, or one that is secondary to an underlying condition.

This is a heartbreaking but not uncommon experience since the symptoms of ADHD resemble those of other conditions, and vice versa. A community member shared with me that they were diagnosed and treated unsuccessfully for depression for *two decades* before their ADHD was recognized—and that treating the ADHD ultimately helped with the depression, too.

Another community member and friend—a fierce, brilliant trans woman and coder—suspected she was Autistic as well as ADHD. When she was finally able to access a neuropsych evaluation, however, she was shocked to learn the rigidity she'd been attributing to her suspected autism was actually due to severe OCD (obsessive-compulsive disorder). Because she assumed it was due to autism, she didn't know to seek treatment for her OCD until her magical thinking and agoraphobia had gotten so bad that she couldn't leave the house.

While psychology is an imperfect science, there is still a science to it. To maximize your chances of an accurate diagnosis, find a provider who has training in (and, ideally, specializes in) the conditions you suspect you have, as well as understands the cultural nuances that may impact your presentation/experience. Someone who specializes in your condition and population (women, LGBTQIA+, BIPOC, etc.) will be most likely to accurately identify whether you fit the parameters of that condition, as well as educate you on your options for minimizing the impairments associated with it.

This may not always be possible. If you feel as though a provider you do have access to is ruling out something prematurely or that they've misdiagnosed you entirely, don't be afraid to ask, "Why are you ruling this out?" or "Why this diagnosis and not that?" If their answer feels off to you, get a second opinion. My first doctor told my mom, "She can't have ADHD. She's too smart." ADHD kids can also be gifted. They can even grow up to be authors.

Finally, even if you don't officially qualify for a diagnosis, you can still struggle with *some* of the symptoms of a condition. Use strategies that work for you, regardless of what you're diagnosed with (or not)!

2. THINK HOLISTICALLY

When looking for tools and treatment, it's important to consider all the factors involved. Effective treatment and support take the whole person into account, not just a single condition. It's also important to consider what works from a variety of different sources. You don't have to get all your tools from the same store.

- **Get curious.** When you're trying to support yourself, don't assume every struggle is rooted in ADHD alone. Could it be ADHD *and* cultural expectations? Anxiety? Do you really have to pee? Approaching a problem from another perspective might open your mind to tools and strategies you might not have considered otherwise.

- **Understand that you may need to treat other conditions first.** Maybe you have ADHD, but it's hard to tell through the fog of depression. Or maybe you'd benefit from an ADHD coaching group, but you won't be able to participate effectively until you get support for your PTSD.

- **Keep other factors in mind when considering strategies.** It's true, using TrendyCool! New System™ *might* help you with your time management issues, but can you afford it? Is your anxiety going to be a barrier to using it? Is it compatible with *waves hand* the rest of your life? On the flip side, what resources do you have access to that others do not?

- **Look for care that is informed about your intersectionalities.** Examples of this type of care include trauma-informed care, disability-informed practices, BIPOC- and LGBTQIA+-affirming care. Research shows that the therapeutic relationship is the greatest predictor of success, and the most productive therapeutic relationships are based on trust, support, and understanding. While it might take longer or be more difficult (or expensive) to find such care, there is often a better return on your investment.

- **Make a plan for when things aren't okay.** My favorite example of this is a Wellness Recovery Action Plan (WRAP). This was designed by a group of people struggling with mental health challenges and has since been recognized as an evidence-based practice. Creating a WRAP plan can help you "to identify the tools that keep you well and create action plans to put them into practice in everyday life." I'll share a link for you to learn more in the "Support Organizations" section (page 431).

3. SEEK COMMUNITY WITH PEOPLE WHO SHARE YOUR COEXISTING CONDITIONS, IDENTITIES, AND BACKGROUND

There is robust literature showing that for ADHD brains, interacting with others who share your diagnosis can increase support and reduce stigma. I've seen this again and again in the How to ADHD community.

Our community is intentionally built to be as inclusive to those who are neurodivergent as possible. It includes Brains and Hearts from all around the world who have enthusiastic conversations about shared experiences, individual factors, and their individual intersectionalities, which serve to normalize those experiences, help us practice self-advocating, and increase compassion and understanding of other stigmatized differences.

Of course, there are going to be limitations to any community in terms of finding the understanding and social support you need. For example, the main purpose of the How to ADHD community is to facilitate discussions about—well, ADHD, and to be accessible for ADHD Brains and the Hearts who love them not just in the US but internationally. Our community guidelines are built with those goals in mind.

Each community serves a purpose, and even the most experienced community managers and moderators have their hands full trying to meet the needs of the group as a whole in service of that purpose. Because of that, no one community is likely to meet all of our individual needs for understanding and belonging. As social creatures, we all need and deserve understanding and belonging, not for one aspect of our identity but for all of them. If we have multiple stigmatized identities, we may need more than one community, too.

There are, however, also communities designed to support specific intersections of ADHD *and*. You can scan the QR code in our "Support Organizations" section (page 432) to find a list of the ones we're aware of; we don't vet these groups, but each one is contributed from someone in our community who has found it helpful for them.

I encourage people to, when they can, also find supports dedicated toward whatever else they're going through. We have other life experiences that deserve specific connection and support, too. Personally, I attend a peer support group for those who may need to use third-party donors to be able to conceive.

It's often worth finding more than one group when you're going through more than one thing.* Connection with others who get it is healing.

---

* This is especially true if you're seen as a leader in your group. If people are used to leaning on you for support, they might not be able to switch to giving you the support you need. It's good to have groups where you can just participate, too.

4. RESPECT YOUR OWN JOURNEY

Again, to effectively manage our ADHD, we sometimes need to zoom out and consider the interplay of other factors involved. We might also zoom out so we can look around and see what others are doing. How have they made it work?

After that, though, we need to zoom in to check in with our inner compass. Where do I want to go from here? What makes sense for me?

Sometimes societal pressures to use or not use a particular strategy or treatment override our own sense of what we need or want to try first—or whether we even want to work on our stuff right now. Maybe we need a break! We can't make others agree or cooperate, but as adults we can decide what to try—or not try—ourselves. What we choose might look different from what "research suggests." It also might look different than others expect. What others do or suggest is often based on their needs and experience and values. It's important to do what makes sense for ours.

LABELS

I talk about a lot of labels in this chapter. For some, these labels can get overwhelming—especially when it comes to communicating them to concerned family, friends, and colleagues.

A lot of people aren't even comfortable with the label ADHD. I hear from parents who hesitate to get their kids diagnosed because they're afraid of their child being limited by labels. There is an understandable fear there.

To those parents, I gently say: your child already has labels. Teachers, peers, and family all apply labels to your child as an attempt to explain behaviors they don't understand. Labels such as *lazy, messy, spacey,* and *irresponsible* are more stigmatizing, more shame inducing, less accurate, and much, much less helpful than any diagnostic term will be.

Having an accurate label for our experience helps us understand it. It shows us what we can do about it. It gives us access to treatment, accommodations, and other supports. While the label itself may seem limiting, the understanding and treatment that we can access as a result can make us more functional and capable, not less. It's important to understand how any piece of equipment we work with works—and our brain is one we have to work with every day, in everything we do.

In 2022, René Brooks, creator of *Black Girl, Lost Keys,* gave the Lived Experience keynote address at the International ADHD Conference. Those keynotes are typically 75 minutes long. René's was only ten minutes, but in those 10 minutes, she gave a keynote so powerful it didn't need the other 65.

The title of her talk was "Relabeling Yourself after an ADHD Diagnosis." She told the audience that it was the label ADHD that had given her access to the labels she wanted: good partner, good employee, good friend.

"Too often," she said, "people gatekeep those labels for us. This label, ADHD, gives us *access.*"

More than that, she said, it had given her access to a community of others who shared that label—people she could call when she was struggling, isolated, or breaking down.

We were all crying by this point of the keynote. Hugging each other. Glancing knowingly across the room, connecting with one another—people we'd never met, people who carried other labels we did not, but who shared this understanding.

We all knew what it was like to be denied access to the labels we wanted. We knew how important it was to see and be seen by people who *understood*.

ADHD has a remarkable ability to connect people with different types of intersectionalities, all around the world, through a single label. There is a kinship, empathy, and shared understanding that requires no words to describe while also making space for way too many. Stereotypical media portrayals may paint us all with one brush, but connecting with one other is opening our eyes, not only to our own unique journey, but to the journeys of others.

After René's keynote, some of us recorded an episode about the experience for Brendan Mahan's podcast, *ADHD Essentials*. What you might not notice in that episode is the way we truly saw one another for the first time. We saw how lonely each of us had been, despite our connection to one another, because we each had struggles that the others knew nothing of. We hadn't felt it was appropriate to share them, since we were at the conference to talk about ADHD. But keeping them hidden had caused us individual pain and kept us from relating to each other as authentically as we might have otherwise.

We made a commitment to one another that we wouldn't have to be alone in our struggles, ADHD-related or otherwise. Not anymore. Although recognizing the label we had in common had connected us, we had learned that true authenticity meant listening to the "and" in one another's stories. Many of us still talk about our struggles beyond the ADHD, reach out when we think to, and respond when we can.

That doesn't mean it's always easy to connect. In deeper discussions months later, René and I observed how some of the conditions I discuss in this chapter can decrease access to one another. Anxiety can keep us from reaching out. Trauma can trigger pain and distrust. As René showed me in one brave and vulnerable conversation, labeling our experiences (with terms such as "anxiety," "rejection," "sensitivity," "trauma," "grief"), just like labeling our emotions (see "How to Feel," page 216), can make them easier to understand; and communicating those experiences can build trust and connection, restoring access to what humans need most: one another.

Chapter 12

How to Heart

If it is true that there are as many minds as there are heads,
then there are as many kinds of love as there are hearts.

—LEO TOLSTOY, *ANNA KARENINA*

WHY CAN'T THEY JUST . . . ?

A few months after I started the channel, I began to realize it wasn't just ADHD "Brains" who were watching. Those who cared for them and wanted to better support them were, too. I nicknamed these people "Hearts" because it was their heart that brought them to my videos.

I felt gratitude and awe that they would take the time to understand a brain that wasn't their own—and one that seemingly contradicted all logic and reasoning on a regular basis. I empathized with their frustration, too.

I know what it's like to be in a relationship with someone with

ADHD. I've been in one my entire life. My brain won't do what I want it to do a lot of the time. It promises me it will remember to put the clothes in the dryer, and then it doesn't. It tells me I need to run back into the house for something "real quick," and an hour later I still haven't left. It insists that I need *all the supplies* for a new hobby, then gets bored of it in a week. As much as I love how impulsive and creative and *fun* my brain can be, there have been many times when I wished it would just *cooperate.* Thankfully, I've developed a much better relationship with my brain since learning how to work with it effectively.

When I started dating someone with AuDHD—both ADHD and autism—and became a Heart to him, I *totally expected* that knowledge to translate.

I saw my partner run into brain-based challenges, and equipped with six years' worth of knowledge about how to work with my own brain, I *aggressively* tried to help.

I'd (mostly) figured out how to work with my brain—he could, too!

I patiently listened to his struggles and offered suggestions.

I sent him articles and put sticky note reminders all over the walls.

I tugged at his mask, encouraging him to "be himself."*

I read articles about how to be a better partner and "work on your relationship." I learned about autism and alexithymia, trying to understand his brain the same way I'd done with mine.

---

* The idea of unmasking, meanwhile, terrified him because being himself had not gone well, historically. Showing his neurodivergent traits didn't feel safe. It had led to being laughed or yelled at. It led to breakups.

I did all the things that felt as if they "should" work, though I never knew what would. I felt as if I were throwing spaghetti against the wall and hoping something would stick.

I was determined to make it work. He was worth it. I appreciated his comedic timing, his quirks, his enthusiasm for his hobbies, his sense of justice, and his way of cutting through the noise and speaking directly to the heart of a matter. Our values were aligned, our hopes, our dreams.

I loved him. I also felt lonely.

Once the new relationship hyperfocus wore off, he'd get distracted while we talked, or interrupt me, or change the subject abruptly. He'd miss my bids for attention. He'd agree to do something and then completely forget about it. I yearned for him to care for me as attentively as he did his espresso machine, hat collection, or cast-iron pans.*

He wanted to do better, and I wanted to help. But communication between us was a challenge.

I couldn't tell when he was listening and when he was lost in his own world. I never knew what to expect from him. Was what he was doing or promising to do actually what he wanted to do? And could he do it sustainably? Or was it what he thought he was "expected" to do? And he couldn't keep up?

When I tried talking to him about my frustrations, his emotions ran high, and I couldn't get through. Mine escalated, too.

---

* Which, in retrospect, were not only his special interests—they were also activities he needed to engage in to cope with the stress of trying to meet relationship expectations. I was special, too. He just sometimes needed a break.

I found myself biting my tongue, almost blurting out the comments that countless people have said to me and others with ADHD: "Why can't you just . . ." "What do you mean you forgot?" "If you cared about me, you'd . . ." I even found myself thinking, "This relationship would be amazing *if* . . ." (Yes, I heard the irony in that. *This relationship has so much potential.*)

Eventually, we found ourselves trapped in a relationship death spiral: He was terrified to "mess up" and spent all his energy contemplating what he should be doing, and I'd grow frustrated about his apparent inaction. I'd need something, but he wouldn't do it soon enough, consistently enough, or he'd forget (or miss) the part that mattered the most. Because he'd feel bad about letting me down, the stakes felt higher the next time I asked him for something. He'd already "failed," and he was terrified of getting it wrong *again*.

I'd notice his hesitance, and as much as I wanted to reassure him, my patience was wearing thin. I'd tried all my neurodivergent-friendly relationship hacks and communication tools, but the harder I tried, the *less* my needs were getting met.

I've seen these relationship issues play themselves out over and over in my community and in my own life. Unmet expectations. Frustration. Trying to manage day-to-day life on behalf of your Brain. Trying to manage *them*. Guilt and shame. Loss of respect—or even the relationship.

My neurotypical mom took on more and more of the household, familial, and financial responsibilities and burned herself out. I watched my dad (who likely had ADHD) get into intense and terrifying power struggles with my brother (who definitely does).* I watched my dad fall into a depression, too, painfully aware he wasn't contributing as much as my mom was but not knowing what to do about it. The more areas of responsibility she took over, the more he accepted her role as the caretaker of everything, and the more she had to do to keep everything from falling apart.

> When I tried talking to him about my frustrations, his emotions ran high, and I couldn't get through. Mine escalated, too.

I've been on the receiving end of this type of support with executive function. In past relationships, especially before I knew how to manage my ADHD, my partners ended up taking care of me, cleaning up my mess as I gave over my autonomy and passwords to them, ashamed I couldn't "adult."

I hear all the time from community members who share how their partners treat them like a child that their parents treat them like a problem to be solved. I see their friends make jokes out of the struggles they face in ways that are hurtful, even cruel.

My partner had an ex who once asked, point blank, "Why can't you just be *normal*?"

We can't be "normal." We can only be ourselves. We wonder if we can ever be enough.

---

*   For the record: you can't "punish away" ADHD. Resorting to punishment just made my brother more defiant, and it taught him that the way to respond to people who aren't doing what you want is to force them. It didn't fix his mental health struggles but worsened them.

The Hearts that love us wonder that, too. They wonder if they are doing too much for us or too little. They wonder if they overvalue our struggles or undervalue our gifts.

Eventually we all wonder what it is we're doing wrong. *Why can't we just make it work?*

WHAT I LEARNED

Every relationship, neurodiverse or not, runs into challenges with unmet expectations, either because they aren't expressed or because there's conflict in the ways each person is trying to get their needs met.

ADHD exacerbates this issue by interfering with our ability to meet expectations, even once they're agreed upon. In fact, relationship problems are one of the most common reasons why adults with ADHD seek treatment.

So, Brains, Hearts, take a breath. Whatever frustration, anger, guilt, or shame you're feeling is *normal* if you and/or your loved one has ADHD, and your relationship challenges aren't ones that "everyone goes through." And it's not due to a lack of effort. It's because of ADHD. Not only are there executive function challenges that make it difficult for us to "do our part" consistently, there are also aspects about neurodivergence that look very different from the inside than they do from the outside. This can

> We can't be "normal."
> We can only be ourselves.

make it look as though we don't even care, especially when we're pushing back against expectations we're struggling to meet.

WE CARE WAY MORE THAN IT LOOKS

When we continue to "mess up" even after apologizing for the same thing a hundred times, it might seem like we don't care. After all, if we were so sorry, why wouldn't we change our behavior?

We Are Trying

We are taught that accomplishment comes from effort. If someone is not accomplishing something, they must not be putting in enough effort.

This isn't true for those of us with ADHD. We often must put in significantly *more* effort than our neurotypical peers to achieve the same results—and frequently our effort doesn't look very effortful.

Sometimes our effort isn't obvious. We may have forgotten the instructions, misunderstood what was being asked, or put our effort toward the wrong task. Much of our effort might not be visible at all because it is happening internally. (Check out Chapter 7, "How to Motivate Your Brain," page 156, to learn more.)

Improvement takes time, and progress is rarely linear.

It's not unreasonable to want the person you love to improve in the areas where they struggle. They probably want that, too! What is often unreasonable, whether we're trying to change ourselves or support someone we love, is our expectations of the rate and magnitude of the change.

First of all, we can't change our symptoms. Unlike conditions like anxiety or depression, which can improve or worsen over time, ADHD symptoms generally don't. Our impairments can improve, we can improve how functional we are *given* those symptoms, but we can't get rid of the symptoms themselves. If it seems like we have, we're masking them (see "A Note on Masking," page 273).

Also, most people are only capable of one degree of change at a time. Even if we can manage to change quickly and in multiple areas at once (which is often what's asked of us or what we ask of ourselves), it's generally impossible to sustain change that extensive.

Supports Aren't Designed with Us in Mind

Many common solutions to relationship issues—from couples therapy to those "how-to relationship" articles on the internet—are designed based on neuronormative standards that assume typical cognitive function in most or all areas. Not only do our executive function impairments make it challenging to implement any strategy; the strategies themselves (or many aspects of them) are often inaccessible due to the way our brains work.

In some cases, trying to make solutions or systems designed for neurotypical brains work for a neurodivergent one can backfire. This can lead to a lot of frustration (and can even be retraumatizing!) for everyone involved.*

---

* This is why there's an entire industry designed specifically for those who are neurodivergent—we need solutions that are designed to work the way our brains do.

We're not struggling on purpose.

This point might seem obvious, but it's easy to forget in the moment. Struggling is *not a choice* or something we can opt out of. It's a given. If we didn't struggle with ADHD-related challenges, we wouldn't have been diagnosed with ADHD. The same goes for any other co-existing conditions that we've been diagnosed with. While we might struggle in ways that don't make sense from a neurotypical perspective, it's *not weird* that we're struggling; given our diagnosis, it would be weird if we didn't.

The Double Empathy Problem

In 2012, autism researcher Dr. Damian Milton created the "double empathy" theory as a way of understanding communication breakdowns between Autistic and Allistic (non-Autistic) people. Previous theories proposed that people with autism struggled to communicate due to impaired empathy and "theory of mind," a term used to describe the ability to imagine what might be going on in another person's head. Milton posited that these difficulties resulted from lack of empathy and understanding on *both sides*. In other words, because Autistic and Allistic brains function differently in many ways, an Autistic *and* Allistic person have trouble understanding what the other is feeling and thinking.

While the studies aren't specific to ADHD, there are traits that overlap between the conditions, and research has expanded to demonstrate how the double empathy problem may apply to autistic traits, regardless of specific diagnosis; and we know that difficulties with empathy and understanding are complicated by differences in lived experience.

In neurodiverse relationships, missed connections, misunderstandings, and miscommunications are bound to happen, and the resulting stress on the relationship can be significant. Thankfully, just being aware of this issue can be a good first step in learning how to interface together more effectively—and help you look for supports.

THERE ARE REASONS WHY WE CAN'T "JUST"

Many of the expectations we place on those we love rely on the idea that they *should* be able to do The Thing. As a society, we tend to assume people's intelligence and capabilities based on characteristics such as their verbal ability, long-term recall, or even the work they do for a living. If my partner is a well-spoken psychologist who can name the exact title of season four, episode eleven of *Star Trek: The Next Generation* (it's "Data's Day," he just informed me), he should be able to figure out how to buy me *flowers,* right? Not necessarily.

Cognitive Ability Is Actually Cognitive Abilities

Tasks such as buying flowers require multiple cognitive abilities—and we need to use different combinations of these abilities to produce a given result.

We've gone over many of these in previous chapters already, so I'll just drop in a quick list: processing speed, working memory, pattern recognition, set-shifting, response inhibition, verbal comprehension, visual spatial ability, perceptual reasoning.

Several of these cognitive abilities are significantly impaired in ADHD brains—at least relative to our areas of cognitive strength. In addition, some combinations of abilities are more challenging for some brains than others.

For example, I might have no trouble understanding a recipe I'm reading—my verbal comprehension is extremely high—but my poor response inhibition makes it hard for me to stay focused (and in the kitchen) long enough to prep and cook dinner. Even if I stay focused, my relatively weak working memory means I will one hundred percent forget the instructions two steps in.

My AuDHD partner describes his experience in computer terms. He might have a high-capacity solid state hard drive and twin-linked high-end graphic cards, but a Pentium II processor and about a half a gigabyte of RAM (random access memory). He's capable of doing high-level work with visual/spatial processing or pattern recognition, but his processor is slow and he can only hold on to small chunks of new data at a time.

How does this affect our relationship? The more I explain how important flowers are to me, describing how Suzy's husband bought her flowers and wasn't that romantic, and running through all the tangential topics that come up for me while talking about flowers, the less likely he is able to process—and remember—the part that matters to me: "*Hey, I think it's romantic when someone buys me flowers.*" Because my own brain makes it hard to organize my thoughts, I also have trouble communicating this point succinctly, without going off on tangents. *Le sigh.*

Inconsistency Is Part of the Deal

One of the most common frustrations for those with ADHD and those who love them is knowing we're *capable* of doing the thing—and still for some reason aren't doing it when we're expected to.

Yes, just because we could take care of something yesterday doesn't mean that we can today. Maybe we were hyperfocusing for twelve hours yesterday and now our brains are too exhausted to focus. Maybe we didn't sleep well and our emotional self-regulation went completely out the window. Maybe there were more distractions today.

What helped me a LOT in my own relationship was recognizing and embracing these inconsistencies. I learned that just as sometimes I can focus and sometimes I can't, sometimes my AuDHD partner could make the connections between what I was saying and the context of the situation—and sometimes he couldn't.

Emotions Get in Our Way

Emotions like shame and anxiety can be powerful obstacles to completing even seemingly simple tasks. On top of our struggle to do a task, we also have all the shame and negative emotions of past failures getting in our way—because we know the task isn't "supposed" to be "that hard."

The fact that we care deeply about the task, know how important it is, and feel bad about the fact that we haven't done it yet—and are having trouble getting ourselves to do it—can add to the struggle. (To learn why, flip to page 164.)

ADHD Traits Are Two Sides of the Same Coin

A lot of ADHD traits are strengths in the right situation. For instance, the same emotional sensitivity that can make it difficult for us to have hard conversations also makes us quick to be enthusiastic, understanding, and generous. As my partner tells me, many qualities of mine that frustrate him are, in different situations, also the things he loves. And honestly, same.

Here are some of the fantastic ways ADHD traits can show up in relationships with others:

- Impulsivity → Spontaneous romantic gestures!

- Motivated by urgency → Great in a crisis!

- Divergent thinking → Innovative problem-solving skills!

- Hyperactivity → Infectious energy!

- Shorter time horizons → Ability to find joy in the moment!

- Motivated by novelty → Often trying, learning, and sharing something new! (The relationship will rarely get boring.)

- Emotionally sensitive → Caring deeply! (Even when it doesn't seem like we do.)

The frustrations that come with ADHD and other mental health struggles make it easy for the benefits of building a relationship with someone with ADHD to get lost. But when we get support for the ways in which we struggle, the potential positives have a chance to truly shine. That two-sided coin of ADHD traits can flip more often to the positive side than the negative one.

 Amanda, 20s, USA

"When I was bored, I would turn to my husband for stimulation, which he ultimately could not keep up with. He wouldn't respond with the adoration and interest I craved, so I felt lonely and unloved. He felt overwhelmed and like a bad person for hurting me."

Chad M., 36, Texas

"ADHD almost ended my marriage. My wife didn't know what she was getting into. It became a perpetual cycle of me trying my best while she felt like I couldn't care less. I finally got on meds, and it changed everything. My wife could see the sudden and significant change, which helped her see that it wasn't that I didn't care; I just couldn't show it. There was still a lot of pain to work through, and my ADHD is still a challenge for us. But we learned to differentiate actions from motives."

Amelia B., 35, Arizona

"My ADHD has caused a lot of little frictions in our day-to-day life, like when I repeatedly forget to put the keys back on the hook or put the wash in the dryer. It's also caused a few major disasters that have definitely affected how my partner sees me, I think. After making such big mistakes, it's like I have to prove again, every single day, that I can be a functioning, capable adult and partner."

Lee D., 39, Massachusetts

"I tend to easily get hyperfixated on another person when there are signs of good chemistry, a similar experience to what's been termed 'limerence.' If I don't keep it in check, it leads to broken boundaries, hurt feelings, and diminished or even ruined relationships."

THE TOOLBOX

One of the best ways to support those we love is to support their efforts to find treatment for their ADHD. (I include options for this in Chapter 2, page 29.) We don't expect other medical conditions to manage themselves without treatment—why would it be any different for ADHD? Besides, most of us aren't trained to support others with their health conditions or mental health struggles, and even if we are, we aren't objective enough to do so effectively for those we love. That said, there are ways to strengthen your relationship (or friendship!) with your Brain that are appropriate for the role you already have.

1. ENGAGE IN EMPATHY

So many of us with ADHD—and those who love someone with ADHD—feel alone in our struggles. While you may never fully understand your Brain's experience, you can certainly open your mind to learning about it, which can make empathizing easier and helps to dismantle the shame we've built up over a lifetime of feeling "weird" or "wrong." It also makes it safer and easier to talk about our brain's differences, so we can collaborate on solutions that are more likely to work. And learning more about ADHD's impact on loved ones can normalize your experience, too. So you, too, can feel less alone—and better understand what you need.

- **Ask about their experience.** While those with ADHD often have very similar stories, strengths, and struggles, there are also profound differences in its presentation, how they feel about their diagnosis and challenges, what they've tried, and what works for them. Getting curious about someone's individual experience—and accepting their answers, even if they're surprising—is key to understanding them *and* helping them feel understood.

- **Ask about their inner world and thought processes.** You might think you know what your loved one with ADHD is thinking or why they did (or didn't) do a thing, but if their brain works very differently from yours, there's a decent chance you'll be wrong. Remember the double empathy problem (page 332)? Instead of assuming, ask. And this goes both ways. Asking about each other's thought processes and inner world can increase empathy and make it easier to connect. It can also help us understand where their priorities are. We often assume that what others want for themselves is the same as what we want for them. But that's not necessarily the case.

- **Be an advocate.** Some behaviors and actions aren't problems—they're strategies or coping mechanisms. If your loved one suddenly leaves the room during a family dinner, see it as an opportunity to recognize and advocate for their needs. Shrug and normalize it. "They get overwhelmed sometimes and need to step away." Encourage them to do things in a way that works for them—even if it's "weird"—and have their back if they do it. This models understanding and empathy so that others can engage in them, too.

What If They Don't Want to Talk about It?

There are many reasons someone with ADHD may not want to talk about their ADHD:

- They've had it weaponized against them.

- They don't understand their ADHD, or don't know they *have* ADHD.

- They don't want to be "fixed."

- They don't feel safe talking about it with you, at least right now.

- Talking about it brings up feelings they'd like to avoid.

If you want to broach the subject, you can start the conversation with the help of these tips:

- **Start with respect.** Remember, we're not a broken version of normal. We have a brain that works differently. If you can respect the challenges we face as a result of trying to meet neurotypical expectations, it's easier to respect us, too. This mutual respect also makes it easier for us to trust that you're trying to support us, not fix us.

- **Be mindful of tone.** There's a big difference between a frustrated *"Seriously?* Why did you do it *THAT* way?" and a genuinely curious "Seriously, why *did* you do it that way?" When you can, use a tone that expresses you're ready to listen, not to judge. Then *listen.* There's often a reason we did something differently.

- **Try a different approach.** Conversations don't always have to be verbal. Communication can happen by drawing or sharing videos, or via emojis or GIFs. Asynchronous communication such as texting can be easier for many Brains, because it's easier to discuss important topics at a pace that lets us self-regulate and think through what we want to say.

- **Let us be done if we need to be done.** It's important not to force these conversations. We all have our limits, especially when it comes to talking about aspects of ourselves that we may not love, ADHD or not. It's also perfectly okay for you to set boundaries for yourself so the impact of unresolved issues doesn't fall unfairly on you. (See page 345 to learn about the milk carton rule.)

Jessica H., 30, Ohio

"My partner and I were both diagnosed later in life. Our struggle to moderate our emotions (combined with a processing disorder in one of us) means silly fights happen. Being aware that there is something *causing* those emotions to get a little rowdy means we are more understanding of each other's struggles—and because we think outside the box, we can find solutions where others might not."

Colleen H., 41, Pennsylvania

"Instead of pointing at things, I asked my now husband to gesture at the things he's talking about with his palm up. I thought it was a silly request, but he immediately complied and we had zero confrontations about our then new cohabitation. I start to panic if I'm afraid I've done something wrong and then I go into analysis paralysis. Pointing, even conversationally, triggers feelings of 'oh no, what did I screw up?' Open palms let me know what he's talking about, and it invites me in instead of calling me out."

Colin K., 35, Colorado

> "When I told my dad that I was recently diagnosed with ADHD, he asked what it's like. When I told him how a normal day, a good day, and a bad day was, he said he was sorry he never noticed. It was nice that he just understood. Even when I told him I was nervous about the meds 'cause I didn't want to lose my career, he told me, 'Don't sweat it. Being better is better, and you'll find a new one.' That mattered a lot."

2. CHOOSE YOUR BATTLES

If we have ADHD, we'll struggle with many different things—and in multiple areas of our lives. And that's without adding other coexisting conditions into the mix. We can't work on everything all at once—at least not effectively. We'll need to decide what needs our focus now and what to set aside, at least for now.

- **Prioritize.** Those with ADHD often have trouble prioritizing. If there are ten things to work on, we might choose one that's not as important—or the least taxing on our executive function. We might get overwhelmed and not work on any of them at all. Choosing one thing to focus on at a time (maybe two) improves the likelihood that we'll make progress on it. What task, if left undone, is affecting the relationship the most? What would create the most positive impact if it were to change?

- **Let us fail.** This one is especially important for parents. Many parents are afraid to let us do things our way because they're worried we'll fail if they do. We might! But having the space to try—and fail—while we have a safety net in place is *important.* It gives us the opportunity to figure out what does work for us before we're off on our own and taking on even more. It also builds our resilience. Let us practice doing things on our own now that we'll *need* to do on our own when you're not around.

- **Let some stuff go.** Maybe we never get around to removing the bathroom wallpaper—*whatever, it's kitsch.* My boyfriend's learned to accept that if I'm making dinner, I'll need to use a recipe, which means we're probably going to have leftover fennel taking up space in the fridge. As Dr. Ari Tuckman put it in an interview on my channel: "Yeah, I don't love this thing about my partner, but whatever—there's a lot of things in my life I don't love."

- **Find other solutions with the "milk carton rule."** The milk carton rule is inspired by a story of a real-life couple. The wife leaves the milk out after pouring some for her morning coffee, and when the husband comes downstairs for breakfast, he has to use warm milk for his cereal. The husband asks the wife to put the milk back in the fridge, but she keeps forgetting—and leaving it out. One way to resolve the issue is to keep reminding the wife to put the milk back, but the husband has another option: buying his own carton of milk. Many times, a problem can be solved in a way that does not depend on us being able to change our (often ADHD-related) behavior.

 Margaret, 46, Washington

"I wish this was something more parents supported each other with. There's so much judgment—*why did you let him take on so much when you knew he would likely struggle?* Or, on the other hand—*why are you still doing xyz with them? They should be able to do that independently by now!* I do a lot to support my neurodivergent kids and help them succeed, but I've learned my kids will eventually tell me when they don't need or want that amount of support, and they'll tell me if and when they need it again."

 Rebecca C., 43, United Kingdom

"My partner swaps executive dysfunction jobs with me because we're more motivated to complete a task for one another than for ourselves. For example, I find it hard to get myself to the post office, and he finds it hard to pick up his prescriptions."

 **Jessica K., 28, Florida**

"When my family members started working on not taking my quirks, like leaving the refrigerator door open, personally, it made me feel so much less ashamed."

3. COLLABORATE ON SOLUTIONS

When it comes to ADHD-related challenges, it's not you versus your loved one. It's both of you versus the challenges. Tackle them together! The way in which you collaborate and the degree to which you do it will depend on the type of relationship you have with the person—but the most effective solutions usually involve *some* level of collaboration.

- **Be clear on the goal.** Make sure everyone agrees on what the goal is—and understands why you're working toward it. This way, you're on the same team. Defining together what success looks like ahead of time for a goal, week, or outing can also make it easier for everyone to recognize when it's been achieved. This can build our confidence, which is critical for those of us who have internalized the idea that we aren't "enough."

- **Allow us to achieve the goal in a way that works for us.** ADHD Brains are capable of accomplishing a lot; we just might go about it a bit differently. Allowing for *equifinality*—achieving the same result through different means—can be the difference between us being able to accomplish tasks and leaving them undone. (Or you having to do them all yourself.)

- **Look for the *"and."*** I love this concept from the book *Crucial Conversations*. Don't compromise if you can help it. That can lead to resentment on both sides, because both people are having to sacrifice something that matters to them. Instead, look for a solution that fully meets your needs—*and* theirs.* While we might struggle at executing, we often excel at ideating. We can come up with lots of potential solutions, especially if we're given time to let them percolate. You just might wanna help us narrow them down.

- **Stay in your lane.** At the end of the day, you are your Brain's partner/friend/parent/roommate, not their coach or therapist. It's incredibly easy to get caught up with someone's mental health struggles, but being someone's main source of support inevitably comes at the expense of the role you already have. Parenting a partner kills desire. Playing therapist to a friend requires removing yourself from the equation so you can be objective, which comes at the expense of

---

*   One of my favorite *"and"*s: instead of being soft or hard on yourself, you can be gentle *and* firm. ADHD coach Dusty Chipura taught me this one from a book I totally don't remember the name of.

connection. Rather than *being* someone's support system, support them in building one. If they don't want to, or can't, make it clear that their need for support can't fall entirely on you.

Lyndall C., 30, Alberta

"One of the best things people have done to support my ADHD is feed me. I eat supper with my parents twice a week, which helps free up the brain space that would have gone toward meal prep for other things. An example: I had supper with my parents one evening, which meant I had enough energy and brain space to do all my own dishes later that night—three sink loads full."

Christie H., 38, Colorado

"My partner will remind me I wanted to shower, turn it on, and wait with me while I get in or even sit and talk with me while I'm in there. He also sets easy food on my desk while I'm working."

Laura S., 37, Indianapolis

> "My time blindness means I'm perpetually late to every-
> thing. When I get ready, my partner checks in and gives
> me T-minus updates as our leave time approaches.
> What's really special is there's no judgment or frustration
> in his tone. He's just sharing information."

4. LOOK FOR THE GOOD

Everyone's brains, by default, are designed to notice (and remember!) what's wrong more often than what's right, making it easy to
miss what's actually going well. This can be discouraging in any relationship, but it's especially problematic in relationships where there's
likely to be more going wrong. Seeking out the good not only provides much needed encouragement for everyone involved. It can
also make it easier to, you know, *enjoy* the relationship.

- **Notice their effort.** Failing doesn't mean someone isn't
  trying—in fact, it's often evidence that they *are*. Yes, your
  roommate started the dishwasher without soap—but they
  started the dishwasher! If you're not sure if they are making
  an effort, ask—and if they tell you they are, believe them. According to Dr. Tuckman's research, actively looking for—and
  recognizing—the ADHDer's effort is one of the most important things you can do to improve your relationship. (Brains,
  you can help by flagging your efforts for your Hearts!)

- **Flip the coin.** Remember, the things we love and the things that frustrate us are often two sides of the same ADHD-trait coin. Appreciating ADHD traits when they're enjoyable makes it a lot easier to accept those same traits when they happen to get in the way. Look for the ways their impulsivity shows up in ways you love!

- **Assume best intent.** When you assume that someone with ADHD cares about an issue they agreed to address, you'll be right more often than wrong. If you know they care but their actions are telling you they don't, it might be helpful to ask for clarity: "Hey, I know you care about this—can you help me understand why it's not happening? I'm not seeing it." Asking invites them to show you what you're missing—or to explain what's getting in their way.

- **Celebrate their successes.** Specific, immediate positive feedback is incredibly motivating to ADHD Brains. When we make progress on something important to us, give us a high five! Throw a mini dance party! Do whatever makes us feel good! While we might get praised for going above and beyond on a project, coming up with a brilliant new idea, or crushing it in sales, it's rare that we get celebrated for putting effort into the things that are hard for us because they seem "easy" or "obvious" to everyone else.

Scott D., 46, Washington

"My dad taught me the importance of looking at something you've done and appreciating it. He called it 'Admire Time.' Mowed lawn, clean car, new fence, etc. After we finished a task, he would say, 'Okay, Admire Time,' and we'd stand there and look at the thing we just did."

 Ron W., 50, Detroit

"I often go through my day just trying to survive, putting out one figurative 'fire' after another, and desperately hoping I haven't missed anything that will cause everything to burn down. When my wife says to me, 'Hey, I really appreciate that you did X' or 'This thing that you built really makes things easier for me,' I suddenly feel truly seen and my feeling of self-worth is revived, plus it gives me renewed energy to keep going!"

5. TAKE CARE OF YOURSELF

Having a loved one who's struggling, for any reason, can be emotionally draining. While almost no one with ADHD intends to make your life more difficult or make you feel neglected, intent isn't the only thing that matters. How it's impacting you matters, too. Putting your own oxygen mask on first can help you be there for the person you care about in a sustainable way.

- **Set boundaries.** It's important to set limits that allow you to maintain your own peace. It's okay to make requests of other people, but *boundaries* should focus on your actions, not the actions you want from someone else. This is because we can't control other people's behavior. If your boundaries involve someone else's behavior—such as yelling—a boundary that you might have is that you don't participate in the conversation while they are.*

- **Engage outside support.** Therapy, peer support, friends who are navigating similar situations, even articles about neurodiverse relationships can validate your experiences and help you process the emotions that come up. They can also offer guidance so you don't have to figure it all out on your own.

- **Allow yourself to have feelings.** It might feel wrong to be upset about ADHD-related behavior because it's unintentional. But you're allowed to have feelings, regardless of why something is happening. There's a difference between *understandable* and *acceptable*. You don't have to accept behavior that hurts you just because someone has ADHD.

---

* If you are concerned that expressing your boundaries could escalate the situation, please talk to a mental health professional before trying this. While boundaries are important and can create a greater sense of safety in relationships for everyone involved, those who aren't used to boundaries can get angry and even lash out when others begin to communicate them.

Feel your anger, your hurt, your sadness. Allowing yourself to feel can help you understand what you need, regulate those emotions, and communicate more effectively with your Brain. It helps you focus on your feelings and needs,* as opposed to their behavior.

- **Take a break.** Make sure you're both getting time apart to pursue other social connections, hobbies, or even just to recharge. Getting time away from each other is what many (even neurotypical couples) find important to the sustainability and happiness of their relationships. You can also take a break from the relationship completely if you need to. Just because someone has a disability doesn't mean you can't break up with them. I ultimately had to take a break from my relationship. (We got back together after a year—and lots of therapy.) It's unhealthy for you to feel chronically neglected. It's also unhealthy for them to be in a relationship where they're constantly failing. Sometimes, the place you're both at right now means the relationship isn't serving you, even if you really love each other. It's okay to step away.

---

* Michael Rosenberg, the creator of nonviolent communication, describes criticism as a "tragic expression of an unmet need." It's tragic because complaining about someone's behavior is much less likely to enact change than expressing your own feelings and needs. The person we criticize often feels attacked and winds up on the defensive.

❝ Claudia B., 26, Mexico

"I'm a Heart, my boyfriend's a Brain. We've been together almost nine years, and one of the things that has helped us both so much in our relationship is understanding the way we each communicate and reminding ourselves of our boundaries. Sometimes he gets so excited, he just flat out interrupts me and goes off on his own. So I firmly stop him and say, 'I'm not done.' At first, it felt incredibly uncomfortable to have to do this, because I didn't want to interrupt *him,* but this is something he has asked me to do countless times, and he doesn't take it personally because it's about our communication with each other and not so much about who is saying what."

❝ Castor S., 24, United Kingdom

"When we are having trouble understanding each other, we change modes of communication. We suggest things like 'Let's take turns and chat over messages. I'm not upset, I don't think I'm portraying the emotion I'm feeling, and it is not your fault.' My partner and I have anxiety and ADHD, and using a tool to find space helps. We've recently celebrated a decade of dating; being clear that we don't always show or interpret how we are feeling well is a linchpin."

WHAT'S THE PLAN?

Those who live with and love those with ADHD often find themselves picking up after them, managing more and more of the responsibilities, and becoming hypervigilant about their mistakes.
Those with ADHD often find themselves feeling less-than in the relationship, in constant fear of messing up, or not doing or being
"enough." We slip into these patterns almost without realizing it. It's
not the choice either person would have made, but due to our executive function challenges, it is often what happens by default.

These arrangements work well for absolutely no one involved.

There is, I have found, a better way. It starts by asking one simple
question: What's the plan?

I knew I didn't want to repeat my parents' (and grandparents')
patterns. I didn't want to parent a partner. I also didn't want to be
parented by mine. I wanted an actual partner, someone I could respect. I also wanted to be respected—and to be able to respect myself.

When I first moved in with my partner, we asked ourselves:
What's the plan for housekeeping? What do we care about maintaining and cleaning? Who's doing what? What's left? Do we let that stuff
go? Do we get outside help?

This conversation helped us split up
the mental and physical loads of housekeeping more evenly. We checked in and
tweaked the plan as needed, and it worked
out wonderfully. We now both knew who
was doing what, and if something didn't

> There is, I have
> found, a better
> way. It starts by
> asking one
> simple question:
> What's the plan?

get done, we didn't feel the need to step in and do it for them. We could just remind each other of what we'd agreed to. We worked together as equals and split up the work equitably.* We both took pride in our contributions and appreciated the other person's efforts. And we didn't stress about what we couldn't get to. We outsourced or let it go.

Three years later, somehow stuck in the relationship death spiral I mentioned earlier in the chapter, I was humbled to realize I'd still been parenting my partner—just in a different way than I'd anticipated.

Turns out, the emotional parts are also a huge chunk of any romantic relationship, and you might find yourself managing all of that for both of you! I took on these responsibilities without realizing it.

To make sure our relationship was emotionally healthy, I tried to understand what he needed and accommodated my own ADHD so I could meet his needs; I also tried to understand what I needed and accommodate his AuDHD so he could meet my needs.

When I told my partner how exhausted I was from my efforts to support his mental health and maintain our relationship, he replied, "I didn't ask you to."

And you know what? He was right.

I took it upon myself to do all of this because I thought it needed

---

* It's unrealistic to expect partners to be able to split work exactly down the middle. What if someone is working longer hours? What if housework takes one of you twice as long due to a disability? Don't aim for equality; aim for equity: Instead of looking at "how much is each person doing," consider how much free time/energy each person has to be able to pursue their interests, hobbies, etc. How well are each person's needs getting met?

to be done. And not only could he not consent to my efforts to support, he also couldn't appreciate them. It turned out, he was doing a bit of the same for me as well—reminding me to pick up my medication, picking up after me, trying to be present for me through grief even when he was overloaded and needed time alone. And I hadn't even realized it.

My partner and I started making time for relationship check-ins every week. Again, we asked, what's the plan?

When are we spending time together, time apart, and time with friends? What are we doing for date night? Let's get that on our calendar.

What's going on with your mental health? Do you need support, and if so, how are you going to get that support? What part do you want me to play?

It's naive to think ADHD (and the coexisting conditions we have along with it) won't impact a relationship. While acceptance is lovely, it's a place to start—not a place to end.

Whether it's about managing housework, buying a car, raising a child, working on the relationship, or supporting someone's mental health, the path to true partnership is the same. If you make a plan—*together*—you can discuss what's yours and what's theirs and decide what to do, as adults and partners, not as someone who has to manage the other.

> While acceptance is lovely, it's a place to start—not a place to end.

The plan won't always go perfectly, but

things can only get so far off track in a week. If it's not working for either person, it can be tweaked.*

It's hard to change old habits. It wasn't easy for us to learn (and we did have to learn) to communicate our needs instead of just offering solutions or complaints. It wasn't easy to learn how to support each other's efforts instead of replacing them. Oh! Did I mention we both have anxiety?

Having a shared plan can be helpful for keeping anxiety in check, too. Before, my anxiety kept trying to make new plans, and he kept wandering off somewhere to anxiously ruminate on potential solutions for eight hours . . . at which point I'd already come up with a better plan! This, it turns out, was a large part of the cycle we'd fallen into.

We've now been together for four years. Our relationship is better than it's ever been, and it's a *much* healthier relationship than either of us have ever had. Do we actually meet every week? No. We both have ADHD. But we do check in

> If you make a plan—*together*—you can discuss what's yours and what's theirs and decide what to do, as adults and partners, not as someone who has to manage the other.

---

* Also, write it down. One or both of you have ADHD. Someone *will* forget. "Don't worry! I can remember!" you might think. No. No you can't. Especially when you're stressed or anxious. Bring a notepad. Have your calendar at the ready. Come with pens in tow. There's a link to the "What's the Plan?" worksheet I made for us on the online resources page (scan the QR code on page 432).

with each other when we miss these meetings, and we have honest, nonjudgmental conversations about how to get back on track.

Interestingly, when we plan together, it's actually less work for both of us because the work we're each committing to is more helpful and meaningful to the other. It's work that is working. It helps us feel more optimistic, more empowered, and more appreciated for our efforts, too.

How to Change the World

We never touch people so lightly that we do not leave a trace.

—PEGGY TABOR MILLIN

A CHANGE OF PLANS

I started my YouTube channel—and my journey toward self-empowerment—with the premise that I could "overcome" my ADHD struggles. I didn't think I wouldn't have ADHD anymore, exactly—but I thought I'd keep the parts about it that I liked, figure out which impairments were getting in my way and what to do about them, *and then* I would be successful. I would finally be the person I was *supposed* to be—someone who had friends I could remember to keep up with, a clean house, and perfectly managed finances.

There are all kinds of suggestions for ways we might "overcome" the obstacles we face, reach our potential, be this person we're "supposed" to be. "Just do ____," they suggest. "Buy this planner, set a timer, make a list." We can "life hack" our way over our hurdles and not struggle anymore. So, this was my plan. I was willing to accept that if I was different, I might have to do things different*ly.*

What I hadn't been willing to accept was the limits of this approach. Turns out, even doing things in a way that works for our brains and equipping ourselves with tools that make the world more accessible to us isn't a panacea. If anyone could have "overcome" their ADHD, it would have been me. I had the time, energy, and resources—I made it my entire *career.* Unfortunately, that is not how it works.

There is a limit to how many of these tools we can use at any given time. And none of them amount to a "get out of struggling free" card.

Almost every tool we need to use costs us something—time, money, energy. We have to find them, learn how to use them, adapt them so they work for us, defend our need to use them, reapply for them, pay for them, and—oh yeah!—find ways to remind ourselves to use them. And the time, energy, and other resources we spend on tools that others don't have to use is time, energy, and other resources we can't dedicate to going out with friends, enjoying our hobbies, or experiencing the other parts of life that we value.

And those with ADHD don't need just one tool. Flip back through this book, and you'll see hundreds of them. Dozens of these tools may be crucial for any given person with ADHD, and they may need to use them on a *daily basis,* just to get by.

> There is a limit to how many of these tools we can use at any given time.

Because ADHD is a chronic condition, these aren't tools we need temporarily, either. I collected these "simple" tools one at a time, but seeing them all laid out, it's clear managing ADHD is not a simple task. "Just do this. And this. Oh, and these fifty other things." What . . . *forever*?

At the end of my journey, my toolbox was overflowing! I understood how and when to use which tool, and why. I'd equipped myself with what I needed to be able to function reasonably well in a neurotypical world, and I was incredibly fortunate to be able to afford many that used to be out of my budget.

But no matter how many tools you have access to, and no matter how good you get at using them, it doesn't cancel out the struggle. Not entirely. Ask any wheelchair user.

No matter how great their wheelchair is, there are places that aren't wheelchair accessible. There are also biases, stigmas, misconceptions, and moral judgments placed on those who use them.

Tools are not enough. Our tools need to interface well with our environment. We need to be able to access them, use them. We need to feel safe enough to disclose that we need them. In an ideal world, we don't even have to think about them. The tools we need to function effectively would be built into our environments, available for anyone to use without having to explain why, in the same way we have built services such as electricity, sidewalks, and internet into our public infrastructure.

This is possible.

At the same time I was discovering the limits of my ability to "overcome" my ADHD and live the (very neurotypical) life I'd always imagined I would—just as I was realizing there is only so much a human can change about who they are and what they are capable of—I realized that the world could change. And the world could change fast.

> Systems are far more flexible and adaptable than people are.

The world is made of systems. And systems are far more flexible and adaptable than people are. They can be built, undone, re-arranged.*

As I learned more about systemic issues, I came across the social model of disability, which argues that disability isn't inherent to a person's medical condition—it results from living in a world that doesn't cater to their needs the way it does the needs of those who are non-disabled. Where the systems aren't built with them in mind.

Systemic issues were, I realized, the reason why I even needed half the tools I was using—and I was not alone.

Those with ADHD turn to extensive and elaborate systems to help them be consistently productive, manage their time, and keep their house relatively livable, not because it's fun but because we don't have a choice. We can't opt out of trying to manage our ADHD, no matter the cost, because the whole world is telling us we have to figure it out. We aren't good enough if we don't. We're not acceptable if we don't. We're going to get fired if we don't. The cost is even higher if we don't.

---

*   For example, how many of us were suddenly able to work from home during the Covid-19 pandemic?

I realized that it was far easier to create an environment that accounted for neurodiversity than it was for people to not be neurodiverse. So why weren't we starting there?

If I wanted to reach my potential and to help those in my community do the same, I realized I needed to help build a world in which we reasonably could. In which the entire cost of making a system accessible didn't fall to the person who was already struggling.

We're not only expected to provide our own "wheelchairs," we're also expected to build our own individual "ramps" when we clearly aren't the only ones who need them. This mental, emotional, and physical labor is costly, and not just to us, but to those we love—(see "How to Heart" on page 323)—and to society as a whole. Employers deal with high turnover rates and burnout. Our prisons are disproportionately populated with those who have untreated ADHD. Studies have shown ADHD costs society billions of dollars a year in the United States alone, while treatments and supports for ADHD are only a tiny *fraction* of that cost.

This plan isn't working out well for anybody. Expecting those with ADHD to "overcome" their ADHD is hurting us, it's hurting those we love, and it's hurting society as a whole.

We need a better plan. One that relies on change that is possible, sustainable, and good for everyone.

I decided to change course. I set out to change the world.

> It was far easier to create an environment that accounted for neurodiversity than it was for people to not be neurodiverse.

What I Learned

Like many people who set out to change the world, I discovered change was already in progress.

The world was already a far cry from what it had been when I started the channel. In the years since, it has become much more neurodivergent friendly.

I also learned how what I had already been doing had played a part in that change—and how the changes we needed were not only possible, but good for *everyone*.

INDIVIDUAL EMPOWERMENT CONTRIBUTES TO SYSTEMIC CHANGE

I didn't realize this at first, but I was trying to trade one simple solution in for another—we can't change the fact that we have ADHD, so it's the world that needs to change. (What can I say? Humans like simple solutions.)

There *is* a limit to how much we can reasonably empower ourselves in a world that isn't built with our needs in mind. But that didn't mean my journey of self-discovery had been a waste of time.

Learning about ADHD Helps Close the Self-Discrepancy Gap

Before I started learning about ADHD, there was an enormous gap between the person I was and the person I thought I "should" be.

The person others thought I "should" be. It was this gap—not the ADHD—that made me feel inadequate. It's what led me to accept the judgments others placed on me when they told me I wasn't living up to my potential, and run myself into the ground trying to. I see this over and over again in our community, too.

I learned there is a term for this gap—"self-discrepancy"—and it is responsible for a great deal of the emotional turmoil and negative mental health outcomes anyone can experience when who they want or feel they're supposed to be doesn't match up with the person they actually are. It's not unique to ADHD.

But self-discrepancy in those of us with ADHD can be a straight-up *chasm*. The expectations we and others have of us are often wildly inconsistent with our reality; sometimes we can perform on a very high level, and sometimes we struggle with "simple" tasks. Our self-discrepancy is also more profound because ADHD is an "unseen" disability that is not accommodated or even accounted for in most environments.

The tools and information I collected and shared didn't allow me to overcome my ADHD, but they did help me close this gap. What I learned allowed me to let go of unrealistic expectations and understand that, for example, the variability in my performance was normal given my ADHD. My "potential" wasn't a set point—it was a *range*. I now had tools that allowed me to perform at a higher level more consistently, and understood that some of my ADHD behaviors (like fidgeting) were actually healthy coping mechanisms for me. This changed how I interacted with the world, and how I advocated for myself. It helped me accomplish what I wanted to accomplish more often. I was able to adjust my understanding of who I "should" be to something closer to the person I already am, while still moving toward the version of myself I *wanted* to be.

Learning about ADHD has helped many in this community do the same.

It's changed how we interact with ourselves. How we speak to ourselves. How we allow ourselves to be spoken to. Our mental health (and self-esteem) is better for it. We're slowly beginning to let go of and refuse to listen to the internalized messages that we're not *enough*, not *doing enough*, not *good enough*, or not *"reaching our potential."* We're understanding and subsequently educating others that we already are who we're supposed to be.

Individual Empowerment Has Ripple Effects

I thought setting out to change the world meant starting over on a new journey. I thought that, once again, I would have no idea what I was doing and would need to learn from scratch. What I discovered was what I had been doing all these years, instead of pushing for systemic change, had *led to systemic change.*

Turns out, I was part of the system. The work I had done accepting and understanding my own ADHD, talking about it openly, and sharing what helped had had ripple effects that expanded far beyond my immediate reach. Maybe I had *intended* for people to watch my videos, learn about their brain, and create a toolbox of strategies for themselves, but I didn't realize how many in my community would go on to create their own ripples. I'd known about a few examples:

A Scottish MP sent me a video of himself at Scottish Parliament requesting action be taken regarding a dangerously misleading "documentary" about ADHD.

A middle school teacher told me about a weekly support group she'd started for her ADHD students. Some Brains who watched the channel became advocates and built their own platforms, even wrote their own books.

But when I started talking to my community about wanting to focus on systemic change, even more people reached out to share how they had started employee resource groups, worked with political leaders about initiatives that could benefit our community, or asked for accommodations that their boss was now providing to other ADHD employees.

It slowly dawned on me that for every ripple I learned about, there were many more I didn't. And all these ripples created others. They didn't stop at the person they were intended to reach. They *kept spreading*.

I looked back at the ripples that had reached me. I wasn't just influencing others. I had also been influenced by the work others had done and the work of those before them. The researchers whose papers I read probably didn't expect me—a random person with ADHD who accessed their paper through a nursing student I knew—to present their work on YouTube, but here we were. Professional and grassroots efforts have long been making ripples in the world of ADHD, long before How to ADHD or ADHD TikTok was a thing.

Other advocacy groups and organizations and communities have been making ripples, too. The LGBTQIA+ community laid the groundwork for how people can disclose important parts of their identity safely. Autistic advocates and disability advocates have been initiating discussions about neurodiversity, ableism, and cognitive accessibility. Researchers and mental health providers have been more open about their own conditions, and pushing for greater collaboration and more effective support of the communities their work is meant to benefit.

As I looked around me, I realized all of these ripples were converging and turning into *waves* of significant change: Open conversations about neurodiversity. Improved care for adult ADHD. Environments that account for neurodiversity and are more equitable for those who have it.

These changes don't apply to everyone—*yet*. As cognitive scientist Dr. Deirdre Kelly puts it: "The future already exists in pockets around the world. When we embrace this fact and learn to see the good, we can make decisions and take actions that bring us closer to who and where we need to be. Look for what's possible, and realize it."*

---

* In order to encourage more products and services to be designed in a way that's ADHD-friendly, and help those with ADHD connect with those that already are, we also collaborated with Dr. Deirdre Kelly to create a (free!) accessibility rubric. You can find a link to the online resources on page 432.

Phases of Acceptance

Unfortunately, even after so much progress, you may still have people in your lives—family, friends, co-workers, even healthcare providers—who view your ADHD struggles with skepticism. Maybe you still do so yourself!

Those working in the LGBTQIA+ community often refer to stages someone may go through when coming out. These rely significantly on the original model developed by Dr. Vivienne Cass in 1979. It has expanded to apply to those who are navigating their journey of acceptance for others. People navigate the stages at their own pace, often bouncing among them. These stages can also apply to acceptance of stigmatized disabilities. Below I adapted the acceptance model by Monica Luedke to demonstrate the stages I've seen in the acceptance of ADHD:

- **Anti:** Is in denial about the existence of ADHD, or of you having it. (*"It's just laziness and poor discipline!"*)

- **Acknowledgment:** Recognizes ADHD is real, but still has misconceptions about the condition. (*"You don't 'seem' ADHD." "ADHD doesn't have to limit you!" "Why should she get [insert accommodation here]? That gives her an unfair advantage!"*)

- **Acceptance:** Recognizes that ADHD brains work differently from most and that those differences create real impairments. Believes your experience of it. (*"Huh, okay, I didn't realize emotion dysregulation was an aspect of ADHD. That makes sense."*)

- **Affirming:** Asks you about your experience (and *listens to your responses*), encourages you to get the support you need, and offers accommodations. (*"Thank you for telling me that you have trouble prioritizing when multiple parts of a project are due at the same time. Would it help to have separate deadlines so you can focus on one at a time?"*)

- **Advocate:** Speaks up for those with ADHD, even when they're not in the room; offers support to those who have it without them having to ask. Speaks up for themselves and what they need to others. (*"Class, we are moving through this material pretty quickly, and some students might have trouble taking notes. I will be emailing everyone the lecture outline, and my TA has compiled notes you can refer to as well."*)

I imagine you can think of people in your lives who fit into many of these categories, for better and for worse. Someone at a different point in their journey doesn't mean they're a terrible person who will never support you. If you're like me, you can think of times when you were in a different stage than you are now.*

A journey involves motion, and even when people don't always move at the pace we would like them to, most can become more accepting and supportive with more information and experience. I will never forget someone who commented angrily on my videos about how ADHD was fake and none of what I was saying was true only to come back a few years later and apologize. They shared how they had been diagnosed with ADHD and hadn't been ready to accept it—and how my videos had helped them do so.

THE CHANGES WE'RE CREATING BENEFIT EVERYONE

Motivation matters, whether we're trying to convince ourselves or someone else to make a change. Thankfully, the changes we're creating have clear benefits for ADHD Brains, the Hearts who love and care for us, our employers, and society as a whole.

---

* We also may be at a different stage for ourselves than we are for others. (*"It's fine if others need accommodations, but not me! I should be able to do this!"*)

Open Conversations About Neurodiversity

As we talk, we normalize and improve our understanding of one another and the diversity within neurodiversity. And for the first time, many of us are starting to feel like we don't have to settle for *fitting in.* In more and more spaces, we can *belong.* Coping mechanisms and tools that work for us are becoming more normalized and expected. This allows us the ability to use strategies that help us effectively cope with our challenges, rather than hiding them. We're finding each other, offering each other support, and even inspiring those who didn't realize they had ADHD to seek diagnosis and treatment when what we're saying sounds *really familiar.* Without these conversations, many more would go years or even decades longer without the support they need to speak up, get support, and thrive. And as we speak up about our ADHD, our loved ones, employers, and friends can connect with each other about their role in supporting us, too.

Improved Care for ADHD Adults

Adults with ADHD have always existed but have gone untreated, undiagnosed, and undersupported. In fact, as of this writing, there are currently no guidelines for treating ADHD in adults. As a result, there is a wide discrepancy of care. This makes it difficult for those of us who don't know what to expect when we go to a new provider, and leaves providers guessing at the best treatment options. This is changing. There is now a professional consensus that people do not typically "grow out" of ADHD, and right now, the American Professional Society of ADHD and Related Disorders (APSARD) is working on guidelines for diagnosis and treatment. Not only is this good for those who treat (and need treatment for) ADHD, it's good for society as a whole. Better care for adults with ADHD can positively impact all kinds of societal change we'd like to see: better mental health outcomes, safer roads, decreases in obesity and addiction rates, and improved general life expectancy, to name a few.

Workplaces and Higher Education Offer More Supports for ADHD

Those with ADHD feel more fulfilled in their jobs and in school when they can perform at their best and contribute in a meaningful way. More and more colleges are offering programs to support those whose brains work differently and encouraging students to use the accommodations available to them. This not only improves our sense of belonging and our mental health but also graduation rates. Many employers have initiatives in place to hire for neurodiversity and are learning how to effectively support their neurodivergent employees and set them up for success once they're hired.

Accommodations in the workplace are often a bargain compared with the high cost of absenteeism, presenteeism, burnout, missed deadlines, and employee turnover. When effectively supported, many of us excel. ADHDers are often characterized as "doers," "go-getters," and "problem-solvers." We can be swift decision makers and pursue achievements without letting challenges or obstacles deter us. In many cases, the harder a problem is, the *more* we want to explore and solve it. When we can spend less time slogging through paperwork, we can spend more time inventing things, problem-solving, collaborating, and enthusiastically taking on projects that would be daunting to others.

Increased Accessibility for Everyone

In Canada, there's a push to have the tools we need in school readily available, not as accommodations we have to fight for and complete paperwork to access, but as standard features that are available to anyone who needs them. This is an example of universal design, which takes into account the diversity in human capabilities.

---

universal design (n.)
The design of a product, service, or environment to be as accessible as possible, to as many people as possible, without the need for adaptation or accommodations.

Universal design works well because what creates *accessibility* for one group often makes everyday life *easier* for everyone. Consider curb cutouts. They allow wheelchair users to navigate crosswalks, but they are also helpful for those who are traveling with luggage, delivering packages, or riding those dope little electric scooters.

With universal design, supports are seamlessly integrated into our environment. We don't have to go out of our way or call attention to our challenges to obtain them. It also offers end user choice. Just as we can decide whether or not to turn on our desk lamp to work, we can decide whether to use a standing desk or to sit. And *so can everyone else.**

ADHD-friendly spaces often have whiteboards, notepads, and other office supplies readily available. There are quiet spaces we can use to focus or step away from our work when we get overwhelmed. The tools we need are placed at the point of performance so we don't have to remember to bring them or to hunt them down. And there are meeting-free days when we can allow ourselves to get into flow without worrying our hyperfocus will get us in trouble.

These are all examples of how universal design creates greater accessibility for those with ADHD and other cognitive challenges, while offering helpful tools for everyone else. Everyone has limited working memory, loses and forgets stuff, and experiences moments when there's too much demand on their executive function. As Microsoft's guidebook on cognitive inclusivity explains, "For any task to be successful, motivation must equal or surpass cognitive load." By reducing cognitive load, we make the bar for success lower, which makes it easier for *everyone* to clear.

---

*   This also cuts down on judgment and jealousy from those who may misunderstand the accommodations we need as an "unfair" advantage as opposed to creating the accessibility we need due to the impairments we face.

THE TOOLBOX

There's a joke kicking around the ADHD community that I hear often: Those with ADHD could change the world—if we could just remember what we wanted and organize ourselves well enough to go after it.

It's endearing, and every time I hear it, I laugh along with everyone else. I truly appreciate how it conveys a loving acceptance of our limits.

I also call bullshit on the conclusion that we can't change the world just because we're too ADHD to do it.

We *are* changing the world. And we're doing it without "overcoming" our ADHD. We're doing it while being distractible, while running out of meds or facing barriers to accessing them, and while dealing with chronic pain. We're building a more ADHD-friendly world intermittently, imperfectly, sometimes unintentionally—but we're *doing* it.

How? By working with our brains, not against them—and by putting our efforts where we can create the most impact.

1. FIND YOUR FUEL

Those with ADHD tend to get discouraged more easily: "*I tried to change the world (in five minutes) but it didn't work.*" Change often happens over time. It starts by planting seeds that take time to grow. Or casting a stone and seeing where the ripples go. We need to stock up on fuel for what can sometimes be a long and frustrating ride.

- **Keep an "inspiration for a rainy day" file.** When I started posting videos, I read every comment, and saved the ones that made me feel appreciated or showed me I was making a difference. Rereading them on days when I was exhausted or discouraged kept me going. Making an inspiration or feel-good file can help you stay positive as well as tap into your emotional "why" when you (inevitably) forget why you thought this was a good idea.

- **Be the person you needed.** Many advocates doing incredible work are able to sustain it because we're creating what we needed and didn't have. If you create the kind of support you needed, chances are it will benefit others, too—and you'll be able to tap into the memory of how important it was for you.

- **Spend some time ideating.** Our brains excel at being creative, generating new ideas, and thinking outside the box. Dream up the future you'd like to help build. What does it look like? Who does it serve? How so? What is happening in other pockets of the world, and what might make sense to implement in ours?

Conserve Your Fuel, Too

Changing the world doesn't mean trying to change the world in all the ways it needs to change. Many people in our community are exhausted just trying to keep their heads above water. So our efforts are better spent in areas we can have the most impact. Everyone has stuff they can control, stuff they can influence, and stuff outside their sphere of influence, places where only the ripples can reach. As much as possible, put your energy into what's within your sphere of influence. And take breaks. This is a marathon, not a sprint.

 Nik K., 40s, New York

"My secret weapon is crowdsourcing. I understand myself better through others who are like-minded and find their perspective helps me appreciate who I am. Feeling a sense of community and connection can break away stigmas and redefine what were once considered cultural norms."

Emmanuel A., 30s, Georgia

"Support groups for neurodivergents (e.g., ADDA) did a lot to help me understand myself and my ADHD. It helped bridge the gaps of loneliness and isolation, helping me to understand the power of having representation and telling my story."

 Chris L., 37, Washington

"I wrote Soft Focuses, a game to help non-neurodivergent people better understand what those of us with ADHD experience on a daily basis. A number of people have told me how much it has helped their loved ones understand them better. It has even helped some people realize they have ADHD. It's a very niche game, but I'm really proud of it and glad to have helped others with it."

2. FOCUS ON WHAT YOU WANT, NOT WHAT YOU DON'T WANT

When J2, our operations director, was learning how to ride a motorcycle, she received this advice: Don't look where you *don't* want to go. You'll crash. Same with horseback riding, according to our community manager, Harley. There is robust research to support the same is true when pushing for change. Looking where you want to go, and encouraging people to go there, is much more effective than trying to correct people on what you don't want.

- **Set constructive goals.** Without a positive goal to work toward, both small and big picture, it's easy to fall into the trap of trying to avoid negative outcomes, which can lead us to avoid taking the action that would lead to a positive one. You can't make a basket if you're so afraid of missing the hoop you never shoot the ball. (If you keep forgetting your goals, that's ADHD normal. Flip back to "How to Remember Stuff," page 187.)

- **Frame requests in the positive.** People are generally more willing (and able!) to do something than to stop doing something. And most requests to *stop* doing something negative can actually be *framed* in the positive. For example, if you want someone to stop being a judgmental jerk to the new ADHDer at the office, instead ask them to use welcoming and encouraging language. This framing gets better results because it helps them understand what successfully meeting your request looks like.

- **Respond to the people who add to the conversation.** I learned early on in my YouTube career that your attention is like a spotlight. Shine a light on what you want seen. Ignore, delete, or block comments that don't move a conversation forward (or respectfully contribute a different perspective!) so you can focus on responding to and signal boosting those that do. In other words, don't feed the trolls.

- **Vote.** You can vote by casting a ballot in an election, and you can also vote with your dollars. Support ADHD-friendly initiatives, products, and services as well as businesses that prioritize mental health or are taking steps to do so. You can even vote with your attention by curating what you listen to, what you share, and what you repeat.

 Alexis M., 30, Oregon

"My favorite way to help is on a small scale: I'm the oldest diagnosed ADHDer in certain branches of my family tree. As such, I can advocate for the younger ones, who are less eloquent and/or less respected. Sometimes I'm asked for advice (which I give with disclaimers and encouragement to listen to the kids). Sometimes I can give context for a frustrating situation. Sometimes I help avert a meltdown by identifying and addressing a need that the other adults may be too dysregulated and/or naively neurotypical to address themselves.

I know these things bring peace in the moment. I think they contribute to an understanding family culture. And I hope they help counter the negativity I know these kids will experience as they grow."

Jacob K., 27, Australia

"Earlier in life, I was so adamant to prove what I could do and what I was capable of. Now that I'm on the other side, I want people to understand that a lot of what I achieved was done at the expense of my own health, and that a need for accommodation doesn't equate to a lack of value.

"Going forward, I want to use my achievements as leverage to effect change: 'Oh, you like what I can do now? Well, imagine how much more I could achieve if I didn't have one hand tied behind my back.' If nothing else, I want to fight for people, no matter their needs, to be able to live up to their full potential."

3. JOIN FORCES WITH THE PEOPLE DOING THE WORK

Someone may already be working toward the change you're hoping to see in the world. Joining forces with them makes the work of advocates and organizations more efficient because they don't have to compete for the same resources or start their advocacy work from scratch. It also helps you see where there might be gaps and how you can fill them with your own efforts. There are also many ways you can support the work that is already underway:

- **Donate or fundraise.** This book would not exist if it weren't for my Patreon Brains. Their donations have allowed me to quit my day job to focus on How to ADHD full-time, hire a team, and take time away to write this book. Many organizations with which I've spoken stress that the best way to support a cause is to provide them with the resources they're requesting—money, supplies, volunteers—and let them take it from there.

- **Signal boost.** Commenting, sharing, reposting, and sharing a message with people an organization or advocate wouldn't otherwise reach is another way to make serious ripples. It can be especially helpful to signal boost to others in the position to make change, such as your employer, school board, or local representative.

- **Share resources.** Don't underestimate the power of sharing what you know! You might connect someone with information that they in turn can use to inform and improve their own work. When doing so, it can be helpful to vet your info. In the "Support Organizations" section (page 429), I include a bonus tool of how to do that.

- **Collaborate.** In the ADHD and neurodiversity advocacy circles to which I belong, collaboration is welcomed and encouraged. While we tackle ADHD from different angles and using different mediums—and we may not always agree on everything—we're all working toward the same goal: a better life for those who have it.

Todd H., 44, Australia

"I started a support group at work of just five people, which over eighteen months grew to thirty-five. We share knowledge, advice, and experiences of all things including diagnosis and treatment paths."

Claudia S., 32, Mexico

"I've had the opportunity to organize a couple of panels for PAX conventions, where we talk about intersectionality in video games and TTRPGs [tabletop role-playing games]. It's been great for me and my fellow panelists, and I think we had the good luck of talking in front of open-minded audiences."

John Y., 75, Texas

"I work with teachers and counselors to help create more ADHD-friendly policies and spaces in our schools. I have thirty-five years of classroom experience and fifteen years as a journalist, and I now understand how to advocate for ADHD diversities. So I write novels with ADHD characters, I write op-eds, I mentor reading programs and students in need or with neurodiverse conditions."

4. SHARE YOUR STORY

According to research on reducing stigma about mental health, telling stories is one of the most impactful ways to lay the groundwork for change. Humans don't respond to data or how right you are. They respond to emotion—to how something makes them *feel*. By speaking to even one person about your ADHD, or shining a light on one small positive action toward an ADHD-accessible world, you may be creating ripples that will lead to change in someone you will never meet and in systems you will never even see.

 Joseph, 22, Ohio

"One of the best decisions I ever made was to come out as neurodivergent. I feel so much more like myself, and I've been able to connect with other people who share my experiences and even speak publicly about neurodivergence. Being told that my words make a difference is why I continue to write and speak publicly about neurodivergence."

 Julia F., 39, California

"I'm unapologetically open about my AuDHD in both my personal and professional life. When the Adderall shortage hit me, I was up front with my boss and team. I speak in open public work channels. I'm raising my daughter to be proud of how her brain works, to never be ashamed."

Tawny F., 43, Colorado

"I create art that touches on mental health and 'societal divergence' as an opening to have deeper conversations on what it means to be human. I ask the question, 'Who made the (socially acceptable) rules this way, why? What if we chose not to follow them?' I believe it has helped the Divergents feel less alone, with the added benefit of having conversations with Typicals that may expand their understanding of others as well as themselves."

 Alanna G., 30, Pennsylvania

"Whenever I require an accommodation, I try to openly state it's for ADHD, even when it's not necessary, to help let people know that this diagnosis requires accommodations in adulthood."

 Jenn R., 32, USA

"As difficult as it is, I disclose whenever I feel safe enough. When people see AuDHD in someone they interact with every day (in person or online), they see it doesn't make them a monster. It's not just extremes or stereotypes. There is power in demystifying 'other.' By existing as authentically as I can and being open and honest about my struggles and triumphs, I hopefully help return a human element to the cold and clinical. Different is not less."

PERSPECTIVE

As you set out to change the world, know that you aren't approaching it with the same perspective as someone else. People may be convinced change is impossible, want a different kind of change, want change to happen faster, or think things are fine as they are. There are many reasons why you may perceive the world differently.

One is that brains are just glitchy. We see the world skewed *all of the time*. I learned this from *The Skeptic's Guide to the Universe*, but I was reminded of it by one of the quotes I collected while writing this book. Brian, a grief counselor living in Washington, described how he lost a finger in an accident:

> After I lost my finger, my brain couldn't accept that it was missing, so it assumed there was something wrong with the world. When I would rest my hand on a table, my brain perceived that there was a hole in the table where my finger should be, rather than recognizing that there was no finger anymore. It took at least half a year before my brain started to accept that the world wasn't broken or missing, part of me was.

Our view of the world comes in through our senses. Our brain encodes this information by comparing it to what we already know, and fills in any gaps. When the information coming in makes sense to us and fits with our current perspective, we're able to incorporate it. When it threatens our self-esteem and self-concept, however, we often reject it. This is important to understand, because what it means is this: the way people change their minds isn't by replacing what they know with what we are telling them. It's by incorporating it, when they can, into their existing perspective.

Perspective shifts can't be forced. If you're sharing information with someone that contradicts what they currently believe, it can take time for their perspective to shift—if it happens at all. This is the case even if the information is true and you can show them evidence that it's true. Sometimes, people build fortresses around their perspectives and find evidence to reinforce them so that no one can kick them over.

What can make it easier for someone to see what we see is connection. In an Italian poem called "Quattro Occhi," the poet describes how when you're in love, you get to see the world through four eyes instead of two.

I adore this poem because it captures some of the main reasons why loving someone can be life-changing. We get to see ourselves through the perspective of someone who thinks we're beautiful, or brilliant, or brave. Who can see our strengths, even when we may only see our struggles. And we get to experience the rest of the world through their perspective, too. The danger here, of course, is that if we trust others more than we trust ourselves, we can still end up experiencing the world through only two eyes—theirs.*

The same can occur if you spend a lot of time in a space where

---

*   This can be especially common with an abusive relationship in which you are isolated, manipulated, or experiencing gaslighting (talked out of your own perspective and into one that benefits them to the point that you feel like you're losing your mind).

everyone hears and repeats the same perspective. This is what happens for too many of us with ADHD. We don't have the chance to view the world through our own two eyes because, for most of our lives, we've experienced and internalized the neurotypical perspective on how we should exist in the world.

Back when I was trying to be an actress, I had all of these people—agents, managers, casting directors—telling me how they saw me and what they thought I needed to change in order to be acceptable in their world. When someone in the industry finally told me that it was okay to take up space as the shape that I am, I was able to begin to shift my perspective of who I was and who I had to be. In turn, I've been able to do that for others. How I have changed the world has not been through demanding that it change, but by sharing my perspective and listening to the perspectives of others. By learning to see the world through four eyes instead of two.

Opening our minds to other perspectives when we feel safe enough to do so exposes us to new ideas and gives us new choices. It can help us change the world. We can share what we each know with one another, which gives us access to new information and new tools. Plus, people can hear our perspective more clearly when we talk *with* them and try to understand theirs. What this means, though, is you can't just change the world; you also have to be ready to *be* changed. Having these conversations can expand your perspective, but it can sometimes threaten, even topple it. My own perspective has shifted drastically *many* times in the process of listening to and learning from this community, research, other advocates, my team, and random strangers on the internet.

While the shifts in our own perspective that may come from these conversations can be disorienting, I'm happy to report that they can also be empowering. The more we share perspectives, the more complete ours becomes. It becomes easier to connect with others and hear their perspectives without losing our own. The new perspectives become less threatening to the worldview we are constructing, and our vision of the better world we work for becomes clearer and more achievable.

I'll leave you with a final perspective, one Deirdre shared with me: If you want to change the world, you can. Now. As you are. If you want a world that is more accepting and understanding, accept and understand someone. And the world will already be a more accepting and understanding place. It's inevitable, because you are part of the system. We all are.

Stories and Endings

Two roads diverged in a yellow wood,
And sorry I could not travel both
And be one traveler, long I stood
And looked down one as far as I could
to where it bent in the undergrowth . . .

—ROBERT FROST, "THE ROAD NOT TAKEN"*

BUT AND THEREFORE

Our lives are not stories on a page.

We don't get to determine what comes next or decide what the other characters will do.

---

* I recently discovered I missed the most beautiful thing about this poem. (So do most people, which is why it's often mistakenly titled as "The Road Less Taken.") *The path the narrator took wasn't the road less taken.* As he points out earlier in the poem, both paths were worn the same. But now that he's chosen one, he knows he'll someday tell the story of how he chose which road to take and that he'll tell it in a way that gives *meaning* to his choice: "I took the one less traveled by, / And that has made all the difference."

Our lives are, nonetheless, full of story—the stories we tell our-selves, the narratives we are trying to play out, the pages from the past we're trying to rewrite.

And just as in movies and books, the story paths in our lives aren't linear. It's not "we do this, and then this, and then we do this and this and this." Like all good stories, we are faced with obstacles and choices. A "but" and a "therefore."

Our main character does *this*.

But . . . *this* happens!

Therefore . . . they make a new choice.

Whether the obstacle they faced was internal or external, this is a *choice point* for our hero: they can attempt to continue the way they were going, or they can change direction.

Their choices may be limited; they may not have any ideal choices; they may not even have all the information they need to make the choice that seems obvious to those witnessing the story unfold; but they do *have* a choice. And they make that choice.

As far as my own story goes, spending the last seven years learning how my brain worked has helped me recognize more of these choice points. It helped me understand the "buts"—the invisible obstacles I keep running into—and gave me more effective options to choose from.

I went from this:

I need to fill out this form.

But . . . I keep getting frustrated and overwhelmed.

Therefore...I'll avoid it and play video games while feeling like a terrible human who is incapable of adulting.

To this:

I need to fill out this form.

But...I keep getting frustrated and overwhelmed.

Therefore...oh, this might be a working memory issue. I need to work one step at a time, have the instructions pulled up for reference, or maybe use an active body double who can read them to me as I fill this thing out.

I learned to let go of how I thought my efforts "should" go and make choices based on how they *did*. I made my invisible obstacles visible, which made it *possible* to navigate around them—sometimes. I know what to do when I still run into them. They slow me down, but they no longer stop me.

Because I learned how my brain works, I went from not respecting myself because of my failures to respecting the challenges contributing to them. And this, ultimately, helped me better respect myself.

> I learned to let go of how I thought my efforts "should" go and make choices based on how they *did*.

As with the hero in the hero's journey, or the traveler in "The Road Not Taken," our power doesn't lie in deciding how the story goes. Or even in predicting how it will.

Our power lies in evaluating information as it comes in—and in making new choices.*

Now, I'm learning to give myself choice, not just with how I'm navigating an obstacle on my path, but what path I'm even on.

There have been lots of warning signs that indicate a path isn't working out for me or going to get me where I'm trying to go. But no matter how many warning signs I pass, I still sometimes get stuck on following it, especially now that I have so many options for navigating the obstacles along the way. In a way, I'm still *trying harder*—just with more ADHD-friendly options in my toolbox.

If I want true empowerment, it's not enough to have choice in how I navigate the obstacles on my path.

I need choice as to what paths I follow, too. I need choice in whether to continue *down* them. With the support of a grief and loss counselor, I'm learning to give myself that choice.†

I HAD NO CHOICE (BUT TO GIVE MYSELF CHOICE)

Finishing this book represents, for me, the end of a seven-year journey, one where I put much of my life on pause so I could figure out

---

*   That choice can involve an action, or the meaning we assign to our experiences. As Robert Frost perhaps hinted at in his poem, how we tell our stories is a choice we can make long after our path-choosing days are behind us.

†   As he gently points out to me, we never have complete choice. But learning to unattach from achieving or avoiding a specific outcome gives us greater access to the choices we do have.

how to work with my brain more effectively. At the beginning of my journey, I set out to learn to work with my brain, not against it, and put everything I learned somewhere I could find it again. Then, once I'd accomplished that, I could go back to my life, only this time "successful."*

I planned my journey the same way most people would plan to go to the store for the ingredients they needed to make dinner. *I'll just run out real quick, be back soon. Can you pause the show?*

It quickly became clear this was a much more complicated "how to work with my brain" recipe than I'd expected, with a lot of neuro-spiciness involved.

And until I reached the very end of the path, I didn't totally believe I could get to this point. I kept feeling that someone might realize I shouldn't be here and kick me out of the store. *What's a college dropout doing explaining research on the internet? Giving a TEDx Talk? Writing a book?*

Also, I had never in my life finished a long-term project before, no matter how often people told me I had the "potential" to do it.

I was worried I'd fail, or get bored, or burn out. Sometimes, I did.

But I made it. I basically put myself through neurodiversity university. I turned in the manuscript for this book. I reached the end of this path. And the day I did, I realized . . . I could finally go back to that life.

Excited, I scanned through the goals I'd put on pause:

---

*   Don't worry, Brains. I'm not going anywhere.

- Building the beautiful backyard I was so close to finishing for my mom. It had an optimistically large firepit area that I could use to entertain new friends.

- Planting the organic vegetable garden that was going to be the finishing touch to that backyard.

- Being better about memorizing my lines *before* my acting class so I didn't have to miss half the class trying to remember what they were.

- Spending time with friends without panicking about what I was behind on. Feeling more confident about attending the recurring pool parties at my co-worker's building once I understood how to navigate social situations.

- Impressing my agent and casting directors and finally earning the leading roles my team said I had the potential to book so I could make my mom's life easier and make up for the ways in which I had made it so hard.

A lot of those goals didn't make sense anymore. So much had changed since I set out on this journey.

My mom had died. I had processed that much. It was heartbreaking, the realization that there was nothing I could do to make her life easier anymore when that's why I'd so badly wanted to succeed, and why I went on this journey in the first place. That loss of meaning was one of the main factors that led to the experience I shared at the beginning of "How to Feel," page 216.

I knew we'd sold that house. And with it, the backyard. The place I live now doesn't have one.

I'd quit my job waiting tables; there were no co-workers' pool parties to attend. I live in Seattle now, and I don't know many people here yet. Also, we don't really have pools.

I'd decided I liked what I do now more than acting, so there was no point in going back to class. Besides, *it was a thousand miles away*.

I could go back to my life, *except* . . .

It's been *seven years*. I have nothing of that life left to go back to.

This realization hit me hard.

I'd been so attached to how my journey was "supposed" to end that I hadn't noticed it no longer could.

Obviously, I knew I had a new career, lived in a new city, and had a new partner, and I loved these life developments. I'd known I was giving up *some* of the life I thought I'd be going back to, but all of it? I hadn't chosen that. Would I have?

Would I have chosen to keep going on this path if I had recognized my ability to make a different choice as new information came in? Would I have decided that I'd made enough progress on this path before the life I had known had all fallen away? Would I have resumed some parts of my life if I hadn't been so stuck on finishing what I'd set out to do? If I'd been mindful enough to notice the last bits of my past ambitions slowly disappearing while I was trying to become good enough to deserve them?

Maybe more importantly, was I okay with how this journey

turned out? Was I okay with the fact that I didn't have the chance to return to the life I'd wanted to live? That I was building out my life from the one I'd created along the way?

It is another truth in stories that what a character sets out in search of at the beginning of a story is not what they get in the end. They might not wind up with the thing that is so important and powerfully motivating that they walk through fire and slay dragons to attain it. Yet we still have happy endings. Why?

By the end of their journey, they realize: what they set out to pursue isn't what they actually needed.

I understand now that the same was true for me.

When I set out on this journey to learn about my brain, what I thought I needed were the tools and understanding to overcome my ADHD struggles and become the person I was "supposed" to be. If I could use these tools to navigate around my invisible obstacles, I reasoned, I could finally be happy, live a fulfilling life, and care for the people I love.

What I actually needed was to let go. I needed to let go of rigid expectations of who I was "supposed" to be in order to be happy—because these rigid expectations were a large source of my unhappiness. I needed to let go of the idea that I had to reach a certain level of functionality before I could enjoy my life and care for the people I love.

What I truly had to "overcome" was that biased *perspective,* so I could enjoy my life and care for the people I love in the ways I already could. I needed to accept who I am, where I am, and what I had to give, and find joy and satisfaction in myself and my journey "as is." Even as I'm pursuing "more." Even as I'm trying to grow.

If my sense of worth hinged on being someone I'm not, or somewhere I'm not, I might spend my whole life chasing those things before I allow myself to actually *live*. I might (and *did*) lose the life I wanted. Even as I tried to make it to the starting line of being "good/capable enough" to live it.

I wish someone had told me I didn't need to be good at *everything* to be valuable. That I could be considered a good friend even though I forget to text back, or run a successful business without being able to successfully manage the contents of my car. If anyone told me I was acceptable *as is,* ADHD and all, I forgot, or I couldn't hear it through the noise of the whole world telling me otherwise.

So I'm saying it to you, *writing it down* for you:

You already are the person you're supposed to be. You're *already reaching* the range of potential you have with the tools and skills and resources available to you. That range may change over time, but this is how our brains work.

We'll work better on some days than others and our level of focus will depend on how engaging a task is. We'll get distracted. We'll need things written down so we don't have to hold so much in our head. We'll lose track of time and underestimate how long things will take. We'll

> I needed to let go of the idea that I had to reach a certain level of functionality before I could enjoy my life and care for the people I love.

be impressively good at some things and epically bad at others. We'll have a lot to give, and have trouble consistently giving it. And we are acceptable humans *as is,* not once we stop having ADHD. You do not need to be fixed because you are not a broken version of normal.

Your brain works differently. And the goal *can't be to fix that.* It needs to be, *given* that, what do we do?

What do we want to try? What do we want to give?

What's worth doing?

What *do* I want to do and give? It's kind of cool that now I get to choose.

Because I'm not going back to the life I was "supposed" to live, I can live a life more in line with my values, not with the values I thought I "should" have. I can get curious about what my values are and what a life in line with them looks like. I like that I'm getting to start from a relatively blank slate. And yet. It would have been nice to have *chosen* that.

It took my brain just a couple of days to come up with a new hero's journey. Once again, I'm setting out with a vision that I believe is worth walking through fire and battling dragons to achieve: I want to be a good leader for my team, and make space on my platform for voices besides mine. The journey I'm personally on is no longer about self-improvement—but personal *fulfillment.* (Dedicating seven years to self-improvement was quite long enough.)

Now that I understand how my brain works, I've chosen a new path to take: to drop the compared-to-neurotypical stencil away from myself and start building, toolbox in hand, a life that's based on the shape that I am. I want to learn not just how to do things, but what's *worth* doing. To answer a new question—not "How do we reach our potential?" but "How do we live a fulfilling life as the person we already are?"

> I want to learn not just how to do things, but what's *worth* doing.

This time around, though, I'm also installing a few checkpoints. I'm using what I learned about cued recall to help myself remember: I get to choose my paths. Every once in a while, I can look around to make sure that this is still the one I want. And even though imagining the future motivates me, I'm trying to let go, a bit, of my expectations for how I think it will or should turn out because I understand now that it may not go that way.

I've also learned not to put my whole life and personal fulfillment on hold until I reach a certain outcome.

Many times in my life, I've done this. In seven-year journeys and in "I need to finish this project first" sprints.

But if there's anything I've learned, it's that there are no guarantees. I won't always "have time after." The results I'm hoping to achieve won't always even be possible. I'm never going to be someone who doesn't have ADHD.

Therefore, leading a life in line with my values can start now. It could have started then. Sure, I have limits, but as fellow YouTuber and ADHDer Hannah Hart told me, creativity loves limits.

> You already are
> the person you're
> supposed to be.

Hey, look. A starting line. Turns out, we can draw our own.

You don't have to be who or where you want to be to begin enjoying yourself, accepting yourself, respecting yourself, *caring* for yourself. To begin leading a life in line with your values. And you don't have to be capable of *all of the things* to be valuable. That's a lie we were taught.

You already are the person you're supposed to be. And you, as you are, have plenty to give.

It doesn't mean you can't grow or that you can't pursue goals. But it does mean you don't have to earn the right to enjoy your life, care for yourself, contribute your talents, or take breaks, or do whatever else you've put on hold. You can do all that now. Or just a little part of it. Even if it's a smaller part than you'd like.

I hope what you've found in this book is not just information, but the ability to recognize more of the choice points in your own story.

Wherever you are along your journey, I hope you can put this book down (hopefully somewhere you can find it again!) and go back to a life that is better for us having traveled together for however many pages you made it through. I hope you can let go, a little, of the outcome you're counting on. Of the expectations you've internalized. I hope you can keep making progress in the areas that are important to you while you learn and grow.

And if you need more support, well, you know where you can find How to ADHD. Seven years ago, I decided to put what I learned in a place that couldn't be lost. Turns out, I put my brain and heart there, too.

Whether you found us through a YouTube channel, a TEDx Talk, or connected with us for the first time here on these pages, know that you are never alone. You belong. There's an entire community of us that exists all across the globe. I hope, as we walk our many paths, our brains and hearts keep finding one another.

When I started out, I wasn't really clear on what I wanted; I was trying to do too many things at once, and the way I was navigating the obstacles I faced didn't really make sense. The most powerful tool I got out of my journey was this one: the ability to get clear on what it was I was trying to accomplish and to navigate obstacles as they came up in a way that helped me toward that goal. The "Navigating Obstacles" worksheet on page 419 is designed to help you do the same.

Wait, One More Thing!!!

This is important, I swear.

—ME, BECAUSE I HAVE ADHD AND CAN'T TELL ANY
STORY IN ORDER EVER WITHOUT LEAVING SOMETHING
IMPORTANT OUT, INCLUDING, APPARENTLY, MINE

LEAN INTO YOUR STRENGTHS

As I was finishing this book, I decided to get in touch with Dr. Ned
Hallowell. In his work as a psychiatrist, author, and ADHD advocate,
he champions the strengths that come with ADHD. He's always been
so supportive of me and the work that I do, and I was afraid he'd hate
what I'd written because so much of my journey involved learning
about my impairments. (I might have Hallowell's heart, but I have
Barkley's research.)

When it came to navigating the world and accomplishing
goals that were meaningful to me, acceptance, reassurances, and

platitudes about how my ADHD made me special hadn't helped me at all. What *had* was understanding how my brain worked on an empirical and scientific level. This knowledge gave me the ability to work with it effectively.

I'd found it empowering and validating to learn about my deficits and impairments in bits at a time, but now I had collected all this information in one place. I was worried that the picture of ADHD I painted might be too negative. Would the alternate universe version of me who stumbled across this book find it empowering? Or would seeing all of the tools and strategies we needed to function in the world feel overwhelming and discouraging? Even hopeless?

I knew there *were* positives to having ADHD; I saw them in my community and even in myself. I just didn't know how to highlight them in a book that described the journey I had taken to learn about the impairments. I couldn't say ADHD was a gift, as he so often does, when it's clear from the research it's *not*; at least, not entirely. Even our "superpowers," like hyperfocus, stem from difficulty regulating our attention, and that's not always fun. The struggle is *real*.

I asked Dr. Hallowell if he had any research on the strengths, so I could include it. "Research doesn't really focus on that," he said. "But people mis- quote me. I don't say ADHD is a gift; it's a *potential* gift. It's also a potential disaster. But tell them the stories. Tell them about the stories of those who leaned into their strengths."

He launched into a long list of people

I knew there were positives to having ADHD; I saw them in my community and even in myself.

who wielded their strengths to their advantage. I nodded, took notes. "I mean, look at you!" he observed. "Look at all you accomplished by leaning into your strengths!"

"I did?"

I blinked.

"We often don't metabolize our strengths," he explained. "But we need to." This is *why* he points them out. Because otherwise, we don't see them. A brilliant patient of his hadn't realized she was smart, because she so often felt like she wasn't. Dav Pilkey, the author of the *Captain Underpants* series, had been disciplined harshly for being disruptive in class and making the other students laugh. But he leaned into that *strength,* and because of that, found success; now he makes a lot of people laugh.

I thought back to how my journey began. Before I understood anything about my ADHD, before I knew how to recognize the obstacles, before I had tools, before I had a team, before I had any of the language I'd learned over the last seven years.

What had I done?

What I could, with the tools, traits, values, and skills I already had. Many of which I'd never considered valuable.

I impulsively started a YouTube channel without thinking through other options; it didn't occur to me that this was an outside-the-box idea. I just knew I wouldn't lose YouTube.

I like helping others, so I decided to make those videos public and enthusiastically engaged with this community without considering the potential consequences of talking openly about my ADHD challenges on the internet for anyone to see. My "naive" willingness to trust people helped me be authentic and open and accept help from others.

My insatiable curiosity that led me to spend so much time googling stuff that I was fired from my position as a volunteer receptionist at a yoga studio served me well as I devoured information about ADHD.

When I struggled to figure out how to edit my videos, because I went on so many tangents and kept forgetting what I was saying, I didn't try to get better at organizing my thoughts in real time. I started writing scripts.*

Which, of course, became its own challenge. I have trouble memorizing lines. Well—I love going to Staples! And showing up unprepared to all those acting classes had helped me get really good at cold reading. I bought a poster board, printed out the script in thirty-point font, read each line, and then spoke them aloud to the camera. The reason my videos punch in and out so much is to hide the cuts between each line—which ended up making them more engaging for the community, too.

The whole time, my passion—my *obsession* over something I cared about—was fueling me. As soon as I figured out how to navigate one challenge, another popped up, but because there were no instructions to follow, I did things in ways that seemed easier to me.

---

* I also got an editor. When I couldn't afford to hire one yet, I bartered; turns out, I *like* doing *other* people's laundry.

Intuitively, I steered away from my areas of weakness—and into my strengths—which were often the flip side of my challenges. I hyper-focused a *lot*.

> With the help of my Patreon Brains, we compiled a Bingo board of strengths that those with ADHD often have (and are valued for!) on page 421. No one has all of them, but most of us have more than a few, and they're often related to our ADHD.

I also had strengths that weren't related to my challenges.

My gifted-kid level of reading comprehension came in handy when I tried to make sense out of research papers I had not been trained to read.

I had translatable skills from my acting career: how to sit (rela-tively) still, allow myself to be vulnerable, cope with critical feed-back, and collaborate with other creatives.

As a server, I had a flexible schedule, and I could get someone to cover for me when I was behind and needed to write; I also had a notepad with me constantly while I worked, and often scribbled new ideas down.

I used to be frustrated by my inability to describe simple things in beautiful and complex ways like poets can; I could only manage to describe even the most complex ideas in simple words. Turns out, this is a talent that's useful in science communication. It's a *strength*

to be able to boil down complex information into words anyone can understand without losing too much of the nuance.

I began realizing many of my past successes happened when I'd been allowed to lean into my strengths.

The pizzas I'd earned by reading books (thanks, BookIt!). The little tickets I'd drawn in CorelDRAW. Getting that A in statistics class because my professor was cool with me taking it with my friend-I-wanted-to-impress, even though I hadn't registered for it yet. The papers I'd written beautifully because I was able to choose a topic I was excited about. I was amazing at waiting tables, and that benefited the restaurant that was more forgiving about me showing up four minutes late. I got us many great reviews (and glowing praise calls to corporate!).

I remembered something I'd learned years into my YouTube career, when I'd been confused about how I'd become successful even as I still struggled so much with so many things. When I felt guilty about hiring a housekeeper instead of trying to be better at cleaning, I'd remind myself of this fact:

The most successful people aren't the ones who get good at what they're bad at; they're the ones who lean into their strengths.

It's something we already and instinctively do, when we're given the chance. We can do it not just in terms of learning how to do things that are hard for us, but in doing more of what we're already good at—and leveling up.

We have innate strengths, skills, talents, and aptitudes that others simply *don't*—and in combinations that you can't find anywhere else. Because our brains work differently, we both *already have* and develop strengths others don't. We think to *use* our skills and strengths in ways others don't. Understanding this helped me understand why, despite everything I've learned about how impairing ADHD can be, I still *like* being neurodivergent. As the world is beginning to acknowledge, *interesting things happen in the margins.* Because of my neurodivergence, I've accomplished things others can't, or maybe wouldn't even think to try. And I did that by leaning into my strengths.

This isn't to say we have to be exceptional or do amazing things to "make up for" the fact that we have ADHD. This belief stems from internalized ableism, same as the belief that we "should be" neurotypical. It can be just as harmful, or worse, because now we're expected to meet all the same standards and *outperform,* too.

Like Dr. Hallowell, I want to highlight our strengths because, otherwise, we might live our whole lives focused on what we're not good at. We might not understand that we have strengths at all, because they're not where society expects them to be and because they often exist on the flip side of the traits we've been told are just "bad." We all need to get curious about what our different strengths are. And to learn how to lean on each other effectively, *interdependently,* for strengths we ourselves do not have. This is especially essential for those whose strengths and weaknesses are both far from average. Who exist in the margins.

To use another D&D metaphor, you don't put a mage on the front lines, or expect them to battle a dragon single-handedly. They'll die. You put together a party of people with different skills and strengths so that everyone can focus on doing what they excel at. No one can be good at all the things. This is why you *never split the party.*

Sometimes we need to level up stats that hold us back, but it doesn't make sense to do that at the expense of what we're already good at.

I'm glad I didn't know this when I started out, because I definitely wouldn't have spent seven years focused on "overcoming" my challenges. And I am glad I learned all the tools I shared in this book. We can't totally opt out of the stuff we struggle with. Some of these things are important for living a fulfilling life. Like sleep. Or making friends. Or knowing (roughly) how time works. It's nice to have tools for when I have to do things that aren't ADHD-friendly, like the two-year-long project of publishing a book. I needed to use *many* of these tools in the process. Having tools and understanding how and when to use them can make it easier to apply our strengths in unique and world-changing ways.

But I want alternate universe me and you, the reader, to know this: You don't have to wait until you're good at using these tools to work with your brain, not against it. It's *okay* if you forget about strategies and can't find them again. Working with your brain is something you can start doing right now, even if you don't remember a word of what you've read in this book.

You can do it by leaning into your strengths.

It's not the complete picture of working with your brain, not against it, but as I am humbled to realize, it is absolutely the most important part. Our *strengths* are

> Working with your brain is something you can start doing right now, even if you don't remember a word of what you've read in this book.

where our potential lies. And it makes the most sense to level them up. Also, learning to navigate our challenges effectively takes time; leaning into your strengths can start right now.

You might, like me, not realize what your strengths are at first because, to you, it just feels like the stuff that isn't as hard. It's easy to discount our strengths with "Well, but that's just easy, right?" It's not, not for everyone.

You can start leaning into your strengths by doing the stuff that comes easily to you.

"What do I find easy or effortless? What do people say they admire that I can do? What do people turn to me for help with? When given the opportunity to do it however I want, how do I approach a hard task?"

Those are your strengths. We all have some. Which brings me, finally, to this. One of this community's greatest strengths is *one another*. We all have different strengths. It's often easier for us to do something for someone else than it is for ourselves. We love to help. We know what it's like to struggle. This community is amazing at effective interdependence. And they have taught me that leaning into each other's strengths is a strength. When we're able to do that . . .

It's okay if we're weird.

It's okay if we struggle.

We do not need to try harder.

We are different, we are beautiful, and we are not alone.

Appendix 1

The Toolbox Worksheet

Tools I think sound helpful:

_____

_____

_____

_____

_____

_____

Tools I'm currently trying:

1._____

2._____

3._____

Tools in my toolbox:

Appendix 2

A Permission Slip

_____ has permission to STOP doing the following:
(your name here)

(check all that apply and feel free to add your own)

☐ Trying harder   ☐ _____

☐ Making up for lost time   ☐ _____

☐ _____   ☐ Anything else your brain just
                                       convinced you that NOW
☐ _____   YOU HAVE TIME TO DO!

from _____ until (circle at least one) you have a better
(date)

idea of where your effort should go / you have finished enough of this

book that you feel you know how to work with your brain more

effectively / you have had adequate rest and self-care / and/or

_____.
(insert your own criteria here)

This permission slip does not expire and can be reissued at any time.

SIGNED: YOUR BRAIN

WITNESSED BY: *Jessica McCabe*

Appendix 3

Decisional Balance Worksheet

When we think about making changes to help us achieve a goal, most of us don't really consider all "sides" in a complete way. But in addition to non-motivation-related issues that can get in our way—skill gap, resource gap, we forgot about the goal entirely—we often forget that there is always motivation *not* to change, too.

Instructions: Fill out the worksheet. Then, look at your overall picture, compare each of the boxes. Maybe talk it through with someone and ask for feedback. Finally, ask yourself, "Are the costs of this change worth it? Is this where I want to be putting my effort?"

The goal I want to achieve is:

_____

_____

_____

The change I'm considering to help me to reach this goal is:

_____

_____

_____

	Benefits/Pros	**Costs/Cons**
Not changing	*What are the advantages of the status quo?* *What are the advantages of continuing with the same behavior?*	*What are the downsides of the status quo?* *What are the downsides of not changing the behavior?*
Making a change	*What are the advantages of changing the behavior?* *What are the good things that would happen?*	*What are the downsides of changing the behavior?*

After considering the costs and benefits of changing, remember:

It's your decision—you're the one who must decide what it will take to tip the scale in favor of changing. For example, you can add rewards to the change you want to make; or try this worksheet with a different type of change that may help you toward your goal in a way that's more worth it to you!

It is common to have mixed feelings when making decisions to change.

Appendix 4

Navigating Obstacles

Instructions: Fill out the worksheet. You can make as many copies as you want and practice with it. You can complete it in retrospect or for a future action you'd like to take when you know what the obstacles might be. The same "scene" can often go a more helpful way when we can recognize our choice points and make a mindful choice.

What's something that's really important to me (a hero's journey I'm on/would like to begin)?

_____

_____

_____

Why is it important to me? What am I hoping to achieve?

_____

_____

_____

How does/might it go when obstacles come up in a way that isn't helping me toward that goal? What does the "scene" look like?

I do (action): _____

_____

But (obstacle faced): _____

_____

Therefore (unhelpful action/choice): _____

_____

How could it go differently, in a way that would be more helpful toward your goal?

I do (action): _____

_____

But (obstacle faced): _____

_____

Therefore (potentially helpful new action/choice): _____

_____

Remember that new information coming in can change the choice we make, too. When will you reevaluate to see if this path still makes sense?*

_____

_____

_____

_____

_____

*   Put a reminder in your calendar, set an alarm on your phone, etc.

Appendix 5

Strengths Bingo

If you want a place to start leaning into your strengths, you can go through this grid of strengths and circle ones that you appreciate in yourself or that others have said they appreciate in you. Or play bingo with this list—mark off a strength when you get compliments about it! Your choice!

Creativity	Openness to new experiences	Spontaneity	Empathy	Adaptability
Originality	Being a jack-of-all-trades	Persistence	Intuition	High-energy
Enthusiasm	Cool under pressure		Sense of humor	Problem-solving
Thinking outside the box	Learning quickly	Emotional intelligence	Risk-taking	Flexibility
Curiosity	Pattern recognition	Making connections	Resourcefulness	Resilience

Notes

To access the research that I've cited in the book, please head to https://howtoadhd.com/book or use the QR code below.

Glossary

Finding common language has validated and empowered our ADHD community to have open conversations about experiences we were once too ashamed to discuss. The definitions in this glossary are meant to clarify how these words and phrases are being used in the ADHD community at present, and how I use them *in this book*. That being said, language changes constantly, particularly when you are talking about cutting-edge science and rapidly evolving culture, so these definitions aren't intended to be formal or absolute.

* Asterisks denote terms original to the How to ADHD channel!

ableism (n.): discrimination and social prejudice against people with disabilities, including ADHD, based on the belief that (neuro)typical abilities or those with (neuro)typical abilities are inherently better or more valuable.

accommodations (n., plural): modifications or adjustments to a task, tool, activity, or environment in order to create accessibility for someone with a disability.

alexithymia (n.): the inability or impaired ability to recognize and describe your own feelings or the feelings of others.

Allistic (adj.): a descriptor used to refer to a person who is not Autistic.

Brains* (n.): a term of affection used to refer to ADHD and neuro-divergent persons who are learning how to work with their brain, not against it. (Hello, Brains!)

brain smoothie* (n.): a figurative term referring to the makeup (or current blend) of specific neurotransmitters within an individual's brain.

chronotype (n.): your body's natural disposition to be awake/alert or sleepy/asleep at certain times of the day, based on your circadian rhythm.

circadian rhythm (n.): a natural, internal process that regulates the sleep-wake cycle and body functions within a day; your body's internal "clock."

decision paralysis (n.): the inability to decide what to do out of fear of making the wrong choice and/or overwhelm. In those with ADHD, this commonly presents as feeling "stuck," being unable to start a task, or procrastinating by changing activities.

disability (n.): according to the Americans with Disabilities Act (ADA), "disability" is defined as a "mental or physical impairment that substantially limits one or more major life activities."

divergent thinking (n.): a cognitive process that generates creative ideas by exploring many possible solutions or bouncing from one thought to the next. Divergent thinking generally occurs spontaneously, is seldom linear, and tends to produce abundant and unique ideas.

emotion dysregulation (n.): an impaired ability to control your emotional response, which can lead to extreme and/or disproportionate reactions that are not necessarily appropriate to the situation.

emotional impulsivity (n.): the quickness and intensity with which ADHDers are likely to react emotionally to events and triggers, relative to our non-ADHD peers. This is related to our impairments in response inhibition; stimuli happen and we automatically respond.

executive function, or EF (n.): a set of top-down cognitive processes (executive functions) that help us self-regulate so we can effectively plan, prioritize, and sustain effort toward long-term goals.

extrinsic motivation (n.): the incentive we have to engage in an activity or complete a task that is based on the external consequences of doing (or not doing) it.

free recall (n.): the ability to retrieve information from memory spontaneously, without any prompts or triggers. Also referred to as *uncued recall*.

Hearts* (n., plural): a term of affection referring to those who love, care for, and are looking to learn how to support or have better relationships with those with ADHD.

hyperfocus (n., v.): a state of deep flow or perseveration those with ADHD experience as a result of our differences in attention regulation.

identity-first language (n.): language that identifies a person's neurodivergence as a fundamental aspect of their identity. Disability advocates, especially Deaf or Autistic advocates, often strongly prefer this language, due to the underlying stigma and prejudice involved in the insistence on person-first language by those who consider those conditions something to be "fixed" or "cured."

interoception (n.): the perception of internal signals, such as hunger, thirst, and fatigue.

intersectionality (n.): a term coined by civil rights advocate Kimberlé Crenshaw: "intersectionality is a metaphor for understanding the ways that multiple forms of inequality or disadvantage . . . compound themselves and create obstacles that often are not understood."

intrinsic motivation (n.): the incentive we feel to engage in an activity or complete a task simply because we find it interesting, enjoyable, or satisfying to do so.

masking (v.): performing expected neurotypical behaviors in place of behaviors associated with various neurodevelopmental diagnoses. Masking can be a conscious (or semiconscious) choice, or a habit formed by social conditioning.

neurodivergent (ND) (n.): an umbrella term for describing a person (or group of people) whose neurological development/function differs from what is considered typical.

neurodiversity (n.): term coined by sociologist Judy Singer to create awareness of the diversity that exists in the structure and function of brains (neurotypes). Whereas neurodivergent/neurodivergence refers to individuals with atypical neurological development, neurodiverse/neurodiversity refers to a group of people with different brain types, including those who are neurotypical.

neuro-spicy (adj.): a term of affection used within the neurodivergent community to include all those whose brains work differently, including those who have not been diagnosed.

neurotypical (NT) (adj.): a descriptor referring to 1.) someone who experienced/experiences typical neurological development or functioning, or 2.) something designed with the presumption of typical neurological development or functioning.

person-first language (n.): language that emphasizes personhood primarily, with disability identified as a secondary aspect of a person's identity.

prospective memory (n.): the ability to remember to do something in the future. There are different types of prospective memory; *time-based* prospective memory is impaired in ADHD.

rejection sensitivity (RS) (n.): the tendency to find rejection—or even perceived rejection—profoundly painful. Rejection sensitivity isn't unique to ADHD, but it is a *very* common experience due to difficulties with emotion regulation combined with more frequent experiences of actual rejection relative to our NT peers.

self-discrepancy (n.): the gap between who we believe we are (actual self) versus who we would like to be (ideal self). The self-discrepancy theory proposes that this difference leads to negative emotions, including disappointment and dissatisfaction, fear and feeling threatened, shame, embarrassment, and feelings of moral worthlessness or weakness. Ableism, including internalized ableism, contributes to this self-discrepancy. (See more in "How to Change the World," page 366.)

set-shifting (v.): switching between tasks and activities with different cognitive demands.

time blindness/nearsightedness (n.): inability (or exceptional difficulty) recognizing how much time has passed and/or estimating how long something will take.

working memory (n.): a type of memory that gives us the ability to hold new information temporarily in our head while we work with it.

Support Organizations

You are not alone. In addition to the education and community you can find with How to ADHD (howtoadhd.com) and other advocates and hashtags online (#ADHD!), there are many well-established organizations that offer support to those with ADHD and those who love them, as well as organizations that offer support for some of the difficult topics that I discussed in this book and were part of my own journey. These are just a few; scan the QR code on page 432 for more.

ADHD Resources

Children and Adults with Attention-Deficit/Hyperactivity Disorder (CHADD) (chadd.org) has a wonderful and extensive collection of information and resources not only for adults and children, but for parents, caregivers, educators, and mental health professionals, too.

The **Attention Deficit Disorder Association (ADDA) (add.org)** is an international community made for and by adults with ADHD and houses a variety of resources including workshops, virtual support groups, and a list of professionals focused on ADHD.

The **American Professional Society of ADHD and Related Disorders (APSARD)** (apsard.org) is an organization that works to improve the quality of care for patients with ADHD through the promotion of research and dissemination of evidence-based practices to healthcare professionals. Its members cover a broad spectrum of physicians, psychologists, ethicists, and allied mental health experts who seek to heighten the public's understanding of ADHD, reduce stigma, and promote effective dialogue between healthcare providers and patients.

Understood (understood.org) works to raise awareness and provide resources to help support those with learning and thinking differences across all areas of life.

ADD Coach Academy (addca.com) provides education for those interested in becoming an ADHD coach, as well as a directory of ADHD coaches who are ADDCA-certified.

Centre for ADHD Awareness, Canada (caddac.ca) is a Canada-based organization that hosts a wide range of ADHD resources, programs, and events geared toward those living with ADHD and their loved ones.

Psychology Today **Therapist Finder (psychologytoday.com/us/therapists)** allows you to search by specialty as well as insurance to find a therapist, psychiatrist, or even a support group that may be a good fit for you.

Other Resources

The **American Foundation for Suicide Prevention (afsp.org)** offers a range of resources, from personal stories to resources for those affected directly or indirectly by suicide.

The **National Eating Disorder Association (nationaleatingdisorders.org)** offers support such as helplines, educational resources, and forums for those affected by eating disorders, both directly and indirectly.

Wellness Recovery Action Plan (wellnessrecoveryactionplan.com) aims to provide education and guidance on building a wellness recovery action plan (WRAP), which is a fantastic tool to support your mental health and well-being, even in a crisis.

The **Center for Nonviolent Communication (cnvc.org)** supports the education of nonviolent communication and aids in peaceful and effective conflict resolution in a variety of settings.

The **Job Accommodation Network (askjan.org)** contains resources, information, and lists regarding work and school accommodations in the United States; their list of accommodations can be a great place to start for ideas, no matter which country you live in.

Take This (takethis.org) is a mental health advocacy organization that focuses on providing resources, training, and support to individuals and companies within the game industry.

Speaking Grief (speakinggrief.org) contains resources aimed at helping us get better at dealing with grief, which includes the PBS documentary of the same name.

Modern Loss (modernloss.com) provides insight and solidarity through a collection of essays written by others who are grieving a variety of losses.

Find a Helpline (findahelpline.com) is an international directory of hotlines, online chat rooms, text lines, and resources regarding various crises, including suicide prevention.

Go to howtoadhdbook.com or scan the QR code below for additional resources, such as more organizations, where to find us, links to helpful videos, recommended further reading, the ADHD Friendly Rubric, blogs, individual advocates and hashtags worth following, and more!

Acknowledgments

Thank you to our Brain Advocates and all our Patreon Brains for making this book—and the journey that led to it—possible. It started with Scot Melville, who saw me at the brink of burning out and giving up and offered me the material, support, and words of encouragement I needed to keep going. Scot, and the many wonderful Brains who joined him, are the reason How to ADHD was able to not only survive but thrive. The channel, this book, and everything that comes after is thanks to them.

Thank you to my editor, Elysia Liang, who patiently worked with me, accommodated my ADHD, listened, and learned. When I turned in the manuscript, she didn't point out it was late (or not exactly what most people would call "finished"). You know what she said? "It's a good book. You should be proud." It is and I am, and that is in no small part because of the part she played in helping me craft it, week after week, trusting my vision while lending a guiding hand when needed. Thank you, too, to my manager, Linnea Toney, and the entire book team at Rodale for realizing my vision of an ADHD-friendly tome: Terry Deal, Ethan Campbell, Andrea Lau, Irene Ng, Dustin Amick, Jonathan Sung, and Ray Arjune.

Thank you to my writing buddy, Theresa Weiler, for responding to a frantic call two weeks into me writing this book and staying by my side ever since, offering guidance, mantras ("A-de-quate!

A-de-quate!"), and mac n' cheese as we painstakingly shaped each chapter. Theresa is a shining example of effective interdependence in writing a book: she helps authors say what they're trying to say.

Thank you to Dr. Patrick LaCount for being a huge reason I feel like I know what I'm talking about. As a science communicator, what I share depends on the quality of the information I have access to and how well I understand it; for years, Patrick—who cares deeply about disseminating good information about ADHD—has helped with both. For this book, he has compiled all the citations, dug for studies, had long conversations, dove deep into cutting-edge ADHD concepts, and patiently reviewed every word I wrote.

Thank you to Caroline Maguire, author of *Why Will No One Play with Me?*, who collaborated with me heavily on the "How to People" chapter. She was generous in sharing her knowledge and has supported me as a mentor throughout this entire process. She believed in my ability to publish a book, even when I was scared I would fail. Caroline, you were right!!

Thank you to all those whose work directly contributed to this book: Dr. Carolyn Lentzsch-Parcells, Dani Donovan, Brendan Mahan, Ari Tuckman, and René Brooks. I am in awe of the incredible work each of them has done and continues to do to contribute to this community, and grateful for their contributions to this book.

Thank you to Harley Lohs, community manager for How to ADHD, who sat with me day after day in the last month of writing and editing as an active body double, support, and sidekick. I couldn't have kept going without them.

Thank you to Jessica (J2) Via, How to ADHD's operations director, who is such a badass and so good with tech that for a while everyone thought she was AI. Not a chance: J2 is spectacularly human. Even the most cutting-edge AI couldn't have kept How to ADHD and me moving forward and functioning through this process, but J2 did.

Thank you to the entire How to ADHD production team, now and over the years, who helped bring my videos—and vision—to life. At the helm of it all is our current producer, Eddie Hollenbeck, who has truly created an environment that fosters creativity, who engages with our entire team in creating videos that are as fun to make as they are to watch.

To the moderators, who have taken such good care of the community: Scot Melville, Mike Oerlemans, Chris Hendrickson, M. Svindt, Manon M., and Jaclyn Curler. Thank you for your kindness and generosity in maintaining safe online spaces for Brains to be themselves.

To each and every Brain who has reached out to offer ideas, quotes, support, stories, and encouragement through this long writing process. You are so much a part of what's valuable about How to ADHD, and this book wouldn't have been complete without including you. Thank you for showing me our strengths.

Thank you to my partner and future father of my child, Dr. Raffael Boccamazzo. Raffael, you have taught me so much about how to heart.

And thank you to my mom, for showing me that there's no reason those with disabilities need to be excluded from the activities and work they care about, and for teaching me that everyone has a voice, if only they are given the means to make themselves heard.

Index

About the Author

Jessica McCabe is the creator, writer, and star of the YouTube channel How to ADHD. Since its founding in 2015, the award-winning channel—widely respected by treatment providers, ADHD researchers, and especially the ADHD community—has provided scientifically backed and experientially affirming information on how people with ADHD might work with their brains. Her work has been featured by *The New York Times*, the *Washington Post*, *ADDitude Magazine*, *Today* online, *Upworthy*, and more.